THE SOUTH CAROLINA ADVENTURE

Joel Walker and Donald O. Stewart
The South Carolina Archives and History Foundation

Gibbs Smith, Publisher
Salt Lake City

ABOUT THE SOUTH CAROLINA ARCHIVES AND HISTORY FOUNDATION

The South Carolina Adventure was completed with support of The South Carolina Archives and History Foundation. It is a private, non-profit organization, which supports the conservation, preservation, and education programs of the South Carolina Archives and History Center. The foundation actively seeks the support of corporations, organizations, and individuals who believe in the value of preserving the Palmetto State's vast history. Although the History Center's most obvious functions are the conservation and preservation of the state, county, and local records and the preservation of South Carolina's historic buildings and archaeological sites, it also functions as one of the state's leaders in K-12 history education.

ABOUT THE AUTHORS

Joel Walker has been a state coordinator of National History Day since 1997, serving in Kansas and in South Carolina since 2000. His programs have produced numerous national award-winning students in both states. Prior to his work at the South Carolina Department of Archives and History in Columbia and the Kansas State Historical Society in Topeka, Walker taught middle school for 10 years at Pawnee Heights School in Burdett, Kansas. Presently working on a Master's Degree in Curriculum and Instruction from Columbia International University, Walker's undergraduate degree is from the University of Nebraska at Kearney.

Donald O. Stewart's love for South Carolina history began when he was a student at Windsor Elementary in Columbia. In 1995, he received his B.A. in History from the University of South Carolina. Stewart has worked at a variety of public history institutions, such as the South Carolina State Museum, the North Carolina Office of Archives and History, and Historic Oak View County Park. He currently works at the South Carolina Department of Archives and History as Project Director for Teaching American History in South Carolina, a professional development program for teachers. His prior publications have appeared in the North Carolina Historical Review and the South Carolina Encyclopedia.

Published by
Gibbs Smith, Publisher
P.O. Box 667
Layton, UT 84041
800-748-5439
www.gibbs-smith.com/textbooks

Managing Editors: Carrie Gibson and Jennifer B. Petersen
Associate Editors: Valerie T. Hatch, Susan A. Myers, and Courtney J. Thomas
Cover and Book Design: Alan Connell
Maps and Graphs: Alan Connell

Cover photo: Boardwalk through Congaree Swamp National Monument © Larry Ulrich

Printed and bound in China.
ISBN 10 : 1-58685-425-9
ISBN 13 : 978-1-58685-425-6

14 13   10 9

The authors dedicate this book to their wives, Rose and Karen.

REVIEWERS

Rebecca Dingle describes herself as a teacher and a storyteller who helped her students discover the fascinating stories of history. After teaching 8th grade social studies in South Carolina for 28 years, Dingle served as the Social Studies Coordinator for Dorchester Two Schools in Summerville for four years. She was named South Carolina's History Teacher of the Year in 1993; Dorchester Two Teacher of the Year in 1991; Lowcountry Teacher of the Year (Charleston post and Courier). She also served on the State Teachers Forum's Steering Committee from 1991 to 1994. Dingle currently teaches elementary Social Studies methods to seniors at Charleston Southern University. She also teaches a creativity class and holds workshops on storytelling and social studies around the state.

Archie Vernon Huff, Jr. is Professor of History, Emeritus, and retired Vice President for Academic Affairs and Dean at Furman University, where he taught for 35 years. He holds an A.B. degree from Wofford College, magna cum laude with high honors in history (1959), a B.D. degree from Yale University (1962), and a M.A. and Ph.D. degree (1970) from Duke University. He was a Fulbright Scholar at the University of Edinburgh and a Woodrow Wilson Fellow at Yale. In 2003, Furman awarded him the honorary Doctor of Humanities degree, and he received the Order of the Palmetto from Governor Sanford. Huff is a specialist on the history of South Carolina and the American South and is the author and editor of a number of books, including *Greenville: The History of the City and County in the South Carolina Piedmont* and *The History of South Carolina in the Building of the Nation*, a textbook for 8th grade.

William J. Long is the Curator of History for the South Carolina Confederate Relic Room and Museum, a state museum of military history. His undergraduate education was at the Naval Academy at Annapolis, Maryland, and the University of Georgia (B.A. English, 1991). His M.A. in History is from Georgia College and State University in Milledgeville, Georgia (1997).

Merit Justice has been teaching school for almost 20 years. She currently teaches in the gifted and talented program at McDonald Elementary in Georgetown. Justice received her B.A. in Early Childhood and Elementary Education from Converse College and her M.A. in Education in Reading from the Citadel. She has her National Board Certification as a Middle Childhood Generalist. Justice is a Teacher-consultant for the National Geographic Society's Education Foundation and has been affiliated with them since 1990. She is a member of the South Carolina Geographic Alliance and previously served as the South Carolina Ambassador for Geographic Education.

Lisa Randle currently serves as Site Coordinator at the College of Charleston for the UNESCO Transatlantic Slave Trade Education Initiative where she is responsible for the implementation and enhancement of teaching about the transatlantic slave trade in the K-12 area. She also teaches the Introduction to Historic Preservation class at the College of Charleston. She received her B.A. in International Studies, M.A. in Public History, and Master's Certificate in Cultural Resource Management from the University of South Carolina. Randle is currently completing coursework for a Ph.E. in Anthropology at the University of South Carolina. Randle formerly served as Director of Multicultural and Educational Programming for Historic Columbia and as a 2003 Thomas Day National Fellow, assisted the Thomas Day Education Projects as a consultant.

Kelly Pfiefer is the assistant principal at Stone Academy in Greenville. She is an Executive Board Member of the South Carolina Council for Social Studies and serves as president for the Greenville Council for Social Studies. Pfiefer is also active with the South Carolina Council of Economic Education and is an Education Leader in Teaching Economics.

Monti Caughman completed her undergraduate work at the University of South Carolina. She has also done graduate work in geography at Southwest Texas University through National Geographic's summer teacher institutes. Caughman has taught for several years in Lexington District One, where she has served on numerous committees including Social Studies Curriculum, Maps, Social Studies Textbook Adoption, and Technology. She has also served on many social studies committees for the South Carolina Department of Education, and she has written many social studies showcase lessons. Caughman is currently the Resident Teacher Consultant for the South Carolina Geographic Alliance.

Susan Hoffmann is a Winthrop University graduate and has been teaching for eight years, with most of her time at Greenbrier Elementary School in Greenville. Hoffmann is a member of the technology team and heads up the writing committee at her school. She is on the leadership council of the Upstate Writing Project, the local affiliate to the National Writing Project, based at Clemson University. Her philosophy of education is summed up from a quote by John Dewey: "Give the pupils something to do, not something to learn; and the doing is of such a nature as to demand thinking; learning naturally results."

Contents

Palmetto Detectives

Maps

Charts & Graphs

South Carolina Portraits

SOUTH CAROLINA PORTRAIT

Activities

Blooming on the Vine

Genuine Genius!

Geography Tie-In

Linking the Past to the Present

What do you think?

The Adventure Begins

Photograph of live oak forest on Spring Island, South Carolina
© Eric Horan

Chapter 1

Learning history is an adventure. It is like a treasure hunt. You can find clues that help you learn about the past.

You are beginning an adventure into South Carolina's history. What do you think you will discover?

**WORDS TO
UNDERSTAND**
artifact
biography
cardinal directions
compass rose
culture
decision
document
history
journal
museum
oral history
scale of miles
timeline
tradition

Once Upon a Time

Do you like a good story? The history of South Carolina is a great story! It is a story of people who lived here for many years. It is the story of people who came from faraway lands. It is a story of people who gained their freedom. It is a story of men and women who helped build our state.

You live in South Carolina today. The story of our state is also a story about you. It is about all of us and our future. You can see it is a pretty important story.

What Is History?

Can you remember your first day of school? Think back to when you started kindergarten. It seems like a long time ago, doesn't it? What are some of your other memories? Maybe you remember the first time you rode a bike or played basketball. Maybe you remember a fun vacation you took with your family.

These memories and special things are part of your past and your history. *History* is the record of the past. Everybody and everything has a past and a history. Look at the word "history." Take off the first two letters of the word. What word is left? It is the word "story." Don't forget that history is a story. It is the story of all of us.

Learning From the Past

Think of a time when you made a mistake or got into trouble. Now think of a time when you did something that made you proud. What did you learn about yourself?

By studying history, we learn about the good and bad choices other people made. Knowing history can help us make better *decisions,* or choices.

Ways of Learning History

There are many ways we can learn history. Let's read about some of them.

Timelines

Looking at a timeline is a good way to start learning about the past. A *timeline* uses dates to show the order of when things happened. Most timelines are read from left to right, just like sentences. Sometimes timelines go up and down. Then the first events are usually at the top.

Books

Reading a history book, like this one, is one way to learn history. This book tells stories about many different things that happened in the past. There are lots of other books that tell the stories of the past. One kind of book is called a biography. A *biography* is a story of one person's life.

What do you think?

How can knowing about the past help us today? How does it affect our decisions?

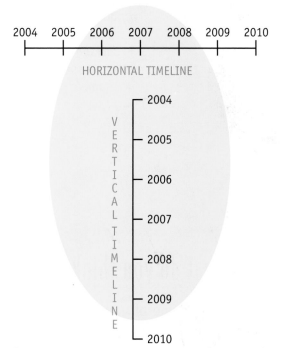

2004 2005 2006 2007 2008 2009 2010

HORIZONTAL TIMELINE

VERTICAL TIMELINE

2004
2005
2006
2007
2008
2009
2010

Genuine Genius!

Keeping a Journal

A *journal* is a book of someone's thoughts and feelings. Reading journals is one way to learn history. People from the past wrote about what happened in their lives.

Find a notebook with blank pages. Write a short journal entry called *The History of Me*. Make a list of your memories. Write your thoughts and feelings, too.

This young boy is playing a fiddle at a bluegrass festival at Andrew Jackson State Park. Bluegrass music is an example of culture.

What do you think?

What are some of your family's traditions? What are some of your community's traditions? What do these traditions tell people about your culture?

Culture

We can learn history by looking at culture. *Culture* is the way a group of people live. It includes the food they eat, the clothes they wear, the homes they live in, and the *traditions* they keep alive. Does your family do something special on certain holidays each year? That is a tradition. Parents pass down traditions to their children. Culture is also about the way people celebrate special events. Songs and dances are part of culture, too.

Artifacts

There are ways to learn about history without reading books. One way is to look at artifacts. An *artifact* is something made or used by people in the past. It might be a tool or a toy. It might be a dress or an old telephone. It could be as small as a button. It could be as big as a steam engine. By studying an artifact, you might learn what people used it for or how it was made. Artifacts help tell the story of the past.

Documents

Documents also tell us about the past. *Documents* are paper records. A document can be a letter, a certificate, or a newspaper. They can tell us what someone in the past saw, thought, or did.

Museums

Visiting *museums* is a great way to learn history. They are places where historical objects, like artifacts and documents, are put on display. Our state has many museums. The South Carolina State Museum is in Columbia. It tells the story of our state. What museums are in your town? What stories do they tell?

Oral History

Sometimes the most interesting way to learn history is to have someone tell you about it. Maybe your grandpa can tell you about your family's first television set, or maybe someone you know took part in an important event. When you listen to someone tell a story about the past, it is called *oral history*.

This artifact tells us that people didn't always have electricity. They used lanterns for light.

Photographs Show Change

Looking at old photographs is another way to learn about the past. They record what was happening at a moment in time. You can often see what people wore, what their homes were like, and how they lived.

This photograph shows a classroom in the 1930s. What do you see in the picture that tells you about the past? How would a photo of your class be different from this one?

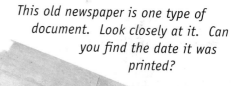

This old newspaper is one type of document. Look closely at it. Can you find the date it was printed?

Maps

Maps are a good tool for learning history. They help us know where things happened. Old maps help us see how things have changed.

There are many kinds of maps. Can you think of some? Maybe you thought of a treasure map. Maybe you thought of the road maps your parents use on trips.

Activity

Reading a Map

Look at this map. It shows roads that went through our state a very long time ago. Use the map to answer the questions.

1. What is the title of the map?

2. What do the symbols on the legend stand for?

3. What direction does the road at Kings Town go?

4. Find the scale of miles. Use a ruler to find how many miles are between Charles Town and Camden?

5. If you wanted to travel the shortest distance, what would your route be between Ninety Six and Beaufort?

6. Look on the Internet or in a reference book to find a map of roads in South Carolina today. Are any of the roads in the same place as the roads on this map? What roads are different?

Cardinal Directions:
A **compass rose** shows the directions north, south, east, and west. We call these the **cardinal directions.**

Legend	
●	Town
▪▪▪▪▪	Road

Legend or Key:
Mapmakers use symbols, so they don't have to print words all over the map. The symbols stand for cities, rivers, forests, and other things. The legend or key explains what the symbols mean.

Memory Master

Lesson 1

1. What is history?

2. Why do we learn history?

3. What is an artifact?

4. What does a compass rose show?

The South Carolina Adventure

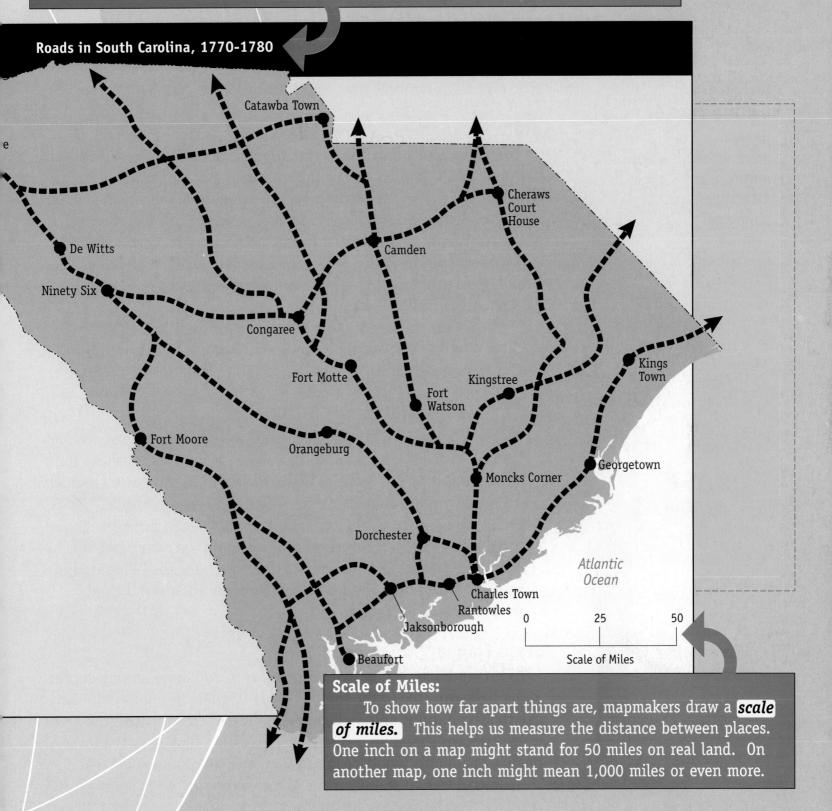

Roads in South Carolina, 1770-1780

Catawba Town

Cheraws Court House

De Witts

Camden

Ninety Six

Congaree

Fort Motte

Kingstree

Fort Watson

Kings Town

Fort Moore

Orangeburg

Georgetown

Moncks Corner

Dorchester

Atlantic Ocean

Charles Town
Rantowles

Jaksonborough

Beaufort

0   25   50

Scale of Miles

Scale of Miles:
To show how far apart things are, mapmakers draw a *scale of miles.* This helps us measure the distance between places. One inch on a map might stand for 50 miles on real land. On another map, one inch might mean 1,000 miles or even more.

WORDS TO UNDERSTAND
flexible
government
motto
nickname
palmetto
seal
symbol

Symbols of South Carolina

The U.S. flag is a symbol of our country. A *symbol* is something that has a special meaning or can stand for something else. We have symbols that stand for our state, too.

State Nickname

A *nickname* is another name for a person or place. South Carolina's nickname is the Palmetto State. The *palmetto* is a beautiful tree. It is very strong and *flexible.* This means it can bend without breaking. Over 200 years ago, some South Carolinians built a fort from palmetto trees to defend themselves from attack. They were fighting in the American Revolution. The attackers shot cannonballs at the fort, but the cannonballs just bounced off the palmetto walls.

Our state nickname means we are very strong and we "bounce back" when times are tough. Do you think the Palmetto State is a good nickname for South Carolina?

State Motto

South Carolina has two mottos. *Mottos* are sayings that tell a goal or an idea. Our state's mottos show the spirit of our state. They are written in the Latin language. *Dum Spiro Spero* means, "While I breathe I hope." It means that as long as we are alive, we can hope for better things to come. Another meaning is, "Don't ever give up." Our other motto, *Animis Opibusque Parati*, means "Prepared in minds and resources." South Carolinians use their minds and resources to face the future.

State Flag

Our state flag is blue with a white crescent shape in one corner and a palmetto tree in the middle. Our flag has not always looked like this. It did not always have the palmetto tree. It was just a white crescent shape on a blue flag. That flag flew over the fort made of palmetto wood. Many years later, our state added the palmetto tree to stand for the great victory at the palmetto fort.

Have you seen a palmetto tree?

D. ERD

The palmetto tree on our flag stands for our victory at the palmetto fort.

Today, you can see the state flag flying over the capitol building in Columbia. It is flown at other state buildings, too. Look at the flagpole at your school. Do you see the state flag flying below the U.S. flag?

The Great Seal

Our state *seal* is a symbol used to mark important *government* papers. The state seal has two pictures on it. One picture shows two trees. One of the trees is a palmetto. It stands for the brave soldiers at the palmetto fort. The other tree is an oak tree. It has fallen down. It stands for the people who attacked the palmetto fort and lost. The other picture is of a woman walking on a beach. She stands for hope.

Look at the state seal again. Do you see the state mottos? Animis Opibusque Parati: Prepared in minds and resources. Dum Spiro Spero: While I breathe I hope.

Our state seal stands for bravery and hope.

State Butterfly:
Eastern Tiger Swallowtail

State
Flower:
Yellow
Jessamine

State Tree:
Palmetto

State Spider:
Carolina Wolf
Spider

State Game Bird:
Wild Turkey

State Amphibian:
Spotted Salamander

State Fish:
Striped Bass

State Bird:
Carolina Wren

State Insect:
Carolina Mantid

State Fruit:
Peach

State Animal:
Whitetail Deer

State Dog:
Boykin Spaniel

State Reptile:
Loggerhead Sea Turtle

Other Symbols

All states choose different animals and plants for state symbols. We have a state bird, fish, fruit, and insect. We also have many other symbols. Each symbol shows something special about our state.

Not all of our symbols are plants and animals. We have a state stone, a state dance, a state opera—we even have a state drink. Can you find out what it is?

Memory Master

Lesson 2

1. What is our state nickname?

2. Draw a picture of our state flag.

3. What are our state mottos? What do they mean?

4. List three of our state symbols.

Palmetto Detectives in SECRET MEANINGS

"Please turn the TV off. You've got homework to do."

"I'm all done, Dad," Kevin said.

"You're all done?" Kevin's dad asked.

"Well, pretty much. It's not due until next Tuesday. It's only Thursday."

"What is due on Tuesday?"

"It's for my South Carolina history class. Ms. Izard said this year our class will be palmetto detectives. We are going to look at clues to learn about our state. Our first assignment is to design a new state seal. Do you think we need a new state seal, Dad?"

"I don't know, Kevin. I don't even know what our state seal looks like. I'm not from South Carolina." Kevin's dad was from South Korea.

"Maybe we do need a new seal. It's really funny-looking. It has a tree and a lady on it."

"What do the tree and lady stand for?"

"What do you mean?" Kevin looked at his dad.

"The state seal is a symbol for the state. As a symbol, it stands for something. It has a secret meaning. Your new state seal should have a secret meaning, too."

"A secret meaning?" Kevin asked. "Wow. That sounds cool."

"I have an idea, Kevin. Let's go to the state museum in Columbia on Saturday. We can find out the secret meaning of the state seal, and you can get an idea for your seal."

Kevin had never been to the state museum before. Now the thought of seeking out 'secret meanings' made him excited. The next day he told his classmates about his planned trip to the museum and his search for secret meanings.

"What do you mean about secret meanings?" Grant asked Kevin as they stood in the lunch line. "Is it like a code or something?"

"My dad said state symbols have hidden meanings," Kevin explained.

"What are you guys talking about?" Christina interrupted. "The state symbols don't have any secret meanings."

"Didn't Ms. Izard tell us that a symbol was something that stood for something else? If it stands for something else it has a secret meaning," Kevin said.

"Well, I've already drawn my state seal," Christina said proudly. "And it doesn't have any secret meanings."

"What does your seal look like?" Kevin asked.

Christina looked at him and said, "I'm not saying. You will copy my idea."

"No, I won't. Just tell me what it looks like."

"Alright. I made a seal with the shape of South Carolina on it, and I drew mountains on one side and a beach on the other," Christina said proudly. "South Carolina has mountains and it has a beach."

"It also has rivers and lakes and trees, lots of trees," Grant added.

"And swamps. South Carolina has swamps, too," another boy joined in. His name was Carter, and he was also in Ms. Izard's class.

"I didn't draw any rivers or swamps. Are you drawing a seal with a swamp, Carter?" Christina asked.

"No, I have a submarine in mine," Carter answered.

"A submarine?" everyone asked all at once.

"Yeah, haven't you ever been to the state museum? They have an old submarine on display," Carter explained.

A submarine? Kevin thought to himself. *This museum is going to be cool.*

YOUR SEAL!

Now it's your turn. If you had to design a new state seal, what symbols would you choose? What are their secret meanings?

Chapter 1 Review

Blooming on the Vine

Using and Making a Timeline

A boy named Jamal has made a timeline to show some things that happened in his life. Use his timeline to answer these questions:

1. What year was Jamal's baby sister born? At that time, how old was Jamal?

2. How long has Jamal had his dog?

3. Which happened later: Jamal joined a soccer team, or the family moved to Greenville?

4. In 2003, Jamal started taking swimming lessons. Where would you place that event on the timeline?

5. Make a timeline of your own life. Decide what year to start and end your timeline. Put the events in the order they happened. Make sure the marks show equal amounts of time.

Jamal's Life

1996	Jamal is born.
1997	
1998	Jamal's family gets a dog.
1999	Jamal's family moves to Greenville.
2000	
2001	Jamal starts kindergarten. Jamal's baby sister is born.
2002	
2003	
2004	Jamal starts third grade.
2005	Jamal joins a soccer team.

Geography Tie-In

Know Your Town

It is fun to learn about the place where you live. What do you already know about your town? As a class, look on a map to find where your town is located. Make a list on the chalkboard of things found in your town. Are there hills in your town? Are there forests or lots of buildings and roads?

Don't worry if your list is not very long. If you do this again when you finish this book, your list will be much longer!

Your History

If you think history is just the story of other people, you should think again! You are part of history now.

What things have people in your family (like your parents, grand-parents, or great-grandparents) done that have changed your life? For example, did any of your relatives come from a place other than South Carolina? Do you know why they came here?

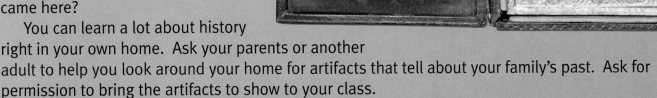

You can learn a lot about history right in your own home. Ask your parents or another adult to help you look around your home for artifacts that tell about your family's past. Ask for permission to bring the artifacts to show to your class.

Remember that old books, magazines, newspapers, journals, photographs, paintings, clothes, quilts, uniforms, medals, and coins can tell us much about the past. What do your artifacts tell you about the history of your family?

Blooming on the Vine

Artifacts Tell a Story

When you need butter for your toast or pancakes, where do you get it? Long ago, people had to make their own butter. They used a butter churn. To make butter, they put cream in the bucket. Then they used the pole to churn the cream. As they moved the pole up and down, the cream got thicker. It took a lot of churning to turn the cream into butter.

Look closely at the butter churn and answer the questions.

1. What is the butter churn made of?
2. Describe how it looks. What color is it? Is it smooth or rough?
3. Who might have used it?
4. Where might it have been used?
5. What does it tell us about the life and times of the people who used it?

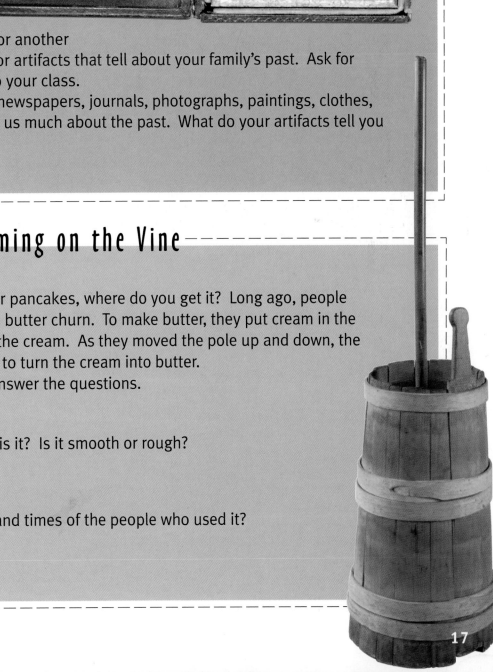

"At the foot hills of the Appalachian chain, Down through the rivers, to the coastal plain, There's a place that I call home, And I'll never be alone, Singin' this Carolina love song . . ."

—*from* South Carolina on My Mind *by Hank Martin and Buzz Arledge*

2

These children are fishing near Hilton Head Island. Do you like to play outside? Have you been to the beaches and mountains? What do you know about the land in our state?

The Story of a Place

Photo © Eric Horan

Lesson 1

PLACES TO LOCATE
Pee Dee River
Santee River
Savannah River

WORDS TO UNDERSTAND

agriculture
basin
climate
economy
geography
goods
human system
hurricane
industry
manufacturing
natural resource
port
precipitation
river system
services
temperature
tourism
tributary

The Land We Call Home

South Carolina seems very large to us, yet it is only one small part of the world. South Carolina is important to us because it is our home. People all over the world live in places that are important to them.

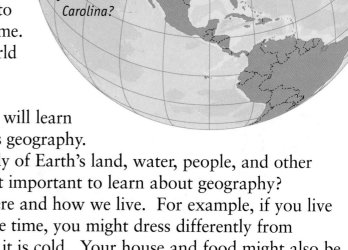

Our world is the planet Earth. Can you find South Carolina?

In this chapter, we will learn about South Carolina's geography. *Geography* is the study of Earth's land, water, people, and other living things. Why is it important to learn about geography? Geography affects where and how we live. For example, if you live where it is warm all the time, you might dress differently from people who live where it is cold. Your house and food might also be different.

Geography Is a Stage

Have you ever seen a play? People decorate the stage to help tell the story. If history were a play, then geography would be the stage. It is the setting for our state's story.

Location is part of geography. Can you imagine what our state would be like if it was not next to the ocean? When we learn about a place, it is helpful to ask certain questions. They are:

• Where is it located?
• Why is it there?
• What is special about its location?
• How is the place related to other places?

Can you answer these questions about the place where you live? To start, look at a map of our state.

20

The South Carolina Adventure

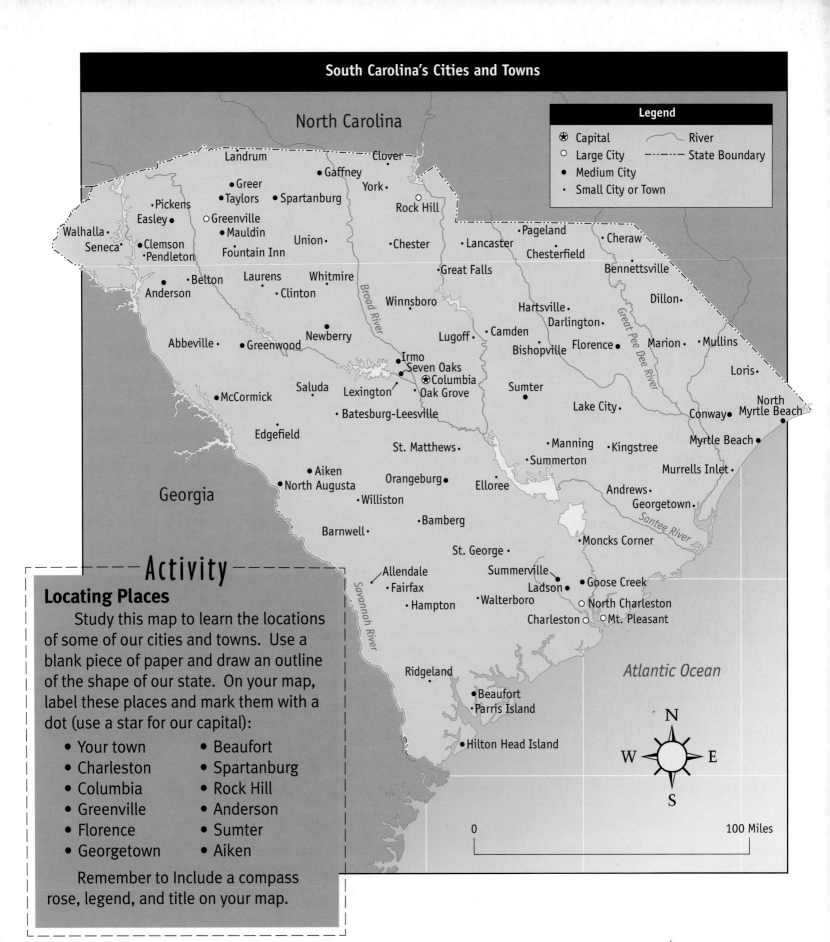

South Carolina's Cities and Towns

North Carolina

Legend
- ⊛ Capital
- ○ Large City
- ● Medium City
- · Small City or Town
- ⌇ River
- —·— State Boundary

Landrum · Clover
· Greer · Gaffney
· Taylors York ·
· Pickens · Spartanburg Rock Hill ○
Easley · ○ Greenville
Walhalla · · Mauldin Union · Chester ·
Seneca · · Clemson Fountain Inn
· Pendleton · Pageland · Cheraw
· Belton Laurens Whitmire Great Falls · Lancaster · Chesterfield
Anderson · · Clinton Winnsboro · Bennettsville
Abbeville · · Greenwood Newberry Hartsville · Dillon ·
Broad River Lugoff · · Camden Darlington ·
Irmo Bishopville · Florence · Marion · · Mullins
McCormick · Saluda · Seven Oaks · Columbia Sumter · Loris ·
Lexington Oak Grove · Great Pee Dee River
· Batesburg-Leesville Lake City · North
Edgefield Conway · Myrtle Beach
St. Matthews · Manning · Kingstree Myrtle Beach ·
· Aiken Orangeburg · Summerton · Murrells Inlet ·
· North Augusta Elloree · Andrews ·
Georgia · Williston Georgetown ·
· Bamberg Santee River
Barnwell · St. George · Moncks Corner
Allendale Summerville · Goose Creek
Savannah River · Fairfax Ladson · ○ North Charleston
· Hampton · Walterboro Charleston ○ ○ Mt. Pleasant
Ridgeland
Atlantic Ocean
· Beaufort
· Parris Island
N
W E
S
· Hilton Head Island

Activity

Locating Places

Study this map to learn the locations of some of our cities and towns. Use a blank piece of paper and draw an outline of the shape of our state. On your map, label these places and mark them with a dot (use a star for our capital):

- Your town
- Charleston
- Columbia
- Greenville
- Florence
- Georgetown

- Beaufort
- Spartanburg
- Rock Hill
- Anderson
- Sumter
- Aiken

Remember to Include a compass rose, legend, and title on your map.

0   100 Miles

The Story of a Place
21

South Carolina's Rivers

You have probably seen at least one river in our state. That's because there are so many of them. Look at the map. Can you see how many rivers we have?

Boats once traveled along our rivers to move supplies and crops. Today, people use our rivers for things like fishing and boating. Some of our rivers help make electricity.

River Systems

Many of our rivers never reach the ocean. Instead, they flow into other rivers. When this happens, the rivers they empty into become bigger. Rivers that empty into other rivers are called *tributaries*.

As rivers empty into other rivers, they make a *river system*. Our state's four main river systems are the Santee, the Savannah, the Pee Dee, and the Edisto. The land surrounding each river system is called a *basin*.

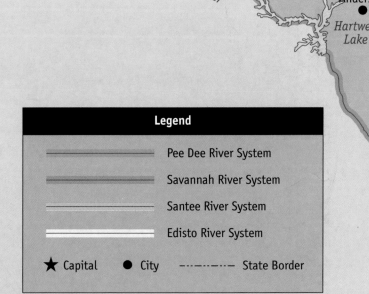

Legend

———— Pee Dee River System

———— Savannah River System

———— Santee River System

———— Edisto River System

★ Capital   ● City   --------- State Border

Activity

Find the River System

The four main river systems are the Santee, the Savannah, the Pee Dee, and the Edisto. Can you find these rivers on the map? Pretend your finger is a fish, and follow these rivers all the way to the ocean. Then answer these questions:

1. Which three rivers form the border between South Carolina and Georgia?
2. Which two lakes are on the Savannah River?
3. Which large lake is connected to the Santee River?
4. Which rivers make up the Pee Dee River system?
5. Which two rivers empty into the Edisto River?
6. There are other important rivers that do not empty into the four river systems. Find the Ashley and Cooper Rivers. What city are they near?

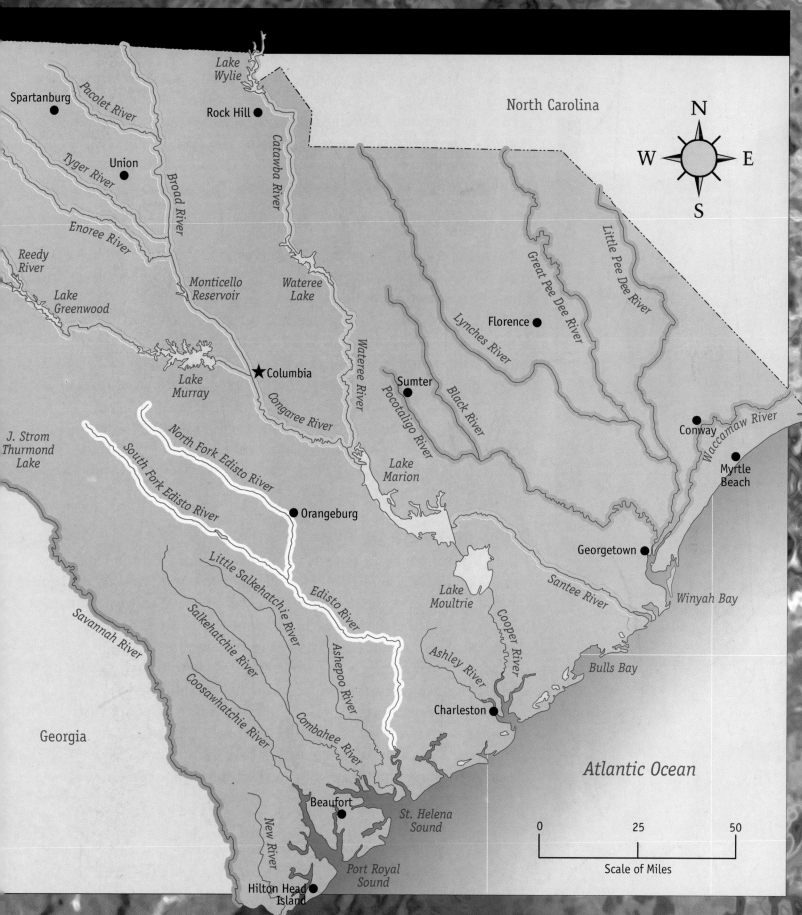

Human Systems

Now you know where some of our towns and cities are located. Do you know why they were built there? Some of our towns were started because they were near rivers, railroad tracks, or roads. Some of our towns were started because the land in the area was good for farming. Towns and cities are types of **human systems,** or the ways people use and change the land.

Using the Land

The land has a lot to do with the way people live. It has to do with the foods and crops people grow, the clothes they wear, and the kinds of homes they build.

Over time, people have changed the ways they use the land. Long ago, people traveled across the land to hunt animals and gather wild plants for food. They cut trees and moved earth and rocks to build shelters. Later, other people used the land to plant rice and cotton. Many more changes took place.

We still use the land to grow crops. We cut trees to make houses and paper. We make bricks from clay. We build roads, factories, shopping malls, and grocery stores. We use the land for many different things.

Choosing Where to Live

Geography plays a part in where people live. People have choices about where to live. How do they make these choices? One thing that helps people decide is jobs. People have to earn money. If you were a fisherman, you might want to live by the ocean. If you were a banker, you might want to live in a big city.

Many other things help people choose where to live. Some of these things are natural resources, climate, and industries. *Natural resources* are things found in nature that people use. *Climate* is the weather of a place over time. *Industries* are types of businesses. All of these things play a part in our state's *economy,* or the way people make a living. Let's read more about how these things affect where and how people live.

One way people use the land is for farming. This farmer is using a computer. It helps him know which crops need care.

Activity

Where Do People Live?

People live all across our state. In some places, there are a lot of people. In other places, there are fewer people. This map shows the names of our state's counties. Counties are part of our state government. Look at this map to learn more about where people live in our state. Answer these questions:

1. What is the title of the map?
2. What do the lines show?
3. Which 14 counties have the fewest people?
4. Which county do you live in? How many people live in your county?
5. Which five counties have over 200,000 people? Can you name one large city in each of these five counties?

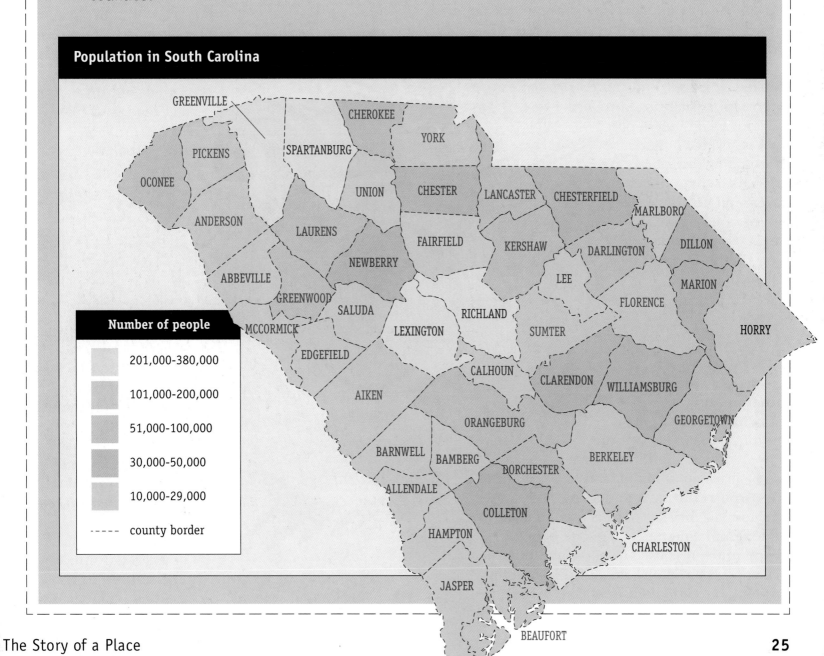

Population in South Carolina

Number of people

201,000-380,000
101,000-200,000
51,000-100,000
30,000-50,000
10,000-29,000
----- county border

Our Natural Resources

In South Carolina, people depend on many natural resources. Let's read about some of them.

Agricultural Products and Timber

Our state is a good place for agriculture. *Agriculture* means raising crops or animals to sell. Farmers grow tomatoes, watermelons, strawberries, cucumbers, soybeans, tobacco, and cotton. They grow a lot of peaches. Have you ever bitten into a juicy peach?

People in South Carolina raise chickens, turkeys, and cattle. These are important agricultural products.

More than half of our state is covered by forests. Forests provide timber. We use timber to build houses, stores, and furniture. People also use trees to make paper. Some farmers grow Christmas trees to sell.

Minerals and Rocks

People use minerals and rocks from South Carolina to build many things. Granite is used to make buildings. It can be crushed to make roads and airport runways. Kaolin is used to make bricks. Marl is used to make cement and concrete. Our state is rich in vermiculite. It is used to make building materials like concrete and plaster. Silica is another mineral found here. It is used to make glass.

Water

Water is one of our most important natural resources. We drink it, cook with it, and bathe in it. We have two types of water: freshwater and saltwater. Freshwater is found in most rivers and lakes. Saltwater is found in the ocean and in some swamps and marshes. Many kinds of fish and sea animals live in saltwater. People catch them for food. People also use the ocean for fun.

Big boats can float in deep ocean harbors. The boats carry tons of goods. *Goods* are things that people make to sell. People need to send their goods to places all over the world. The big boats can do that. They also bring goods from other places to our ports. A *port* is a place where ships can load and unload goods. The boats are loaded with thousands of things, like toys, food, and cars.

Soil

South Carolina has different kinds of soil. In some places the soil is like clay, and it is hard and stiff. In other places the soil is sandy. Some places in South Carolina have good soil for farming. Some soil is also good for forests.

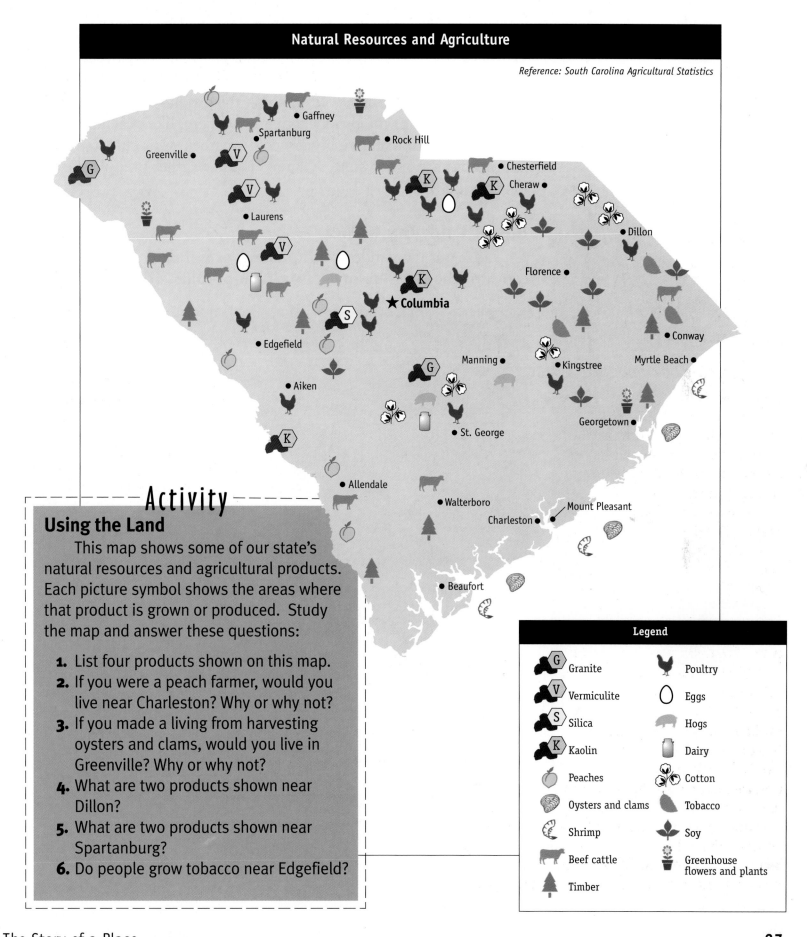

Reference: South Carolina Agricultural Statistics

Activity

Using the Land

This map shows some of our state's natural resources and agricultural products. Each picture symbol shows the areas where that product is grown or produced. Study the map and answer these questions:

1. List four products shown on this map.
2. If you were a peach farmer, would you live near Charleston? Why or why not?
3. If you made a living from harvesting oysters and clams, would you live in Greenville? Why or why not?
4. What are two products shown near Dillon?
5. What are two products shown near Spartanburg?
6. Do people grow tobacco near Edgefield?

Legend

Symbol	Product	Symbol	Product
G	Granite		Poultry
V	Vermiculite		Eggs
S	Silica		Hogs
K	Kaolin		Dairy
	Peaches		Cotton
	Oysters and clams		Tobacco
	Shrimp		Soy
	Beef cattle		Greenhouse flowers and plants
	Timber		

Climate

Can you imagine what it would be like if it were cold here all year long? What if there was snow on the ground for many months? Many of the products that grow here, like peaches and cotton, would not survive in very cold weather. Our climate is an important part of our state. Climate is the weather of a place over a long period of time.

Hot or Cold, Dry or Wet

Look out the window. Is it raining, or is it dry? When you came to school this morning, was it hot or cold? These questions

Tourists at Myrtle Beach help our economy.

Tourism

Our climate is one reason why people like to visit here. They come from places all over the world to see South Carolina. This is called **tourism**. It is a big part of our economy. While tourists are enjoying our nice weather, they spend money at our hotels, restaurants, museums, and stores. Tourism provides many jobs for people in our state. Most of the jobs are **services**. A waiter in a restaurant, a tour guide, and a hotel worker all provide services to tourists.

Hurricanes!

There is one type of dangerous storm that happens in South Carolina. It can happen in the summer and fall. It is called a hurricane. **Hurricanes** are big storms that come from the Atlantic Ocean. When they reach land, they have very strong winds and lots of rain. Because of their strong winds, ocean waves get very high and crash farther onto the land. Some of the strong winds turn into tornadoes, too. There is some good news about hurricanes. Bad ones only hit our state about once every 25 years.

When Hurricane Hugo hit in 1989, the winds were very strong. This boat was blown onto the streets in Charleston.

have to do with our climate. *Precipitation* is water that falls to Earth. It could be snow or rain. *Temperature* is a measure of how hot or cold the air is.

Most of the time, our state gets plenty of sunshine and a good amount of rain. In the winter, some places in our state get snow. Most of the snow falls in the mountains, and in cities like Greenville and Spartanburg. Sometimes those places get ice storms.

Activity

Reading Climate Maps

These maps give information about South Carolina's climate. Use the maps to answer these questions:

1. What is the title of the map that shows how much water falls in South Carolina?
2. What is the title of the map that shows temperatures in the summer? What does the word average mean?
3. What is the average temperature of Florence in January and July?
4. How much precipitation falls each year in Spartanburg?
5. How much precipitation falls each year near Myrtle Beach?

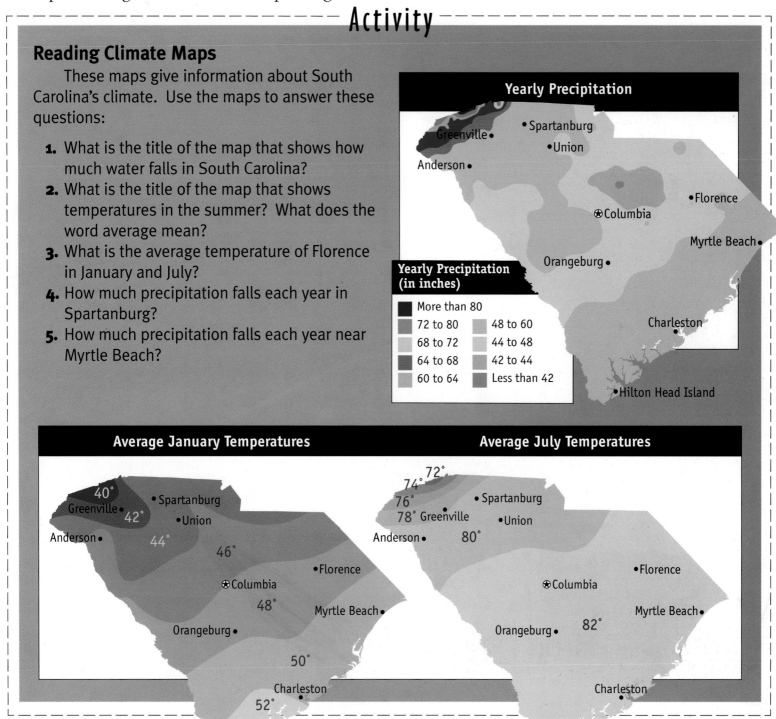

Yearly Precipitation

Yearly Precipitation (in inches)

- More than 80
- 72 to 80
- 68 to 72
- 64 to 68
- 60 to 64
- 48 to 60
- 44 to 48
- 42 to 44
- Less than 42

Average January Temperatures

40° 42° 44° 46° 48° 50° 52°

Average July Temperatures

72° 74° 76° 78° 80° 82°

Top: *Michelin Tire Corporation is part of the automotive industry. Over 6,500 people in our state work for the company. It has factories in Spartanburg, Lexington, Greenville, Laurens, and Anderson Counties.*

Left: *Large boats carry many goods in and out of the port of Charleston. The shipping industry is important to our state's economy.*

Industries

Adults often choose to live in a place where they can have a good job. As you have read, people in South Carolina have jobs in agriculture and tourism. These are types of industries. There are other important industries in our state, too. Construction, shipping, education, banking, and *manufacturing* are some of them. Making paper, car tires, plastic items, and cloth are examples of manufacturing.

Activity

Industries in Our State

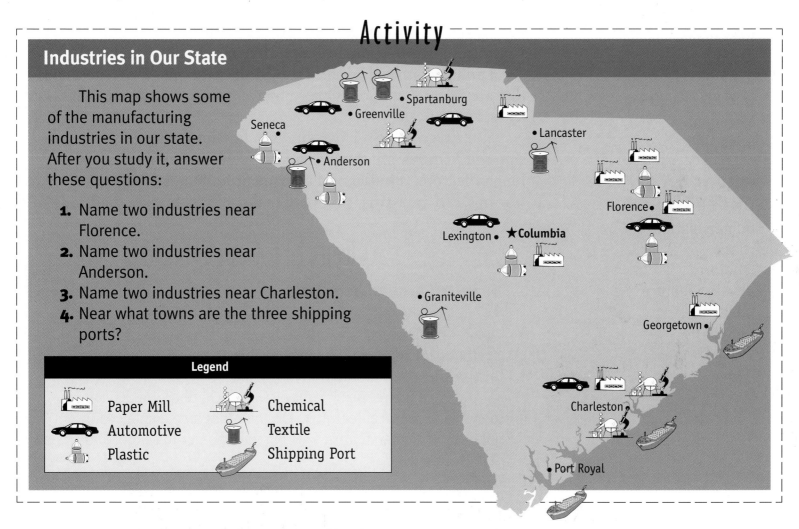

This map shows some of the manufacturing industries in our state. After you study it, answer these questions:

1. Name two industries near Florence.
2. Name two industries near Anderson.
3. Name two industries near Charleston.
4. Near what towns are the three shipping ports?

Legend

🏭 Paper Mill   ⚗️ Chemical

🚗 Automotive   🧵 Textile

🧴 Plastic   🚢 Shipping Port

Memory Master

Lesson 1

1. What is geography?
2. List three of our state's agricultural products.
3. Name our state's four main river systems.
4. What is climate?

Lesson 2

PLACES TO LOCATE
Blue Ridge
Coastal Zone
Inner Coastal Plain
Outer Coastal Plain
Piedmont
Sand Hills

WORDS TO UNDERSTAND
human feature
island
landform
physical feature
plain
region
swamp
tide

What Is a Region?

The world is very big. One way people learn about our world is to think of it in smaller parts. We call these parts regions. A *region* is made up of places that have things in common. Some regions have a wet or dry climate, and other regions have many of the same landforms. *Landforms* are things like mountains or hills.

Landforms are also called *physical features.* These are things that are found in nature. Other physical features are trees, rivers, lakes, and soil.

Some regions also have common human features. *Human features* are things made by people. Your school is a human feature. Houses and apartment buildings are human features. So are barns, shopping malls, roads, bridges, and railroads.

Genuine Genius!

Features Around Your Town

There are many physical and human features in the town where you live. Ask an adult to help you take some pictures of the physical and human features in your town. You can also find pictures on the Internet or in magazines.

Make a poster using your pictures. On one side display your pictures of physical features. On the other side display your pictures of human features. Bring your poster to school and share it with your class.

Our State's Regions

South Carolina's land is not all the same. We have beaches and mountains. We have rivers and swamps. We have salt marshes and thick pine forests. Because our land is not all the same, people divide our state into six different land regions. Look at the map below. What are the six land regions of our state?

Let's pretend we are in a hot-air balloon traveling over our state. We will not see everything, but we'll get a good idea of what the land is like. Hold on tight—we are about to lift off!

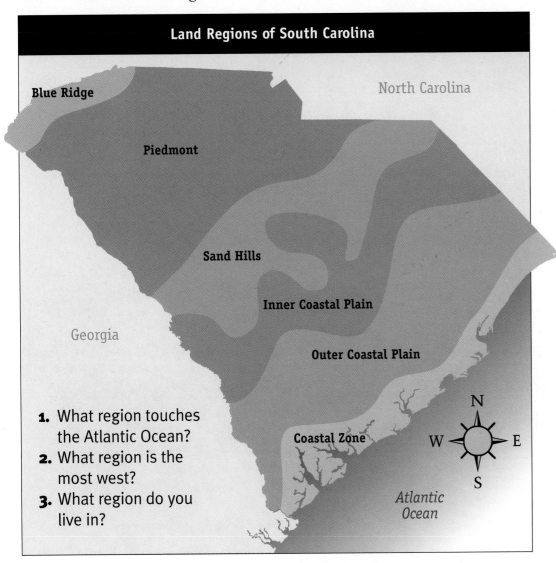

Land Regions of South Carolina

North Carolina

Blue Ridge

Piedmont

Sand Hills

Inner Coastal Plain

Georgia

Outer Coastal Plain

Coastal Zone

Atlantic Ocean

N W E S

1. What region touches the Atlantic Ocean?
2. What region is the most west?
3. What region do you live in?

Table Rock is a physical feature. It is a large rock mountain. It is a gateway to the Blue Ridge Mountains. Can you guess how Table Rock got its name? Does it look like a table?

The Blue Ridge Mountain Region

We'll lift off from the highest point in our state—Sassafras Mountain. Do you see how forests blanket the mountains? If you look closely, you might see some waterfalls crashing to the ground. You might even see people hiking on trails or enjoying lunch at a picnic table. Can you see their campsite nearby?

We are floating over the Blue Ridge Mountain region. It is the smallest land region of our state. The Blue Ridge Mountains make up almost all of this region. There are some small towns, like Walhalla. The air feels cool up here.

What is that roaring sound? It is the sound of rapids on the Chattooga River. Do you see a raft full of people? The ride is cold and fast, but the adventure is great!

Now we see Lake Jocassee. Can you see the large dam there? The dam was built to help make electricity for people living in the region. The lake was made when the river's water built up behind the dam. Today, people enjoy fishing and boating on the lake. They camp at Devils Fork State Park.

Blue Ridge

Physical Features

Blue Ridge Mountains
waterfalls
Chattooga River

Human Features

roads
hiking trails
Jocassee Dam
Walhalla

Can you think of other physical and human features that are part of the Blue Ridge region?

These rafters are enjoying the rapids on the Chattooga River.

The Piedmont Region

We're moving east, and it is easy to see how the land has changed. There are no more mountains, but you can see rolling hills stretch for miles and miles. We are looking at the Piedmont region.

Look at the word *piedmont*. Can you guess what it means? Here is a hint: the first part of the word is *pied*. *Pied* means "foot." *Mont* is short for the word "mountain." Now put the words together: foot and mountain. The piedmont is the land at the foot of the mountains. Sometimes it is called the foothills. One hill called Kings Mountain is near the town of Blacksburg. It is part of a ridge of hills.

In the countryside, you can see apple and peach orchards. Can you see the water tower in Gaffney that looks like a peach? It was built to show how important peaches are in this area.

You might see workers cutting down trees in a forest. Some workers might be cutting Christmas trees. Can you see dairy cows grazing in the fields below? If you listen, you might be able to hear the Savannah River flowing. People like to fish and canoe there.

Some of the larger cities in the Piedmont are Anderson, Greenville, Spartanburg, and Rock Hill. As we travel over these cities, what do you see? Can you see an airport near Greenville? Can you see buildings and roads in the other cities?

Piedmont

Physical Features

Savannah River
Kings Mountain
rolling hills

Human Features

farms	Rock Hill
Anderson	Spartanburg
Greenville	Blacksburg

Can you think of other physical and human features that are part of the Piedmont region?

People grow Christmas trees on some Piedmont farms.

Would you like to visit the rolling hills of the Piedmont?

The Story of a Place

This pine forest is a physical feature in the Sand Hills.

Sand is a natural feature in Lexington County. People mine it and use it to make glass.

Peachtree Rock is a very old physical feature.

Our capitol building is in Columbia. It is a human feature.

The South Carolina Adventure

The Sand Hills Region

We're getting closer to the ocean, but we're not there yet. Wait! Do you see sand below? You might think we are at a beach, but we are not. We are in the Sand Hills region. The ocean was here a very, very long time ago. The Sand Hills were once the beaches of the ocean.

As we float near Lexington, you'll see Peachtree Rock below. It is a good reminder that the ocean used to cover this land. If you look closely, you can see holes in the rock. They were made by ancient shrimp and worms that lived in the ocean.

Moving on, we can see people at Sesquicentennial (SES kwe sen TEN ee al) State Park. They are riding their bikes on the park's trail. This park is a good place to see how sandy the Sand Hills really are. You can also see many plants growing in the sandy soil. Forests of loblolly pines cover the land, too.

Do you see the capitol building in Columbia? That is where our government leaders meet. Many people live in Columbia. You can see houses in every direction. You can also see many rivers, bridges, and roads.

As in the Piedmont region, you can see peach orchards in the Sand Hills. There are many fields of cotton and soybeans. You will also find turkey and hog farms.

Sand Hills

Physical Features

sandy hills
Peachtree Rock
loblolly pines
Fall Line

Human Features

Columbia
capitol building
turkey farms

Can you think of other physical and human features that are part of the Sand Hills region?

People grow peaches in the Sand Hills.

What is the Fall Line?

Have you heard of a place called the fall line? It is the place where the Piedmont drops to the lower land of the Sand Hills. The fall line is easier to see on a river or a stream. You might see a small waterfall or large rocks in the water. Many years ago when riverboats sailed up our rivers, they could not go any farther up than the fall line.

The Inner and Outer Coastal Plain

Now we're really getting closer to the ocean. We're traveling over a plain. A *plain* is an area of flat land. The land here really does look flat. The land near the ocean is called the Outer Coastal Plain. It is very flat. The land closer to the Sand Hills is called the Inner Coastal Plain. It has some rolling hills.

Because the land here is mostly flat, rivers slow down and spread out here. They don't move fast like the rivers in the Blue Ridge region. Slow rivers often form swamps. Can you see the swamps below? A *swamp* is forest that is flooded with water. Do you see a family walking through the Francis Beidler Forest? It is a good thing they can walk on a boardwalk. They would not want to step on a coiled up cottonmouth snake. If they are very quiet, they might be able to watch a spotted turtle on a rock or hear the sound of an owl.

Can you see Lake Marion and Lake Moultrie? They were made when people built dams across the Santee River.

There are many towns and cities in these regions. Some of them are Orangeburg, Sumter, and Florence. As we go over Darlington, can you hear a roaring sound? What do you think it is? It's the racetrack, and cars are whizzing past the finish line.

You can see farms here. There are fields of tobacco, cotton, strawberries, watermelons, cantaloupes, soybeans, and cucumbers.

▶ Cotton photo by Robert Clark

Inner and Outer Coastal Plain

Physical Features

flat land
Francis Beidler Forest
rolling hills

Human Features

race track
Lake Moultrie
Lake Marion
Sumter
Florence
Orangeburg

Can you think of other physical and human features that are part of the Inner and Outer Coastal Plain regions?

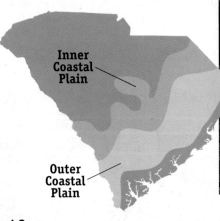

Inner
Coastal
Plain

Outer
Coastal
Plain

Workers harvest tobacco in a field near Conway.

Francis Beidler Forest is a good place to learn about swamps. What human feature do you see here?

ave you seen a field of cotton? This one is in Jasper County.

Visitors come to Charleston to shop
and see historic sites.

People like to
kayak in the
marshes of the
Coastal Zone.

The tide moves in
and out along the
coast.

The Coastal Zone Region

We have arrived at the ocean! Can you smell the saltwater and feel the cool ocean breeze blowing in? This is the Coastal Zone region. There is a lot happening here, so let's go!

Do you see all the people soaking in the sun at Myrtle Beach? It is part of the Grand Strand. Tourists enjoy large hotels, resorts, and shops here.

You can see large ships at the busy ports of Georgetown and Charleston. The ships carry brightly colored shipping containers. Can you see factories? There are large bridges and lots of roads.

Some of the oldest homes in our state are in Charleston. After we're done with our balloon ride, you might want to visit some of them. You'll also see lots of palmettos—our state tree.

If we watch the ocean long enough, you might see the tide change. The *tide* is like the breathing of the ocean. Twice a day the edge of the ocean breathes out, or moves up onto the beaches and into the Coastal Zone. The ocean water rises in the bays and salt marshes. Twice a day, the edge of the ocean breathes in, too. Then the water lowers in the bays and salt marshes.

As we continue down the coast, you will see the Sea Islands. An *island* is a piece of land with water on all sides. There are many islands here. People live on the Sea Islands. Can you see the golf courses on Hilton Head Island? Can you see tomato fields on St. Helena Island?

Look, there is a shrimp boat in the bay. After all this traveling, you are probably hungry. If you like seafood, the Coastal Zone has great places to eat fresh shrimp, oysters, or fish.

Photos © Eric Horan

Coastal Zone
Physical Features
beaches
salt marshes
Sea Islands
Human Features
hotel resorts
bridges
golf courses
historic homes

Can you think of other physical and human features that are part of the Coastal Zone region?

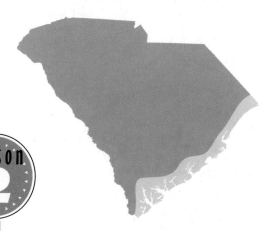

Memory Master

Lesson 2

1. List the six land regions of our state.
2. What is one thing you would see in the Blue Ridge that you would not see in the Coastal Zone?
3. What is one physical feature of the Sand Hills?

Palmetto Detectives
in
SECRET MEANINGS
EXPLAINED

Ms. Izard's class was excited to study South Carolina history. The students remembered the hot-air balloon ride they had taken across the state the day before. Today, they would get to show the new state seals they had made.

Kevin had seen a lot of things at the state museum, but nothing stood out as a perfect symbol for the state. He hoped Ms. Izard and his classmates would understand the secret meaning of his seal.

Ms. Izard asked who wanted to share first, and Christina raised her hand. She held up her seal. It was an odd-shaped triangle. The triangle looked like South Carolina. On the left side of the triangle were mountains. Most of the triangle was filled with little brown and green trees. On the right side, there was a little strip of white next to a big patch of blue.

"When I moved here from Mexico and first saw our state, I thought it was the most beautiful place I had ever seen. I am happy to live in South Carolina. In my seal, I show our beautiful mountains and beaches," said Christina.

Carter showed his seal next. It had two pictures. The first picture was an old sailing ship. It stood for the white settlers who had traveled here long ago on ships. The other picture was the submarine he had talked about. It was a model of the first submarine used in war.

Next, it was Grant's turn to share his seal. His family had lived in South Carolina for many years. Long ago, they had been enslaved. That meant they were owned by other people and were forced to work. Grant was glad South Carolina had changed. He wanted his seal to show people getting along with each other, so he drew a circle of people holding hands.

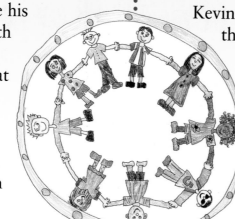

After Grant, Erin showed her seal. It had three pictures. The first picture showed an old plantation where slaves grew cotton. The next picture showed a cotton plant. The last picture showed a cotton mill, where cotton was made into cloth. Erin said her seal showed how cotton had been important to our state.

It was finally Kevin's turn to show his seal. So far, nobody had a seal like his. It wasn't the submarine; it wasn't the mountains; and it wasn't cotton. Kevin held up his seal. It had just one picture.

"It's a telescope!" Erin blurted out. "What does that have to do with South Carolina history?"

Ms. Izard spoke up, "Erin, that is not polite. Kevin, please explain why you picked that for your seal."

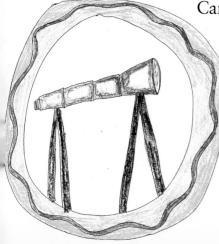

Kevin stood in front of the class. He told them how he and his dad had looked at everything in the museum. One of the last things they found was the telescope. While they were looking through it, his dad said, "Wouldn't it be neat to have a telescope that could look into the past?" Kevin thought it would be neat to look into the future with it, too. When they got home, Kevin's dad remembered he had an old toy telescope. He gave it to Kevin.

Kevin looked at Ms. Izard and then back at the class. He said, "This is my symbol for South Carolina. It stands for how we can look back to the past to understand today."

QUESTION

What did you learn about South Carolina from the state seals the students drew? Answer the following questions:

1. What did Christina's seal show?
2. Name one of the symbols on Carter's seal and tell what it stood for.
3. What did Grant want his seal to show?
4. What did the telescope mean to Kevin?

Chapter 2 Review

Blooming on the Vine

Understanding the Regions

Show what you remember from our hot-air balloon trip. Answer these questions:

1. Read each sentence below, and note if it is true or false:
   a. The Blue Ridge is a beach near the Atlantic Ocean.
   b. "Piedmont" means foothills of the mountains.
   c. The Coastal Zone is next to the ocean.
   d. The Sand Hills are in the middle of our state.
   e. The Inner Coastal Plain has rolling hills.
   f. The Outer Coastal Plain has tall mountains.
2. What region do you live in?
3. Name two physical features and two human features of the region where you live.
4. Read each description and name the region it describes:
   a. This region is flat and has no rolling hills. Rivers run slowly here. There are many swamps.
   b. This region has a lot of beaches and salt marshes. The tide comes in and goes out twice a day.
   c. This region is at the foothills of the mountains. It has rolling hills.
   d. Rivers run fast in this region. They go through mountains.

Blue Ridge

Piedmont

Sand Hills

Inner Coastal Plain

Outer Coastal Plain

Coastal Zone

Genuine Genius!

Make a Brochure

Pretend someone is coming to visit your town, and you want to tell him or her all about the town. Make a brochure about it. Create a page to show each of these things:

- The land and/or water
- Plants and animals
- Things to do
- Different kinds of homes
- The jobs people do
- A map that shows where your town is located

Staple all the pages together into a book, and display your brochure in the classroom.

Geography Tie-In

Common Terms

You might not hear people talk about the Sand Hills very often, but have you ever heard about the upcountry, midlands, and lowcountry? Those are terms that people use to describe the different places in our state. Look at this map. It shows the upcountry, midlands, and lowcountry. Compare it to the land regions map on page 33.

1. What two land regions are part of the upcountry?
2. What two land regions are part of the midlands?
3. What two land regions are part of the lowcountry?

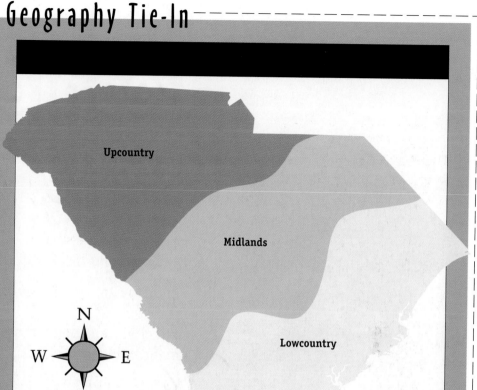

Blooming on the Vine

Why Here?

Have you ever wondered why you live where you do? After reading this chapter, you've learned that geography has something to do with where people live. See how it makes a difference in your life.

1. What jobs do the adults in your family have?
2. Is there another place in our state where they could do the same jobs? Why or why not?
3. Which categories best describe their jobs:
   Natural Resources
   Agriculture
   Manufacturing
   Tourism
   Education
   Other (what?)
4. How does climate affect their jobs?

People of Many Nations

The Eagle and the Rock

I am a Rock and it has an Eagle on it
Like Rock Hill where I live
The Rock is painted by
American Indian artist E. Long
The Rock is green, white and purple
The Eagle is black
I am a Rock on an Eagle
There are Indian words on this Rock
In Cherokee letters
Indians have their own letters
Indians can tell a story
I am a Rock and it has an Eagle on it

—Tyler Beck, Age 6
Member of the Catawba Nation
Rock Hill, South Carolina

Timeline of Events

13,000 B.C.   1000 B.C.   A.D. 1000   A.D. 1100

13,000 B.C.
The first people
enter what is now
South Carolina.

48

Chapter 3

Today, South Carolina is home to many Native Americans. Their ancestors lived here long ago, before any explorers came. The people lived off the land. They hunted animals for food and clothing. They fished and planted crops of corn and squash. The people built homes from bark, logs, or palmetto leaves. They had a rich culture with many traditions. When people from across the ocean came to the land, life for the native people began to change.

1,000 B.C. - A.D. 1700
Native Americans make their homes in the forests and along the coast of what is now South Carolina.

A.D. 1500
Europeans begin to explore North America.

A.D. 1540
Hernando De Soto explores what is now South Carolina.

A.D. 1200	A.D. 1300	A.D. 1400	A.D. 1500	A.D. 1600	A.D. 1700

A.D. 1562
Jean Ribault sets up Charlesfort.

A.D. 1566
Juan Pardo explores what is now South Carolina.

49

WORDS TO
UNDERSTAND
legend
nation

Go Back in Time

Close your eyes for a minute. Imagine you are going back in time. You are going back hundreds of years, before any settlers came across the ocean to South Carolina. There are no cars or highways. There are no airplanes flying in the sky. There are no stores or office buildings. It is very quiet.

All around you are forests. You might smell the ocean close by. Can you see a line of smoke rising from the trees? If you follow the smoke, you might find people cooking food over a fire. The people are dressed in soft deerskins and animal furs. Who are they? They are Native Americans, and they have lived here for thousands of years.

Native People of South Carolina

In the early 1600s, many Native American nations and groups lived here. A *nation* is a large community of people who have many things in common. Some of those things are culture, language, and leadership. Native American nations and smaller groups shared the land we call South Carolina.

Activity

Native American Nations

Study the map to learn where different Native American nations lived. Answer these questions:

1. Name one nation who lived in the upcountry.
2. Name one nation who lived near the coast.
3. Some of our rivers today are named after Native Americans. Use the rivers map on pages 22-23 to help you list three nations who have rivers named after them.
4. Which Native Americans lived closest to where you live today?

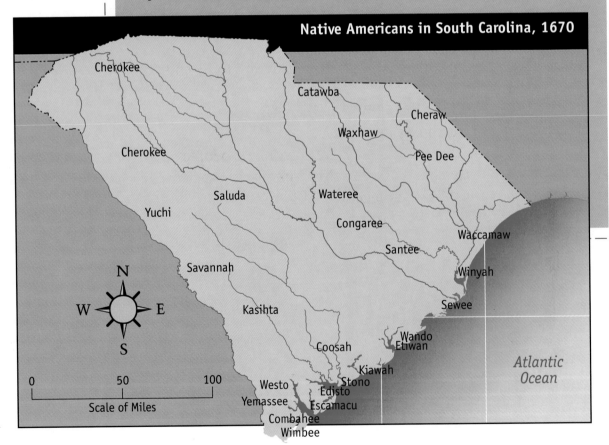

Native Americans in South Carolina, 1670

Cherokee
Catawba
Cheraw
Waxhaw
Cherokee
Pee Dee
Saluda
Wateree
Yuchi
Congaree
Waccamaw
Santee
Savannah
Winyah
Kasihta
Sewee
Coosah
Wando
Etiwan
Kiawah
Atlantic Ocean
Westo
Stono
Edisto
Yemassee
Escamacu
Combahee
Wimbee

N W E S

0   50   100
Scale of Miles

Moving Around

Native Americans didn't always stay in one place. They moved around to find food. They also traveled to other places to trade with other nations. To get to the other places, they followed trails through the woods. They also paddled canoes along rivers or down the coast. Sometimes they traveled hundreds of miles.

The people traded with others to get soapstone. They carved pipes and other things from the soft stone.

Good Times

Native people liked to have fun, too! If they had a good harvest or a good hunt, they celebrated with dances and songs. The Green Corn Festival was an important Cherokee celebration. It lasted for several days, and the people danced and gave thanks for their good harvest.

The people also played games. Stick ball was a game like soccer and hockey combined. Sometimes different villages played against each other. The Cherokee also played a game that was like marbles. They made round marbles by chipping stone.

Learning From Legends

Children learned about their world by listening to legends. *Legends* are stories that tell about the past. Storytelling was a time for sharing and for being close. It was also a time for talking about the good things people did.

Some stories told the history of how a group of people came to be. Some stories explained things, like why there were stars in the sky. Through legends, children learned important lessons. They learned to treat all living things with respect.

In the cold winter months, the people wrapped a warm fur around themselves and passed the time by listening to legends.

HOW FIRE CAME TO THE WORLD

A Cherokee Legend

When the world began, it was a cold place. There was no heat. There was no warmth. Then, suddenly, from the heavens, came a flash of lightning, followed by booming thunder. On an island, the lightning struck inside a hollow tree. A fire started slowly burning.

The animals knew about the fire. They wanted to get it to the mainland. A raven flew across the water and dove down to get the fire, but it was too hot. He was burned forever black by the fire. Reptiles slithered along the water and went close to the flame. They were also burned black by the fire. That is why today they are known as the black racer and the great black snake.

The great horned owl leaped into the air and swooped down to grab the fire, but the flap of his wings stirred the smoke and ash. That is why today the rings around his eyes are white.

Finally, it was the lowly water spider that did what greater animals could not. The spider patiently spun thread. It made a web in the shape of a bowl and placed the web on its back. Inside the bowl, the spider placed an ember from the fire and scurried back across the water. It was that ember that lit the first campfire.

Lesson 1

Memory Master

1. What is a nation?
2. Name one nation who lived in the land we call South Carolina.
3. How did people travel to trade with others?
4. Why did Native Americans share legends?

Living With the Land

Native Americans got everything they needed from nature. They had soil for planting crops. They had forests where they could hunt animals. The forests also gave them wood for making fires and building homes. The ocean and rivers gave the people water for fishing, drinking, cooking, washing, and traveling.

Everything living on Earth was part of a great circle of life. The people saw themselves as part of that circle. They knew if they cared for the land, the land would provide all they needed.

Location

Do you think life was the same for all Native Americans? In some ways it was, but in others it was not. All the people lived off the land, so where they lived affected how they lived. People who lived near the ocean most of the time had things people in the mountains did not have.

PEOPLE TO KNOW
Catawba
Cherokee
Edisto
Yemassee

WORDS TO UNDERSTAND
asi
council
daub
palisade
sapling
tan
wattle
wigwam

Living in the Mountains

Do you remember, from looking at the map, which Native American nation lived in the mountains? It was the Cherokee. They were a large nation with a lot of power. They called themselves *Aniyvwiya* (a-ni-YOO-wi-ya), which means "the real people."

Homes

The Cherokee built villages near rivers and streams in the mountains. They used the rivers for travel. They steered large canoes through the water. If you were a young Cherokee child, you would have bathed in the rivers.

Many villages were surrounded by a tall log wall called a *palisade.* This wall helped protect the people. As many as 600 people lived in a Cherokee village.

The Cherokee had different homes for summer and winter. The summer homes were shaped like large rectangles. They only had one solid wall and a roof made from grass. These homes were mostly open to the air. This kept the people cooler.

The winter homes were round. They were called *asis.* It took a lot of work to build an asi. First, the people had to gather clay and grass. Then they mixed the clay and grass together. This mixture was called *daub.* It was used to make thick walls. Next, they gathered bark and branches, called *wattle,* to use for the roof. The home had no windows. The people hung an animal skin over the small doorway. This helped to keep out the cold.

Inside the asi, the floor was dirt. In the middle of the floor, the women of the house kept a fire going. It helped keep the asi warm. The fire was also used to cook bread and other foods. Smoke from the fire rose up out of the home through a hole in the roof.

The Dugout Canoe

The native people used dugout canoes to travel along rivers, creeks, and bays. People used rivers like we use roads today. Can you imagine riding in a canoe across a river?

Canoes could be up to 60 feet long. How were dugout canoes built? The answer is in the name, "dugout." People dug out canoes from a large tree trunk. Cypress trees made good canoes. So did pine and poplar trees. Look at the pictures. One shows native people building a canoe. You can see a small fire burning inside the log. After the fire burned for a while, the people scraped out the burned wood. They carved the canoes to have flat bottoms and straight sides.

People used canoes to travel along rivers.

The "three sisters"—corn, beans, and squash—were planted close together. The beans climbed up the cornstalks as they grew.

Food

The women of each village worked together to grow crops. They grew corn, beans, pumpkins, squash, and sunflowers. They also gathered crab apples, grapes, cherries, hickory nuts, walnuts, and chestnuts. Young girls worked with their mothers to gather and grow food.

The men were in charge of hunting. They traveled through the forests to hunt deer, rabbits, bears, and turkeys. Young boys went along to learn how to hunt. After hunters brought the animals back to the village, the women cooked the meat.

The men also caught fish in rivers and streams near their homes. The Cherokee sometimes put walnut tree bark in streams and ponds to poison the water. The poisoned water stunned the fish. The fish rose to the top of the water, and the men gathered them.

Clothes

Native people had no stores where they could buy clothes. They made their own clothes from animal hides. Women *tanned* deerskins. First, they scraped off the fur. Then they wet and stretched the skins, so the skins would be smooth and light. The women used needles made from fish bones to sew the skins into clothes.

Winters were cold in the mountains. People wore heavy robes made from thick fur. They wore moccasins on their feet. During the summer, they wore lighter clothes. It was warm enough to walk around with bare feet.

Which man is dressed for winter? Which man is dressed for summer?

Linking the Past to the Present

Native Americans made all of their clothing. They had to hunt, gather, and farm to get food. How do you get your clothes and food?

The South Carolina Adventure

Leaders

There was an important building in the center of each Cherokee village. This was where leaders met as a *council.* They spoke of what was happening in their village. A holy man or woman gave spiritual advice to people.

No one person could make all of the rules. The people of the council had to agree on the rules. There were different leaders who helped the village. The White leader helped during peaceful times. The Red leader helped when the people were at war. Women were part of the council. Older women were honored for their wisdom. Sometimes leaders from many Cherokee villages gathered together. They helped make decisions for all Cherokee people.

Baskets

The Cherokee were very skilled basket-makers. They made baskets from bark, brush, and grasses. They made beautiful patterns on some of their baskets. They used roots, bark, leaves, nuts, flowers, and berries to dye the baskets colors.

The people used baskets to catch fish in rivers and streams. They also used baskets to carry things, much like you use a backpack. The Cherokee also made baskets to hold food. They stored dried corn and beans in the baskets. This helped them have food all year long.

Today, some Cherokee still make baskets. It is one way they keep their culture alive.

People of the village made up the council.

Living in the Piedmont

Like other Native Americans, the people living in the Piedmont region also depended on the land to live. They hunted, farmed, and gathered food. They did some things differently, too.

The Catawba were powerful in the Piedmont region. They called themselves *Ye Iswa*, which means "river people." They built their villages near rivers. They made dugout canoes to travel on the rivers.

Homes

Some Catawba built a palisade around their village. It protected them from attack. Inside the palisade, the people built round homes called **wigwams**. They used wood, bark, and grasses to build their wigwams. In the spring, the people gathered young trees called **saplings**. Saplings could bend easily, so they were good for building wigwams.

The Catawba River is named after the Catawba people. For hundreds of years they traveled on this river in canoes.

A Step-by-Step Wigwam

1

To build a wigwam, the people cut down saplings. They trimmed off the branches. Then they dug holes in the ground and put the saplings in the holes. This held the saplings in place.

2 The people bent the saplings over and tied them together with cord, vines, or animal skins. This made a frame.

3 The people covered the frame with bark or mats made of grasses and reeds. They left a hole in the front for a door. They also left a hole in the roof, so smoke from the fire could escape.

People of Many Nations

Older children helped guard the crops. They scared away birds that came to eat the corn.

Food

The soil next to the rivers was good for growing crops. Like the Cherokee, the Catawba also grew corn, beans, and squash. Women tended these crops. Men hunted deer and other small animals. They caught fish from the rivers.

Clothes

The Catawba wore clothes made from animal skins. During the winter, men and women wore pants and robes. During the summer, men wore something that looked like a leather apron around their waist. Women wore skirts. The people wore special jewelry. They made jewelry from shells, beads, and copper.

Leaders

Like the Cherokee, the Catawba had a council house in their villages. It was where their leaders met. The council spoke about what was happening to their people. They made choices for the village. Near the council house was an open gathering place for meetings, games, and dances.

Catawba Pottery

The Catawba were great potters. They dug clay from the ground. They shaped the clay into pots. This could take many days. Some pots looked like turtles, some were round, and some had animal faces on them.

The people built a very hot fire and put the clay pots inside the fire. The heat made the pots stronger. The Catawba also made special glazes to decorate the pots. Some glazes were made of crushed shells.

Today, the Catawba carry on the tradition of making pottery. The tradition is thousands of years old. The people still dig clay from the ground near their homes. They form their pots and put them in hot fires. The pottery masters teach their children and grandchildren how to make pottery. This is the way the tradition goes on.

Mildred Blue, one Catawba pottery master, learned how to make Catawba pottery from her mother. Her family has passed on the skills for many generations. Mildred taught her nephew how to make pottery. She said "We are keeping alive the only true Catawba craft we have. It won't be forgotten."

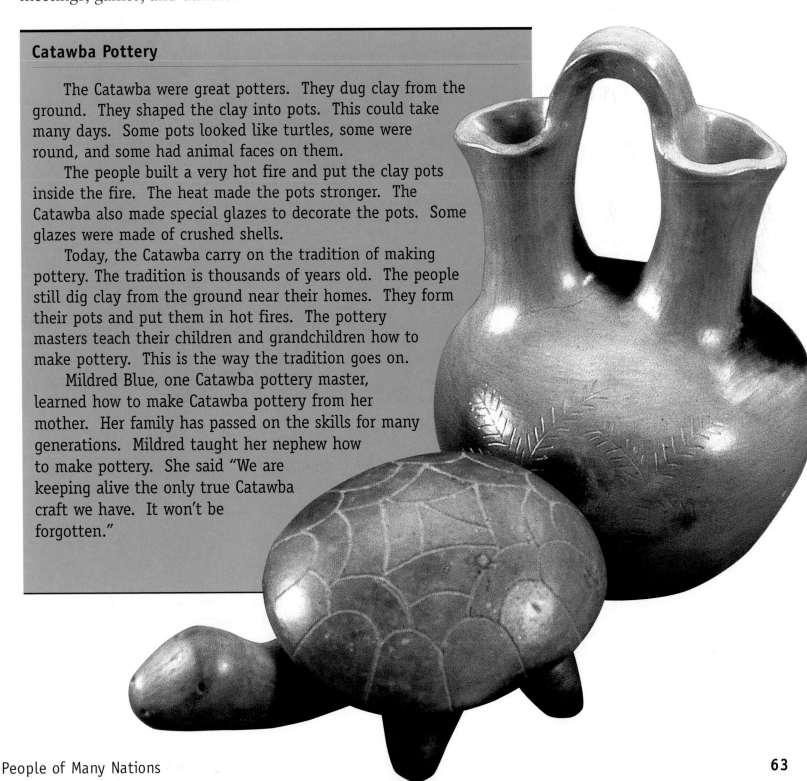

Coastal people spent a lot of time fishing for food in the ocean.

Using Fire

Fire was important. One way the people used fire was to clear a forest. By burning a strip of bark around a tree, people could kill the tree. This made it easier to clear the forests and make new fields for farming.

The people kept fleas and ticks away by burning the brush around the village. Burning brush helped in another way, too. It kept the brush short. If the brush got too tall, it was easier for enemies to sneak up and attack.

Women used fires to cook corn, bake bread, and roast meat. They used fires to make pots. The people built fires for important celebrations.

Living Along the Coast

Many native people lived along the coast. Can you remember who some of the people were? The Edisto and the Yemassee were two of the nations. Which other nations can you find on the map on page 52?

Homes

Most coastal people, like the Edisto, had two types of homes. During the summer, they lived on the beach. They enjoyed the cool ocean breezes. The people built wigwams. Instead of using grasses and bark to cover their homes, they used palmetto leaves. Can you guess why they used palmetto leaves? Palmettos grew all over the coast, so there were always plenty of them to use.

During the rest of the year, the people lived in villages farther inland. They built wattle and daub homes like the Cherokee. Instead of using bark and branches for the roofs, the coastal people used palmetto leaves.

Food

Like all native people, the coastal people hunted animals. They caught fish from the ocean. They gathered clams and oysters, too. They cooked fish and meat on sticks above a warm fire. Women grew corn, beans, and squash.

Clothes

The coastal people made their clothes from animal skins, too. It did not get as cold near the ocean as it did in the mountains, so people did not have to wear heavy robes. They could wear the same clothes all year long. Women wore skirts, and men wore leather aprons around their waists. Some women wore dresses made from Spanish moss. Have you ever seen Spanish moss hanging from large oak trees? The moss grows very well along the coast.

Leaders

The coastal people had leaders, too. If the leader made good decisions, then the people listened to him. They also followed the advice of the council. Many men, and sometimes women, made up the council.

Some coastal people made clothes from Spanish moss.

Memory Master

Lesson 2

1. What type of home did the Cherokee live in during the winter?
2. Where did Cherokee leaders meet?
3. What type of home did the Catawba build?
4. What tree leaf did coastal people use to cover their homes?

Lesson 3

PEOPLE TO KNOW
Christopher Columbus
Hernando De Soto
Gentleman of Elvas
Lady of Cofitachiqui
Juan Pardo
Jean Ribault

PLACES TO LOCATE
Africa
Asia
Caribbean
Europe
France
Spain

WORDS TO UNDERSTAND
conquer
explorer
mica
motive

Searching for a Route to Asia, 1400s

New World
Europe
Asia
Africa
The Indies

- - - - - Traders' Route before 1492
- - - - - Columbus' Route 1492

Explorers Come From Far Away

Many native people made their home in this land. They built villages here. Then people from other places came to the land. The people were *explorers* from far away. They traveled across the Atlantic Ocean from countries in Europe.

The New World

Europeans had been trading with people in Africa and Asia for many years. They got rugs, silk, gems, and spices from those lands. But they had to travel a long way to get the things they wanted. The trip to Asia by land was long and full of danger. Explorers wanted to find a shorter route.

One of the first explorers who looked for a shorter route to Asia was Christopher Columbus. The king and queen of Spain paid for his journey. Columbus did not find a shorter route. He landed in islands in the Caribbean.

Columbus claimed the land for Spain. It did not matter to the European explorers that native people lived there. Soon, other explorers followed. Many Europeans felt that the native people were not important because they looked different and had different beliefs. Europeans felt they had a right to *conquer,* or take over, the native people.

How New Was the New World?

Europeans called the land Columbus claimed the "New World." But it was not really new. Thousands of people, like the Cherokee and Catawba, had been living there for thousands of years. The land was only new to the Europeans.

For King and Country

Kings and queens in Europe wanted to send explorers to the New World. New land and riches were big *motives,* or reasons, for exploration. The kings and queens of Spain and France paid explorers to make the journey. They bought ships and supplies. They paid sailors to work on the ships.

When the explorers claimed land in new places, they claimed it for their king and queen. Their travels were "for King and Country." This meant that when explorers found land, it belonged to their king and country.

We are going to read about three explorers. They are Hernando De Soto, Jean Ribault, and Juan Pardo. Look at the map to see where they traveled.

Activity

Explorers' Routes

Before you read about each explorer, look at this map to see each man's route. Answer these questions:

1. Which two men explored for Spain?
2. Which man explored for France?
3. Which two explorers traveled inland?
4. Which explorer only traveled along the coast?

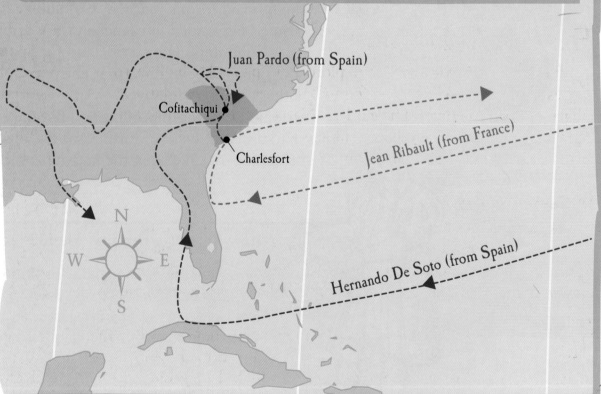

European Explorers to South Carolina

Juan Pardo (from Spain)

Cofitachiqui

Charlesfort

Jean Ribault (from France)

Hernando De Soto (from Spain)

De Soto and his men wore shiny armor. What do you think Native Americans thought when they met the Spanish explorers?

Hernando De Soto

Hernando De Soto was an explorer for Spain. He had heard stories about Cofitachiqui (ko-fe-ta-CHEE-kee). It was a large village of native people. His guide, a Native American named Pedro, told De Soto there was gold and silver in Cofitachiqui. De Soto wanted to find the village and take its riches.

In Search of Gold

De Soto sailed from Spain on wooden ships with an army of 600 men. They landed in what is now Florida. As they marched north, they heard more stories of Cofitachiqui. This made the explorers even more excited. Pedro kept telling his story of gold and silver.

No one knows for sure where the men marched, but we do have a good idea. A man known as the Gentleman of Elvas kept a journal, where he wrote down the events of each day. From the journal, we have a good idea of where De Soto marched with his army.

Disease

As De Soto marched toward Cofitachiqui, the Gentleman of Elvas wrote about seeing empty villages.

Why were the villages empty? Even before De Soto came, other people from Spain had visited the land. They brought diseases that were common in Spain. The native people in the New World never had the diseases. When they got sick, their bodies could not fight off the germs. Many of the native people died. Sometimes everyone in a whole village died.

Finding Cofitachiqui

When De Soto found Cofitachiqui, he sent men to the village to see what was there. They went out during the night. The men saw the twinkling of fires. They heard children playing and dogs barking. They heard men and women talking. They crept closer and closer to the village.

The next day, De Soto went to a place on the river across from the village. Pedro shouted to the men on the other side. He told the men to cross the river and visit De Soto.

The native men climbed into dugout canoes and paddled across the river. De Soto told them he had come in peace. He also said his army needed supplies to keep going on their journey. Men from Cofitachiqui told De Soto that their people would help.

A Lovely Lady

A woman was carried across the river in a canoe. The canoe had a roof and two cushions for the lady to sit on. In his journal, the Gentleman of Elvas called her the Lady of Cofitachiqui.

This might be what Cofitachiqui looked like.

The South Carolina Adventure

The lady gave gifts of animal skins and cloth to De Soto. She also took a necklace of pearls from around her neck and gave it to him, but she gave him no gold or silver.

After De Soto and his men visited the village, the Lady ordered her people to welcome them. They fed the men turkey and deer meat. It wasn't long before De Soto asked them what was on his mind. Where was the gold and silver?

The Lady told her people to bring De Soto what he wanted. They brought out their pearls and shiny rocks. De Soto and his men looked at each other. They were not happy. It was not gold. It was not silver. The shiny pieces were copper and *mica,* a rock that sparkled in the sunlight.

De Soto Behaves Badly

The people of Cofitachiqui had been kind to the explorers, but De Soto and his men began to act badly. They took all the pearls they could find. They took much of the native people's corn.

The people grew angry with De Soto. The Lady tried to run away into the forest. De Soto heard of her plan and captured her. He told her she would be their guide to new lands.

De Soto and his men marched on. Guided by the Lady, the native people gave De Soto's army everything it asked for. Then the Lady escaped and returned to her people.

This was the first time many of the people of Cofitachiqui had seen the white people from across the ocean. They had welcomed the explorers, but they had been treated badly. Little did the people know that more and more white people from across the ocean would come.

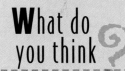

What do you think?

How would you feel if you welcomed strangers into your home, and they treated you badly?

The Gentleman of Elvas

Thanks to people like the Gentleman of Elvas, we know more about the past. His journal tells us many things. De Soto crossed the Blue Ridge Mountains. Elvas wrote about that. De Soto was the first person from Spain to see the Mississippi River. Elvas wrote about that, too.

Because the Gentleman of Elvas wrote about what he saw and heard, we know the story of De Soto and his journey. We also know how some of the explorers felt about things.

When you read about De Soto capturing the Lady, how did you feel? Did you feel sad for the Lady? Read what the Gentleman of Elvas wrote about that part of the story. How did he feel about the Lady's capture?

[De Soto] ordered a guard to be placed over her and took her along with him; not giving her such good treatment as she deserved for the good will she had shown him and the welcome she had given him.

This drawing shows Ribault's ships arriving at Port Royal. It shows the stone that Ribault placed on the island to claim the land. What other things do you see that show what the place was like? Can you see animals, trees, and berries? Can you find Native American homes?

Charlesfort ●

Jean Ribault

Not long after De Soto explored our land, other explorers followed. France didn't want Spain to claim all the land in the New World. A wealthy man in France had an idea. He was part of a group called Huguenots, who had different beliefs than others. They were not well-liked. The wealthy man thought the Huguenots could move to the New World. He sent Jean Ribault to start a settlement.

Port Royal and Charlesfort

Ribault led a group of 150 men, and they sailed on two ships. It took two months for the men to arrive in the New World. First they landed in Florida. Then they traveled up the coast. They came upon a harbor and decided it was a good place to build a village. Ribault named the place Port Royal.

Within five days of arriving, Ribault's men cut down enough trees to build a fort. It was a place where they could protect their settlement from attackers. It was named Charlesfort, in honor of the French king.

Ribault traveled to a nearby island. He set a large stone on the ground. A symbol for France was carved on the stone. The stone showed that France had claimed the land.

Leaving

Soon, Ribault and many of his men returned to France. They wanted to get supplies to help the men at Charlesfort. But Ribault faced troubles in Europe, and he was not able to return to Charlesfort.

Some of Ribault's men had stayed behind at Charlesfort. They were not happy when Ribault did not return with supplies. They got some food from nearby Native Americans, but they were not able to grow food of their own. They had built Charlesfort in a swamp. After a while, they gave up. They headed back home to France.

● Santa Elena

Juan Pardo

Spain did not like the idea of the French claiming land in the New World. They heard about Charlesfort, and they sent men to check things out. When the Spanish men arrived, the French men had already left. The Spanish removed the stone that Ribault had placed on the island, and they burned what was left of Charlesfort.

A while later, Spain built a fort of its own where Charlesfort had been. The fort was called Santa Elena. From this fort, Juan Pardo began his journey into our state. The Spanish wanted to learn more about the land beyond the coast. They wanted to see if there was any gold or silver. They also wanted Juan Pardo to meet Native Americans, and let them know that Spain was their friend. The Spanish wanted good relationships with the Native Americans because they needed to trade furs and other things with them.

Look back at the map of explorers on page 68. Can you see that Juan Pardo traveled inland? What town did he travel through that De Soto also visited?

Some scientists learn about the past by digging in the dirt. Here they are looking for clues about Santa Elena.

Memory Master

Lesson **3**

1. What does "for King and Country" mean?
2. What Native American village did De Soto visit?
3. Name the fort that Jean Ribault built.
4. What country sent Juan Pardo to explore the New World?

Palmetto Detectives
in
A VISIT TO COFITACHIQUI

"So what should we do?" Grant asked Kevin.

It was Saturday afternoon, and the boys were sitting outside. Grant's mom had dropped him off at Kevin's.

"Want to watch TV?" Kevin asked.

"No, I can always do that at home," Grant said. "What about that telescope your dad gave you?"

"What about it?"

"Let's play with that. Come on!"

Kevin got the telescope and gave it to Grant. Grant put it up to his eye.

"Yes, there it is!" Grant shouted.

"There's what?" Kevin asked.

"It's De Soto's army. And there's the Lady of Cofitachiqui!"

"Let me see that." Kevin grabbed the telescope out of Grant's hands.

"Wow!" Kevin said, "I can actually see the native people crossing the river! They are going to talk to De Soto." "Yeah, I see them too!" Grant said.

Chapter 3 Review

Activity

Write a Story About Native American Life

Go back and look at the pictures in this chapter. What do they show about how the native people lived?

Use the pictures to help you imagine what it was like to be a native girl or boy long ago. Then write a story about one day or one event. What would you do for fun? What was happening in the village? What was your house like? These are just some of the things you could write about. You could even draw a picture to go with your story.

Genuine Genius!

Act It Out!

The story of De Soto and Cofitachiqui is full of action! It's your turn to act it out. You can work together as a class or in small groups.

First, you need to write a skit. Your skit should tell the story of De Soto's travels. You can fill in some details from what you read in this chapter. Your main characters should be:

- De Soto
- Gentleman of Elvas
- Lady of Cofitachiqui

You could also have a narrator. What other characters would you choose? Choose people to play the parts, find some simple costumes, and you are set! Enjoy the show!

Living Near Water

Many native people built their villages near rivers, streams, or the ocean. Rivers and streams gave them plenty of water to drink. The people could water their crops more easily if they lived near water. People could also catch fish in the rivers and ocean. Birds and animals came to the water to drink, so hunting was good there. The people also traveled in canoes on rivers.

Can you think of other reasons why the native people lived near water? Why do people choose to live where they do today?

Blooming on the Vine

Comparing Cultures

Native people from different nations had some things in common. They also did some things differently. Much of their culture was based on where they lived. You have read about native people who lived in the mountains, the Piedmont, and along the coast. How were their lives the same? How were they different?

On your own paper, make a diagram like this one. Read through the chapter to fill in the spaces. Look at the types of homes the people in each area built. Look at the types of clothes they wore and the foods they ate.

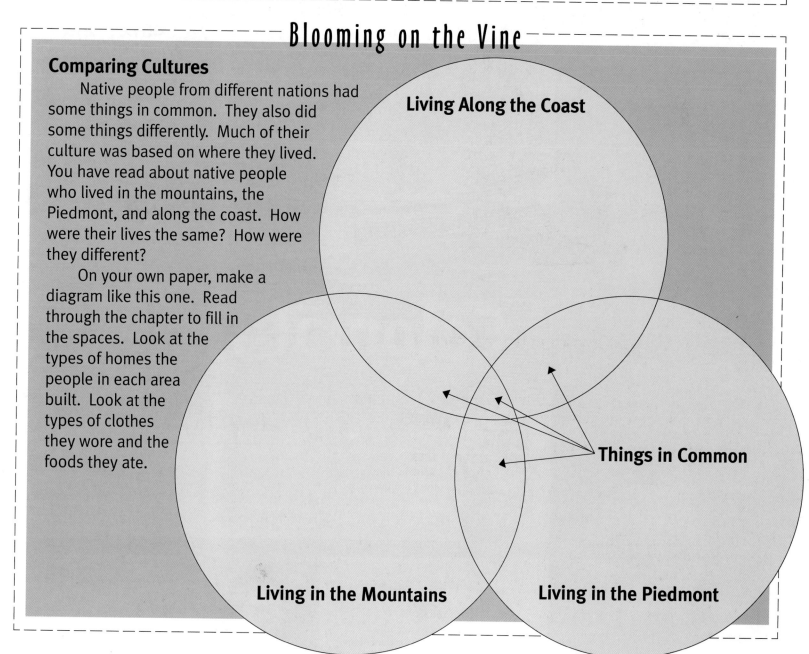

Living Along the Coast

Things in Common

Living in the Mountains

Living in the Piedmont

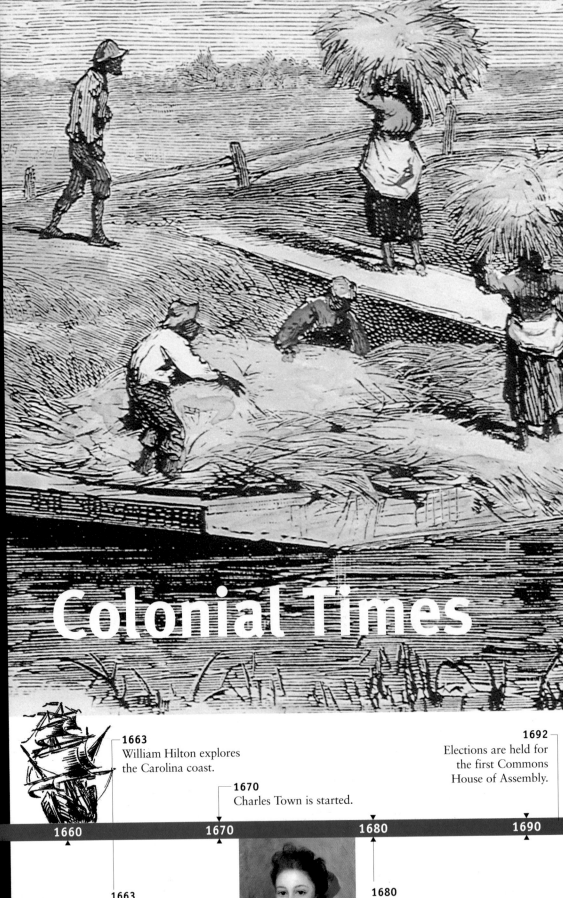

"[*S*wamps are] the Golden Mines of Carolina; from them all our Rice is produced . . . they are the Source of infinite Wealth, and will always reward the industrious and persevering Planter."

—*George Milligan-Johnston*

Colonial Times

Timeline of Events

1663
William Hilton explores the Carolina coast.

1670
Charles Town is started.

1692
Elections are held for the first Commons House of Assembly.

1660　　　　　　1670　　　　　　1680　　　　　　1690

1663
England grants a charter for the colony of Carolina.

1680
Huguenots begin to move to the colony.

Chapter 4

Rice was a very important cash crop in South Carolina. Slaves planted, cared for, and harvested it, but white planters were the ones who became rich from this "Carolina Gold."

1708
Africans become the majority of the colony's population.

1710
Some historians believe this is the year the Carolina Colony split into North and South Carolina.

1739
Stono Rebellion

1740
South Carolina creates new slave laws.

1745
Indigo becomes an important cash crop.

1700   1710   1720   1730   1740   1750

early 1700s
Rice becomes the cash crop for the colony and is called "Carolina Gold."

1715-1717
Yemassee War

1716-1718
Pirates roam the coast and steal ships and treasures.

1730s
German and Scots-Irish people begin moving to South Carolina. Many of them settle in the backcountry.

PEOPLE TO KNOW

Anthony Ashley Cooper
William Hilton
Kiawah
John Locke
Lords Proprietors
Henry Woodward

PLACES TO LOCATE

Ashley River
Barbados
Charles Town
Cooper River
England
Hilton Head Island

WORDS TO UNDERSTAND

charter
colony
experience
experimental
treaty

Charles Towne Landing

Welcome to Charles Towne Landing! This is where the first English colonists of Carolina made their homes. Let's pretend that we have traveled to the past, and we are seeing what it was like when the settlers first arrived.

Arrival!

Do you see the small boats in the Ashley River floating toward shore? They are carrying passengers and supplies from the ship *Carolina*. The land around them is wild. Trees and brush grow everywhere. Snakes and wild animals like wolves live in the thick swampy forests. The settlers have never lived in a land like this. It will be much different from their old land.

The settlers are worried about their safety. They know the native people living here might not be happy about white settlers moving in. Look at the palisade the settlers are building.

A Garden

Let's go inside the palisade and look at the town. Can you see the garden with the plants beginning to grow? Before the settlers left England, they were told what crops they should plant. They were told to plant olives, ginger, and indigo. These plants were hard to find in England, so they would sell for a high price. The settlers were not sure these plants would grow in the colony, so they planted an experimental garden. *Experimental* means something is being tested.

The colonists also needed to plant crops for food. They asked the Native Americans how to do this. Soon they had crops of corn, peas, and grains.

This palisade was built at Charles Towne Landing to look like the one the settlers built.

This home at Charles Towne Landing was built to look like an early settler's home.

A Home

There are men building a house. When the house is finished, it will have one big room. It will have a fireplace for cooking and keeping the house warm. The settlers will have to do everything themselves. They were not able to bring much with them from their old land. They will have to grow and cook all their food. They will make their own clothes and soap. They will have to carry water from the river.

How Did This Happen?

Now that you've looked around Charles Towne Landing, are you wondering how it all came to be? There's a good story behind that question. Let's read about how South Carolina got started.

Linking the Past to the Present

You can visit Charles Towne Landing today. You can see what the settlers' homes looked like. You can see what crops they grew and where the palisade was located. You can also see a forest that is home to black bears, alligators, wolves, and other animals.

Colonists had to provide everything they needed themselves. They even had to make their own thread and cloth.

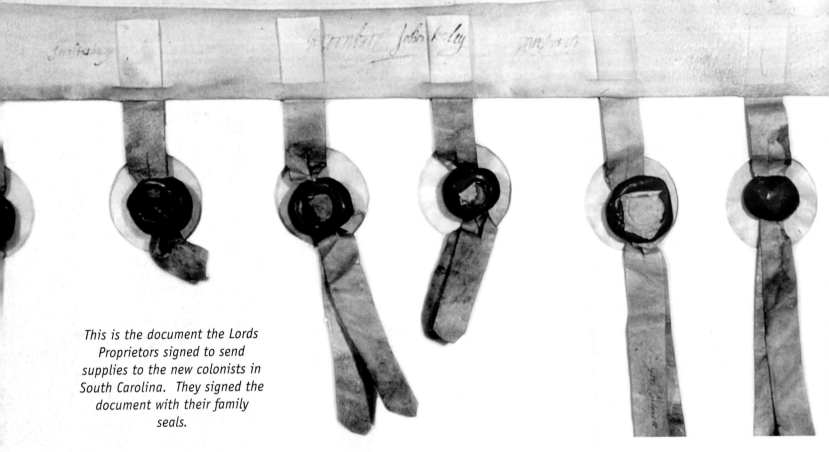

This is the document the Lords Proprietors signed to send supplies to the new colonists in South Carolina. They signed the document with their family seals.

A Colony

People in Europe had known about our land for many years. They learned about it from explorers like De Soto, Ribault, and Pardo. People in England wanted to start a colony in the New World. A *colony* is a settlement under the control of another nation.

The Start of Carolina

The king of England granted a charter for a new colony. A *charter* is a document that gives special rights to people. This charter gave eight men, called the Lords Proprietors, the right to a large piece of land. The land was called Carolina.

The king of England said the Lords Proprietors could rule Carolina. But the new rulers did not plan to live there. Instead, they wanted to send settlers to the colony. They wanted the settlers

The South Carolina Adventure

to grow crops. The eight British men hoped to make a lot of money from selling the crops.

Many of the Lords Proprietors only wanted to grow richer, but one of the men, Anthony Ashley Cooper, really wanted the colony to succeed. He wanted people from all over Europe and other English colonies to come to Carolina, so he came up with a way to get them to make the journey. He wrote a plan for government called the Fundamental Constitutions of Carolina. A man named John Locke helped him write it.

The laws in the Fundamental Constitutions were meant to draw people to the colony. They allowed freedom of religion. They said that if a person went to court and was found innocent, he couldn't be tried again for the same crime. The laws promised free land. They also allowed slavery.

Ashley Cooper's plan worked. People were excited to come to a place where they could practice their religion freely and own land.

Anthony Ashley Cooper wanted the colony to succeed and grow.

Blooming on the Vine

Advertising Land!

The Lords Proprietors wanted people to move to Carolina. They placed ads in newspapers that described Carolina. Here is what one said:

> All those intend to go Passengers to Carolina, with Families or without; or, those that desire to be entertained as Servants, may repair with speed to the Sign of the Barbadoes . . . where they may be informed . . . [of] the Advantage of that Healthful and Plentiful Country.
>
> —The True Protestant Mercury, May, 1681

1. What two words does the ad use to describe Carolina? What do these words mean?
2. If you were living in a crowded city in Europe, and you did not have a job, would the ad make you want to go to Carolina?
3. Is this ad like ones in newspapers today? Explain your answer.

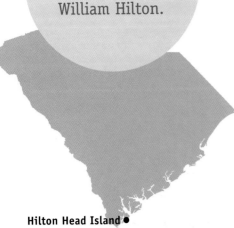

Have you heard of Hilton Head Island? Can you guess who it is named after? You're right! It is named after the explorer William Hilton.

Hilton Head Island ●

William Hilton

Many people in England were excited to start a new life in the colony, but they needed to know where to settle. William Hilton was sent to find the best places. He set out from an island called Barbados to explore the Carolina coast in a boat called the *Adventure*.

What kind of place was Hilton looking for? He was looking for land with good soil, rivers, and trees. All of these things would help settlers build a rich colony. With good soil, they could plant many crops. With rivers and the ocean, they could ship their crops. With trees, they could build homes and ships.

After searching the coast, Hilton found a place that had all of these things. He wrote about it in a book. He made the land sound wonderful. He wrote, "The air is sweet, the country very pleasant and delightful, we wish that all [those people] wanting a happy settlement were . . . here."

What do you think?

Read Hilton's words again. Why do you think he wanted to make the land sound good?

Henry Woodward

An explorer named Robert Sanford was also sent to explore the Carolina coast. On board with him was a doctor named Henry Woodward. The young doctor was interested in the language and culture of Native Americans.

As Sanford prepared to sail back to England, a Native American man decided to sail back with him. The man wanted to learn about English culture. Woodward agreed to stay with the native people to learn their language and become friends with them.

Woodward spent many years exploring what is now South Carolina, Georgia, and Florida. He helped start the fur trade between the English and Native Americans by signing a treaty with the Westos. A *treaty* is an agreement.

Many people believe Woodward was one of the first Europeans to grow rice in South Carolina. They say a ship captain gave Woodward a bag of rice in return for his kindness. Woodward planted the rice, so he could get more seed.

Leaving England

Soon, three more ships left England to head for the colony. On board were more than 100 people. Most of the settlers were men, but women were also on the ships.

A Stop in Barbados

The ships sailed across the ocean, but they were not going to Carolina. They headed for an island called Barbados. The settlers needed to learn some things there. They did not know how to build a town in a new place.

English people had lived in Barbados for a while. They had experience in setting up a colony. *Experience* is what you learn from things you have done. The English from Barbados could teach the settlers how to survive in Carolina. Some of the people from Barbados joined the group, and they all sailed for the new colony.

The English from Barbados had owned and run sugar plantations. They brought their knowledge with them to Carolina.

Colonists' Route to Carolina

England

Atlantic Ocean

N
W ⊕ E
S

Carolina

Barbados

Charles Town Begins

When the settlers got to the colony, some men went ashore. The leader of the Kiawah nation met them. He told them to settle where two rivers flow into the sea. Today, we call these rivers the Ashley and Cooper Rivers. At first, the settlers went to another place. But they were not happy with the land there, so they decided to take the Kiawah leader's advice.

The settlers sailed up the Ashley River. They landed at a place they called Albemarle Point. Soon, the 130 colonists from England and Barbados began to build Charles Town.

Too Close for Comfort

If you were a leader of the Kiawah, would you have wanted the white settlement near your people? You might have heard that the white people were greedy. They carried strange diseases that could kill your people. They had even enslaved some of your men. So why would you suggest that they move near your people?

The Kiawah nation had been attacked many times by another Native American nation, the Westos. The Kiawah leader might have thought that the new settlers would help protect his people from the Westos.

This is a statue of the Kiawah leader. You can see it at Charles Towne Landing.

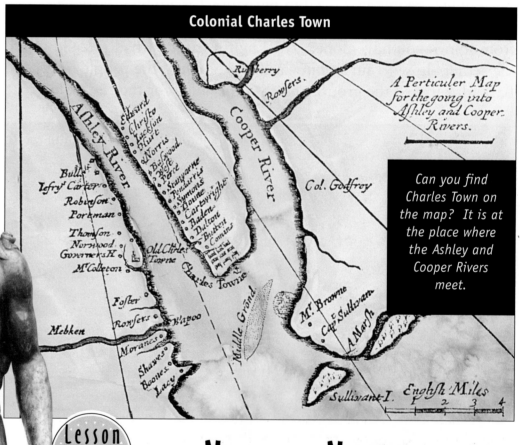

Colonial Charles Town

Can you find Charles Town on the map? It is at the place where the Ashley and Cooper Rivers meet.

Lesson 1

Memory Master

1. Who were the Lords Proprietors?

2. What kind of a place was William Hilton looking for to build the colony?

3. What island did settlers stop at before coming to Carolina?

The South Carolina Adventure

Making Money

The colonists wanted to find ways to make money. They wanted a cash crop. A *cash crop* is a crop that people grow to sell. The settlers tried growing ginger, sugarcane, and olive trees. None of these grew well enough to be a cash crop. But rice and indigo did grow well. *Indigo* is a plant used to make dye. Many people in Europe wanted the rice and indigo. In time, the colony grew rich from these two cash crops.

Colonists also began trading with the native people. There was a need in England for animal skins and furs, and the native people wanted goods from England. To get deerskins, the colonists traded cloth, brass kettles, guns, and gunpowder.

Settling the Colony

Many different people came to the colony. They came for many different reasons. Some came to get rich. Some came to start a new life. Others came because they were forced to come. All of them would play a part in making a successful colony.

English From Barbados

Many of the English men from Barbados were already wealthy when they came to Carolina. They had owned sugar plantations in Barbados. A *plantation* is a large farm. They used African slave labor to grow the sugar, and this had made the English men very rich.

When they moved to Carolina, the English from Barbados hoped to make money from rice. They brought their slaves with them. The slaves had grown rice in Africa. They had the skills to build rice plantations in Carolina.

The English from Barbados brought fancy furniture. It was high fashion in Charles Town. They also liked to eat a big meal in the middle of the day and were known for having big parties.

PEOPLE TO KNOW
William Bratton
Germans
Huguenots
Scots-Irish

PLACES TO LOCATE
backcountry
Barbados
Beaufort
France
Georgetown
Germany
Historic Brattonsville
Ireland
lowcountry
Scotland

WORDS TO UNDERSTAND
cash crop
elite
indigo
plantation

This is a painting of a Huguenot girl named Henriette Charlotte Chastaigner, age 11. It was painted by Henrietta Dering Johnston, who is considered America's first professional woman artist.

Huguenots

The Huguenots came to Carolina from France. They had been forced from their homes because of their religious beliefs. They came to Carolina because there was religious freedom here. They could worship how they wanted. They also wanted to get land.

English colonists welcomed the French settlers. But because the Huguenots were not English, the English settlers did not want the Huguenots to lead the colony or vote for laws. But after a while, the French settlers got the same rights as the English.

Hanover House

The Hanover House was built by a Huguenot named Paul de St. Julien. He carved French words into the chimney: "Peu a Peu." It means, "Little by Little." He meant he was building his house little by little, the way a bird builds its nest.

The whole house was supposed to be made out of bricks. But guess what? After St. Julien built the basement and the chimneys, he ran out of bricks. He had to build the rest of the house out of cypress wood. Cypress is very strong, so that's probably why the house is still standing. Today, it is one of South Carolina's many historic homes.

You can see the Hanover House at Clemson University.

Many families started rice plantations and became part of the *elite* class. They were very wealthy and had a lot of power. Men became government leaders.

As Huguenots became richer, they started social clubs like *The South Carolina Society*. This society started schools for children and helped the poor. It still exists today. It gives money to college students and charities.

Settlers in the Backcountry

Soon more settlers came to the colony. They began to move into the backcountry. They set up townships there. Each settler in a township was given free land. Settlers were also promised supplies to help them survive.

The first thing a family did was clear trees off the land. They also had to build a shelter. Many people built lean-to shelters. A lean-to was made by leaning small logs next to trees. The family could sleep beneath the lean-to and stay somewhat dry when it rained. A real house was built as soon as the land was clear enough.

Farmers raised milk cows, hogs, and chickens on their farms. They grew vegetable gardens to help feed their families. They tried to grow more crops than their families needed, so they could sell the rest for money.

Like today, the area near Charles Town, Georgetown, and Beaufort was called the lowcountry. Almost all the colonists lived there. In colonial days, everywhere else was called the backcountry.

Historic Brattonsville

Brattonsville was started by a Scots-Irish man named William Bratton. Bratton moved to South Carolina from Pennsylvania to start a small farm. Today, you can see his backcountry cabin. It is an example of the homes backcountry settlers first built.

There are many other things you can learn at Historic Brattonsville. It was an important place in our state's history. It is a reminder of what South Carolina's backcountry used to be like.

• **Historic Brattonsville**

These men at Historic Brattonsville are showing how colonists plowed the land.

The Lexington County Museum is a place where people can learn about life for backcountry settlers. This woman is showing a way to make butter.

Traveling to the Backcountry

Settlers did not have cars and roads like we have today. They traveled on foot or in wagons. Horses and oxen pulled heavy loads. When it rained, the dirt roads turned to mud. This made it very hard to travel, and sometimes people got stuck. Sometimes the roads were so muddy that people could not travel on them at all. Settlers had to wait until the mud dried before they could use the roads.

Germans

German settlers moved into the backcountry and built farms. Many came from Pennsylvania, where they had first settled. They often built log homes.

They were given free land in the townships. The land there was good for growing wheat. Soon, they grew enough wheat to feed their families. They sold the rest to others. People began to call German settlements the breadbaskets of the colony.

Germans were known for being hard workers. They were also known for keeping to themselves. They did not get involved in colonial affairs like the Huguenots did.

Scots-Irish

The Scots-Irish came to Carolina for religious freedom. They belonged to the Presbyterian Church. They were a close group of people who were proud of their customs and traditions. They came to the colony in family groups and settled in the backcountry. First the people built a church. Then they built their settlement around the church.

Memory Master

Lesson 2

1. What is a plantation?
2. What type of plantation did English men own in Barbados?
3. Why did Huguenots come to South Carolina?
4. Name two groups who settled in the backcountry.

Problems in the Colony

Everything was not perfect in Carolina. After hurricanes and fires, settlers had to rebuild homes and churches. Settlers also got sick from diseases, and many people died. There were other problems, too.

Problems Over Land

Settlers brought many problems to the native people. More and more new settlers were forcing Native Americans off their land. Since the land had been cleared for farming, it could not give the native people what they needed to live. The animals they used for food were being hunted and trapped by the settlers.

Some of the natives had been treated badly by settlers. White settlers also carried many diseases. Native Americans caught these diseases, and many of them died.

PEOPLE TO KNOW
Blackbeard
Stede Bonnet
Yemassee

PLACES TO LOCATE
Beaufort
Charles Town
Port Royal

WORDS TO UNDERSTAND
plunder
truce

This painting shows how busy and successful Charles Town was becoming.
But not everything in the colony was going well. There were still many problems.

◆ PROBLEMS WITH PIRATES

Blackbeard was a pirate. He grew his black hair long and braided it. He also braided his beard and tied it with colored ribbons. He wanted to be the most feared pirate ever, so he lit pieces of rope on fire and stuck them under his hat. The smoke made him look like a monster. He also wore as many as six guns and swords in his belt.

X

There was another problem in the colony. It came from the sea. Pirates attacked ships sailing in and out of Charles Town. They stole rice, sugar, furs, and other treasures from the ships. Settlers in Charles Town did not like this.

Stede Bonnet

Stede Bonnet was a wealthy English man. He lived in Barbados, where he owned a large sugar plantation. One day, he decided to leave his comfortable life and become a pirate. This shocked everyone on the island. Why would this wealthy man want to be a pirate? No one knows for sure why he did it. Some people say he wanted to get away from his nagging wife. Others say he was tired of living the life of a gentleman.

Bonnet bought a ship called the *Revenge*. He hired a crew of men. Most pirates stole their ships, and they never paid their crew out of their own pockets! Bonnet's ship and crew sailed to colonial cities. Along the way, they stole ships and goods.

Meeting Blackbeard

Bonnet's crew learned that he was not a very good captain. They were tired of working for a captain with no skills. Then Bonnet met the famous Blackbeard, who took him onboard his ship as a "guest." Blackbeard told Bonnet that such a gentleman should not have to deal with the rough life of a pirate captain. He kept Bonnet on his ship while one of his pirates took control of the *Revenge*.

Bonnet was on Blackbeard's ship when Blackbeard plundered ships in Charles Town Harbor. To *plunder* means to steal. They stole goods from 10 ships and took some people as prisoners. The pirates sent a note to leaders in Charles Town and demanded a chest of medicine in return for the prisoners. The demands were met, but angry leaders in Charles Town began a search for all pirates. The leaders wanted pirates to pay for their crimes.

Caught!

After the pirates left Charles Town, Blackbeard gave Bonnet his ship back. Bonnet sailed up the coast. One day, the ship was surprised by an attack from the Charles Town leaders. A great battle took place, but finally the pirates gave up. Bonnet and his crew were taken to Charles Town and put on trial.

The court decided to hang Bonnet and some of his men. People in Charles Town wanted to show other pirates what could happen to them.

The Yemassee fought against the colonists in the Yemassee War. They were trying to protect their land.

Port Royal

What do you think?

Not everyone felt the same about white settlement in the colony. How is this an example of point of view?

The Yemassee War

The Yemassee became angry when settlers started the town of Beaufort. The Yemassee had been living on this land for many years. They had already been pushed off their land in Florida. They were tired of being pushed out of their homes. They joined with many other native nations and planned an attack on the colony. They fought to defend their homeland.

The Yemassee first attacked homes near Port Royal. They killed nearly 100 people. Many settlers left their homes and went to Charles Town. The Yemassee and other native people attacked many other places, too.

Asking for Help

The colonists asked the Lords Proprietors for help, but they got no reply. They asked for help from other colonies, but only a few men came to help. The governor asked all able men to help defend the colony.

The colony also asked the Cherokee for help. The Cherokee had not joined the Yemassee. They decided to help the colonists. Soon, the worst of the war was over. It had been going on for one year. Many of the native people wanted a truce. A *truce* is an agreement to end a war.

After the War

The colony made it through the war, but hundreds of settlers had been killed. Their homes and farms had been ruined. Many of the Yemassee and other Native Americans had also died. Others left their homeland, where they had lived for so many years.

A Royal Government

After the Lords Proprietors failed to provide help in the Yemassee War, the colonists decided they were tired of being ruled by the proprietors. The proprietors had done a poor job of running the colony. They appointed a governor to take care of problems in the colony, but laws, supplies, and taxes were still handled by the proprietors. They often ignored colonists' appeal for help with Native Americans, pirates, money, and new laws. The Fundamental Constitutions did not work as Ashley Cooper had hoped it would.

Groups of colonists started to rebel against the proprietors. They asked for the royal government to take over the colony. This meant they wanted England to control the colony. They wrote a letter to the king of England that explained all the reasons why the proprietors should no longer rule the colony. After many years, Carolina became a royal colony. It was ruled by a royal governor chosen by England.

Memory Master

1. Name two problems the colony had.
2. What famous pirates plundered ships in Charles Town Harbor?
3. Why was the Yemassee War fought?
4. Who helped the colonists in the Yemassee War?

PEOPLE TO KNOW
Olaudah Equiano
Jemmy
Eliza Lucas Pinckney

PLACES TO LOCATE
Africa
Stono River
West Indies

WORDS TO UNDERSTAND
auction
barrel
botany
dike
enslaved
Gullah
husk
mortar
pestle
rebellion
resist

A Wealthy Colony—for Some

Carolina became so large and hard to govern that it was split into two parts: North and South Carolina. Many colonists grew rich from rice and other products. The people who owned large plantations were called planters, but they were not the people doing all the work.

The colonists brought people from countries in Africa to work. These Africans were enslaved. To be *enslaved* means to be made someone else's property. An enslaved person had no freedom and was forced to do what his owner said. Slave owners were called masters. They depended on slave labor.

Some of the enslaved people came from Barbados or other islands in the West Indies. Enslaved people had worked on plantations there for a long time. Other slaves came directly from West and Central Africa.

The Slave Trade

Slaves were worth a lot of money. The work they did made planters rich. For nearly 150 years, crowded ships brought people from Africa to South Carolina. Some slaves were bought by planters here. Some were bought by people from other colonies. This was called the slave trade. Almost one half of all enslaved people brought to North America came through Charles Town.

A Terrible Journey

In Africa, white men or Africans from certain tribes captured men, women, and children. They took them from their villages and sold them to slave traders. The price depended on the slave's age. Young men and women sold for the highest price because they were strong and healthy and could work for many years.

The enslaved people were put on big ships. Many of them didn't know where they were going. They didn't know if they would ever see their families again.

Each ship carried hundreds of people. Africans were chained together and forced to lie down on the floor. Each person had only

By 1708, there were more blacks in the colony than whites. Many enslaved people came from West Africa. Most slaves who came to South Carolina were first sent to the West Indies.

North America

Carolina

West Indies

Barbados

Slave Trade Routes

Africa

South America

N W E S

a few feet of space, so no one could move around at all. They were given small bits of cornmeal, beans, and rice to eat. Sometimes they were given raw, spoiled meat. The water they drank was dirty and made many people sick. There was no fresh air below the deck, so the ship smelled terrible.

Sold!

When the ships arrived in Carolina, the enslaved people were unloaded on Sullivan's Island and checked for disease. Then they were sent to *auctions.* There they were sold to the person with the highest bid. Often, family members were bought by different people. Children were taken from their mothers. Wives were taken from their husbands. Many family members never saw each other again.

SOUTH CAROLINA PORTRAIT

Olaudah Equiano
1745-1797

When Olaudah Equiano was 11 years old, he and his sister were taken from their village in Africa. He was separated from his sister. They would never see each other again. Olaudah was brought to the coast and put on a slave ship. Years later, Olaudah described this experience:

When I looked round the ship [I] saw [many black] people . . . chained together. . . I was soon put down under the decks, and there received such a [smell] in my nostrils as I have never experienced in my life, so that, with the . . . stench, and crying together, I became so sick and low that I was not able to eat.

The ship sailed for many weeks before it reached Barbados. This trip was known as the Middle Passage. It was a trip of horror for all who were forced to make it. Olaudah wrote:

The closeness of the place, and the heat of the climate, added to the number on the ship, which was so crowded that each had scarcely room to turn, almost suffocated us. . . this brought on a sickness . . . of which many died.

Olaudah survived the terrible trip. He was sold into slavery in Barbados, but he was later sold to a farmer in South Carolina. After time, he found a way to buy his freedom. He also learned to read and write. He wrote a book about his life. His book was one of the first books written against slavery.

Colonial Times

These women are using mortars and pestles to smash rice husks from the grain, just like people had done during colonial times.

Rice plants were Carolina's gold.

Carolina Gold!

The Africans enslaved in South Carolina brought valuable knowledge with them from West Africa. They knew how to grow rice. They also knew how to make the tools needed to grow rice. Rice grows well in flooded swampy land. With its many swamps and tidal rivers, the South Carolina coast was a perfect place for growing rice.

Rice came to be known as "Carolina Gold" because it made planters so rich. Have you ever seen the beautiful colonial homes in Georgetown or Charleston? Many of those homes were owned by wealthy rice planters.

Growing Rice

Taking care of a rice plantation was hard work. Slaves cleared the swamps of trees and other plants. They built *dikes* to keep the rivers from flooding the fields. Dikes were like large fences. At times, water was needed for the rice fields. Slaves built gates in the dikes to let water in when it was needed.

Rice fields had to be ready for planting by April. Black men and women carefully planted the rice in rows. This was a hard job done only by the most skilled workers.

Even black children worked on rice plantations. As the crop neared harvest time, birds tried to eat the rice. It was the children's job to keep the birds away.

The South Carolina Adventure

Harvest

When the rice was ready, workers beat the rice grain from its stalk with a stick. Then they used a mortar and pestle to smash the *husk,* or the hard shell, off the rice grain. The *mortar* held the grain, and the *pestle* was a tool used to grind the grain. The last step was to separate the husks from the grain. The people used a fanning basket to do this. They tossed the rice in the fanning baskets, and the wind blew away the husks.

Indigo

Indigo was another cash crop that made planters wealthy. Indigo was used to make a bluish purple dye. Enslaved people did all the work to grow it, just like they did with rice. It didn't take as much work to grow indigo as it did rice, but it took a lot more time to harvest.

First, the indigo plants were soaked in a tub of water for about 12 hours. Then the liquid was drained into another tub and beaten with a paddle. After it was beaten, the liquid was drained into a third tub. The solid goo that was left in the second tub was scooped up and put into small cloth bags to drain. Then the goo was spread out on a table to dry for many days. Finally, the dried cakes of indigo were cut and shipped off to be sold. They sold for high prices in Europe. People used the indigo to dye their yarn and cloth.

Eliza Lucas Pinckney
1722–1793

Eliza Lucas was an unusual young lady for her time. Not very many women were given the chance for a good education, but Eliza went to school in England. Her favorite subject was botany. *Botany* is the study of plants.

Eliza decided to grow indigo in the colony. She knew she could make indigo a cash crop. She tried growing it, but frost ruined the crop. Eliza tried again the next year. This time, the indigo "was cut down by a worm." This meant that worms infected the plants. Eliza didn't give up. Two years later, she finally figured out how to grow it. She and her father helped others grow it, too. They even wrote about it in the newspaper. Because of her success, indigo became a good cash crop.

There are no drawings or photographs of Eliza Pinckney. People made this doll to show what they think she looked like.

Harvesting indigo was hard work. After it was cut, it was carried away in big bundles.

This painting shows two rows of slave homes on a plantation. The homes looked like homes people built in West Africa. Can you also see the planter's house?

Skilled slaves built many beautiful plantation homes like Drayton Hall.

Daily Life

Daily life for enslaved people was not always easy. For most of them, every day was spent working in fields, tending gardens, or doing household chores.

Can you imagine working in a rice field day after day? It might be your job to keep birds and other animals away from the crops, or you might collect firewood. You did not go to school. You could leave the farm or plantation only if you were given a special pass. Let's learn more about what it was like to be a slave during colonial times.

Building Houses and Plantations

Black men were expected to do hard work. If they lived in a city like Charles Town, they might be skilled craftsmen. The men built tall wrought-iron fences. They worked as carpenters, shoemakers, blacksmiths, and coachmen. Some men made **barrels,** which were large wooden containers. Many goods, like rice and indigo, were shipped in barrels. Black men also were experts at steering boats through shipping ports.

The South Carolina Adventure

If they lived on a plantation, most black men worked in the rice fields. They also built homes, fences, and dikes. Slaves built most of the big beautiful plantation homes. Here is what one day may have been like:

> You wake up early and eat a small breakfast of boiled corn. Today, you have been given the task of splitting logs. You will build a fence with the logs tomorrow. You are happy to have something to do besides work in the fields. You spend the hot day splitting logs, and you finish as the sun is about to go down. Your hands are sore.
>
> For dinner, you have a small piece of pork fat and some corn. Then you head to your garden where you grow potatoes, peas, corn, and pumpkins. You gather a bag of vegetables to trade them for other things like tobacco and clothing. Other slaves are working in their gardens or resting in front of their cabins. You visit with them before you go home. You go to bed early because you have another day of hard work ahead of you.

Taking Care of Things

Women were expected to work just as hard as the men. Some women worked in the fields. Many women worked as house servants in their owners' homes. They had to make the meals for the plantation family, take care of the children, make and wash clothes, and do many other chores. Here is what one day may have been like:

> You are a house servant. You wake up early and have a small breakfast. Then you make breakfast for your master's family. Your stomach grumbles as you cook a big meal of pork, biscuits, and cornbread.
>
> You are in charge of taking care of the master's children, so you dress and feed them. After that, you wash and iron the clothes. You have to do everything by hand. Washing clothes is a big job, and it takes you most of the day.
>
> Before the end of the day, you make dinner for your master's family. You have chores to do for your own family, too. You cook dinner for your family and take care of your children. Your husband needs a new shirt, so you sit outside to sew while your family sings and plays instruments. Late at night, after a very hard day of work, you finally go to bed.

The First Cowboys

African Americans helped the colonists in another way. They showed the colonists a good way to raise cattle. In Africa, they had raised cattle on open land. The animals were free to roam around. There was a lot of open land in South Carolina, so it was a good idea to have open grazing here.

Some black slaves were in charge of cattle. They branded the cattle with their owner's mark. Once a year, the slaves rounded up the cattle for market. These black men were the first cowboys.

This painting shows the importance of music to plantation slaves. Can you see the banjo on the left? People in Africa used to play the banjo.

African American Culture

Most slaves lived in cabins built in rows close together. Some plantations had hundreds of slaves. Their cabins were set up like large neighborhoods. This helped black people form their own community. They wanted to hold on to their African culture. To do this, they cooked foods as they had done in Africa. They danced and played music. They dressed like they had in Africa.

Music

One way African Americans kept their culture was through music. Music was very important to them. It was a way for them to express their feelings. It was a way for them to tell stories.

Slaves often sang as they worked in the fields. The speed of their singing controlled the pace of their work. Singing also made the long day go faster. At night, families and friends would gather together to play drums, sing, and dance together. They sang songs and did dances they had learned in Africa. The songs they sang later turned into a type of music we call spirituals. This kind of music is still very popular today.

Hope for Freedom

Enslaved Africans had a strong hope for freedom. Many of their songs expressed hope for a better life. Some songs talked about a place where slaves would be free. They called these places "my country" or "the promised land." Some slaves believed that Africans would one day be freed. Others believed that there was a better world waiting for them after this life.

The South Carolina Adventure

Food

Have you ever eaten gumbo, yams, or hoppin' john? Those foods were brought here by enslaved Africans. Many of the foods we cook in the South have African roots. After all, it was the enslaved people who did most of the cooking. They cooked for the master's family.

Slaves had to do all their own cooking. They weren't given much food, but they worked with what they had. Many slaves grew vegetable gardens, so they could have better diets. Usually, the main dish was cooked outside in a large pot. They used lots of grains and vegetables in their dishes. Everyone sat around the pot and picked up food with their fingers. Then they dipped it in a sauce made from vegetables and spices. They made drinking bowls by hollowing out dried squash called gourds.

Language

Mek yo do' come en shay dis yuh bile pindah wid me? Were you able to read this sentence? It says, "Why don't you come and share these boiled peanuts with me?" Another way black slaves kept their culture alive was through *Gullah.* Enslaved people came from many countries in Africa. They did not all speak the same language, so they created the Gullah language that everyone could speak and understand. Gullah is a mixture of African languages and English. Today, people in Africa speak a language like Gullah called Krio.

Gullah is also a culture. People today celebrate the Gullah culture through art, stories, food, music, and festivals. There are Gullah festivals in our state each year.

Linking the Past to the Present

Many words we use today, like juke (jukebox), gumbo, and yams, are Gullah words. Many people work to keep Gullah culture alive. They want to remember the culture of their ancestors. People speak Gullah, make Gullah foods, and tell Gullah stories.

Making and using handmade fishing nets is one way people keep Gullah culture alive.

Sweet Grass Baskets

If you have ever taken a car ride on Highway 17 through Mount Pleasant, you have probably seen the sweet grass basket-makers. They set up stands along the road where they make and sell their baskets.

Sweet grass baskets are a part of Gullah culture. Do you remember the fanning baskets that slaves used to harvest rice? They were made from sweet grass. The baskets were also used to hold fruits, vegetables, breads, and other things. Enslaved people taught their children how to weave. They wanted to pass down their African culture. People kept passing this tradition on, and that's why we still have it today.

The baskets are now considered pieces of art, and they sell for very high prices. Some people use them to hold fruits or vegetables. Many people collect the baskets and display them.

The sweet grass plant grows in rich soil in marshes or near the ocean. The leaves are very long and shiny on one side. When the leaves dry out, they smell like sweet vanilla. Weavers set the leaves out to dry for several days before they use them.

Sweet grass baskets are very special to South Carolina. This is the only place in the United States where people make them!

Sweet grass basket-makers teach children how to ▶
weave. They want to pass on this special tradition.

The South Carolina Adventure

Slaves worked hard planting and harvesting rice all day long, but they still found ways to keep their culture alive. That was one way of resisting.

What do you think?

How would you feel if someone told you what clothes to wear, what foods to eat, or where you could go everyday? How do you think enslaved people felt?

Fighting Back

No one likes to have his or her freedom taken away. It is not surprising that slaves often resisted against their owners. To *resist* means to go against.

Enslaved people had many ways of resisting. One way was by keeping their African culture alive. When they wore African clothes, beat African drums, and spoke African languages, the people were saying, "We are not just slaves or property; we have our own culture and ways of living."

Other ways of resisting were stealing things from owners, working slowly, and running away. One form of resistance was open rebellion against whites. A *rebellion* is an organized fight against those who are in power.

The Stono Rebellion

The leader of the Stono Rebellion was a slave named Jemmy. He made a plan to revolt, or rebel, against slavery. On a Sunday, Jemmy put his plan to action. He and about 20 other slaves broke into a store near the Stono River. They killed two white people and took weapons and supplies. They planned to go to Florida, where they could be free.

Along the way, they got other slaves to join them. Soon, there were 60 to 80 slaves marching together. For this one moment, the slaves felt free. They began beating on drums and singing chants about freedom.

A leader from Charles Town ran into the group of slaves on a road. He rode into Charles Town and warned the colonists. Then he gathered the colony's army. When the army caught up with the slaves, everyone began firing their guns. By the end of the day, many people were killed. More than 20 whites died, and about 40 slaves died. Some of the slaves got away from the army but were found later and killed.

New Rules

The Stono Rebellion changed life for everyone. White people became afraid that black slaves would revolt again. The next year, the colonists passed new laws about slavery. These laws said that slave owners had to treat their slaves better. Owners had to give their slaves enough food and clothing. They could not punish slaves as harshly as they did before. The idea was that if slaves were treated better, they would not revolt.

The laws also put slaves under tighter control. The "slave patrol" became more common. A slave patrol was a group of white men who looked for runaway slaves or slaves who broke the rules. Slaves could not meet together as a group without permission and the presence of a white person. A slave could not leave the plantation without a pass. It was against the law for a slave to learn to read and write.

Sometimes it was hard for slaves to keep their African culture. It also became harder for slaves to have a chance to get their freedom.

This document told the new slave laws of 1740.

Lesson 4

Memory Master

1. What was the slave trade?
2. What crop was called Carolina Gold? Why was it given that name?
3. Name two ways slaves kept their culture alive.
4. Who led the Stono Rebellion?

Palmetto Detectives in

LEARNING ABOUT SLAVERY

Erin fidgeted in her chair. She didn't like learning about how the Africans had been brought over to be slaves. It wasn't right. She wanted to share her feelings with the class, so she raised her hand.

"Yes, Erin?" Ms. Izard said.

"Ms. Izard, why do we have to learn about slavery? It was such a bad thing."

Other children in the room agreed. Learning about slavery made everyone feel uncomfortable.

"Couldn't we just forget about it?" Erin asked.

"I understand how you feel," Ms. Izard said. "Learning about the good things that happened in history is fun. Learning about the bad things makes us feel uncomfortable. I want you to go home tonight and talk with your parents about slavery. Ask them why they think you should learn about it."

That evening, Erin was sitting on the sofa reading a book. Her parents were in the kitchen preparing dinner. She closed her book and walked into the kitchen.

"Mom and Dad, I asked Ms. Izard today why we had to learn about slavery. She said to go home and talk with you about it."

"Slavery made you feel uncomfortable, huh?" her mom asked.

Erin nodded and asked, "Did our family own any slaves?"

"Not that I know of," her dad answered.

"Erin, even though our family didn't own slaves, it is still important to learn about slavery," her mom said.

"There are a lot of bad things that happened in history. Learning about the bad things can help you," her dad added.

"How can knowing about slavery help me, Dad?"

"Sometimes remembering bad things keeps us from doing them again," Erin's mom said. "We can learn many lessons from slavery. One of them is that all people deserve respect."

The next day in class, Ms. Izard asked, "How many of you talked to your parents last night about slavery?"

Almost everybody raised their hands.

"Does anyone want to share what their parents told them?"

Grant spoke up, "When I learn about slavery, it makes me angry. I don't understand why people treated other people like property. Slavery is a part of my family's past. My parents told me that

I need to remember where my family came from, so I know how far we've come. My great-great grandfather may have been a slave, but my dad's a dentist. Maybe I'll be the first astronaut on Mars."

"Grant is right about learning our family history," Erin said. "I learned that my family probably didn't own slaves, but that doesn't mean I don't need to learn about slavery."

Ms. Izard smiled. Everyone had learned very important lessons about history.

QUESTION

1. In your own words, write what Erin and Grant learned in the story.

2. Write a paragraph about why it is important to learn all parts of history.

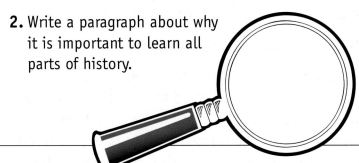

Chapter 4 Review

Blooming on the Vine

Study a Drawing

Look at this drawing carefully. It shows a wealthy Huguenot man and his friends. What does the drawing tell you?

1. What are the men doing? Are they relaxing, or are they working?
2. What kind of clothes are the men wearing? Are they fancy or plain?
3. What can you tell about the men by the way they are dressed?
4. What else do you notice about the drawing?
5. Using what you have learned about backcountry farmers, compare them to the wealthy men in this drawing. Write a list showing differences in their homes, clothing, and way of life.

Activity

A Slave Ad

Slaves did not have freedom. They were someone else's property. This meant they could be bought and sold, just like anything else. The buying and selling of slaves was called the slave trade.

If slaves wanted to be free, they had to buy themselves from their owners. Imagine having to earn enough money to buy yourself. When slaves ran away, they were accused of stealing property.

When a slave trader had slaves to sell, he sent out ads. The ads described all of the good things about the slaves, so other people would want to buy them. Study the slave ad, and answer the questions:

1. What is being advertised?
2. Where are the slaves from?
3. What disease does the ad discuss?
4. What was done to make sure the slaves were not infected with the disease?
5. Why was it important for the slaves to be healthy?

TO BE SOLD, on board the Ship *Bance-Island*, on tuesday the 6th of May next, at *Ashley-Ferry*; a choice cargo of about 250 fine healthy NEGROES, just arrived from the Windward & Rice Coaſt. —The utmoſt care has already been taken, and ſhall be continued, to keep them free from the leaſt danger of being infected with the SMALL-POX, no boat having been on board, and all other communication with people from *Charles-Town* prevented.
Auſtin, Laurens, & Appleby.

N. B. Full one Half of the above Negroes have had the SMALL-POX in their own Country.

Geography Tie-In

A Good Place to Settle

When William Hilton was looking for a place to start a colony, he had a lot to consider. He had to find good soil for crops. He had to find a place with plenty of water and trees. What kind of place would you look for?

On a piece of paper, draw a map of an island. It will be just an imaginary place. Draw it big enough to fill most of the paper. Now add natural features to your island such as deserts, lakes, bays, rivers, mountains, and forests.

Trade your map with another classmate. Imagine you are exploring his or her island. You want to start a colony. Where would you like to start it? Should it be near a river, or mountains, or a forest? Write a paragraph to describe where you will start your colony. Tell why you chose that place. Then mark on the map where your colony will be.

THE TIME
1750–1783

"*If we wish to be free
. . . we must fight!
—I repeat, . . . we must
fight!*"

—*Patrick Henry,
a Patriot in the
American Revolution*

Timeline of Events

1769
The backcountry gets
sheriffs, jails, and schools.

1773
The Tea Act

1765
The Stamp Act

| 1750 | 1755 | 1760 | 1765 | 177 |

1774
Intolerable Acts

◀------ **1750s-1760s** ------▶
Many settlers move into the backcountry.

1774
First Continental Congress

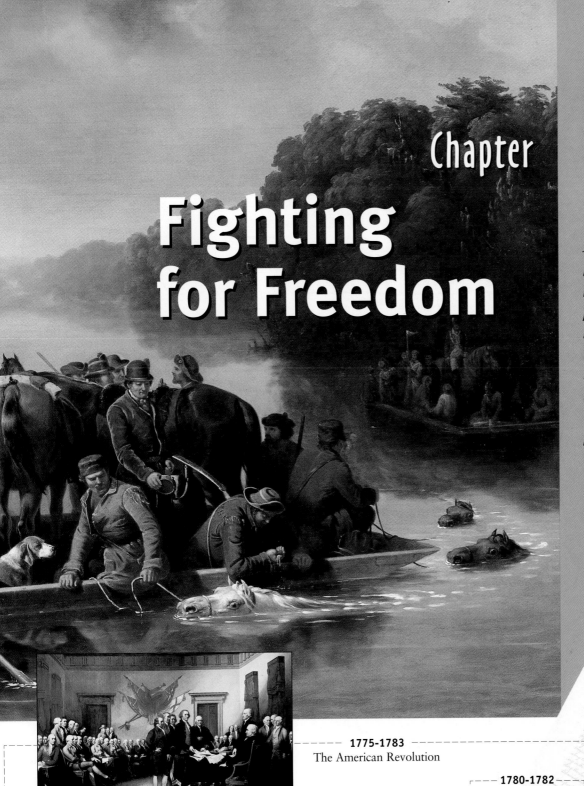

Chapter 5

Fighting for Freedom

During the American Revolution, more battles were fought in South Carolina than in any other state. Many of those battles were in the backcountry, where people like Francis Marion led men in the fight for freedom. This painting shows Marion and his men crossing the Pee Dee River.

1775-1783
The American Revolution

1780-1782
The British occupy
Charles Town.

1783
Charles Town's name is
changed to Charleston.

1776	1778	1780	1782

March, 1776
South Carolina
becomes the first
southern colony
to write a state
constitution.

July 4, 1776
The Declaration of
Independence is approved.

June 28, 1776
Battle of Fort Moultrie

October 7, 1780
Battle of Kings Mountain

January 17, 1781
Battle of Cowpens

October 19, 1781
The British surrender
at Yorktown, Virginia.

PEOPLE TO KNOW
Christopher Gadsden

PLACES TO LOCATE
England
Boston, Massachusetts
Philadelphia, Pennsylvania

WORDS TO UNDERSTAND
boycott
congress
independence
intolerable
Loyalist
Patriot
representative
revolution
tax

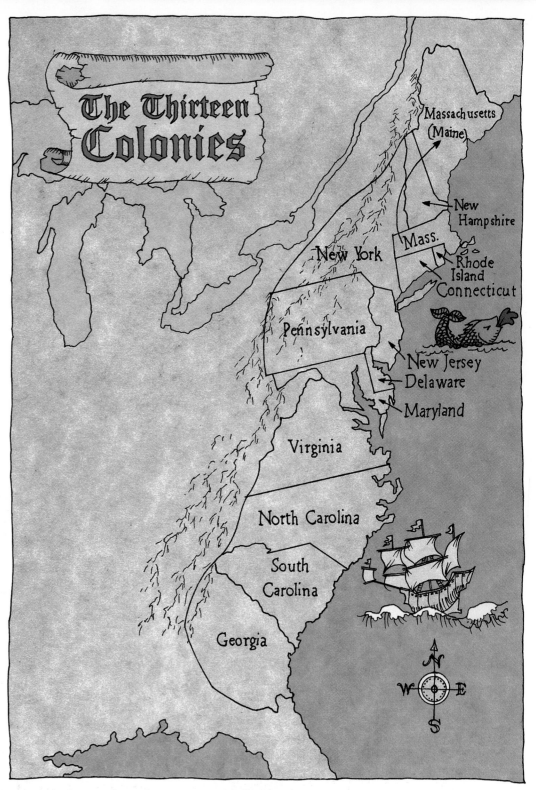

The Thirteen Colonies

By the 1760s, England had 13 colonies in what is now the United States. South Carolina was one of the colonies. Can you find the other colonies on the map?

Freedom

What do you think freedom means? Does it mean that you can do what you want? Does it mean you have the right to make choices? We enjoy many freedoms. But people in our country did not always enjoy the freedoms we have. Long ago, people fought for freedom during the American Revolution. A *revolution* is when people fight to replace one government with a different government.

Leading to a Revolution

For a long time, most people in South Carolina were happy to be an English colony. Some colonists made a lot of money selling rice and indigo to England. Charles Town was one of the richest cities in all of the 13 colonies. For the wealthy planters and merchants, life in the colony was good. They were the leaders, and they had a lot of power. Then things began to change.

The British needed money to pay for wars they had fought. They needed to pay for soldiers sent to America to protect the colonists. To raise money, England taxed the colonists. A *tax* is money the government collects from people. Some of the taxes were on sugar, glass, and paint.

A colony is ruled by a country far away. South Carolina and the other colonies were ruled by England.

No Taxation Without Representation

Since the early days of the colony, England had decided how our government would run. England chose who our governor would be. It set up the Commons House of Assembly. Colonists could elect leaders to serve in the Assembly. Most of the leaders were wealthy men from the lowcountry. They could give ideas for laws, but the English government had to give its approval.

Although the colonists were governed by rulers in England, they did not have much say in what laws or taxes were passed in England. They wanted to send a few people to England to speak for them, but England would not let the colonists send *representatives* to government meetings. Representatives are people who act or speak for a larger group. Many colonists thought this was unfair. They did not think England should make rules for them without letting them have a say. They said, "No taxation without representation!"

Colonists were angry over the taxes. In this picture, they are arguing with the tax collectors.

The Stamp Act

The Stamp Act said colonists had to pay to have a stamp put on all paper items. This seemed silly to the colonists. Why should they pay England to stamp all their playing cards, legal papers, books, and newspapers?

In Charles Town, a man named Christopher Gadsden led the fight against the Stamp Act. Gadsden was a leader of the Sons of Liberty. They fought the Stamp Act with a boycott. A *boycott* happens when people stop buying a product. All over the 13 colonies, people stopped buying the stamped paper.

After a while, the British ended the Stamp Act. They saw that it was not going to work, but other taxes soon came.

A Tax on Tea

When the British decided to tax tea, many colonists were very upset. Tea was a favorite drink. They were not happy that their favorite drink was taxed.

In Boston, Massachusetts, some men decided to show how unhappy they were with the tea tax. They put on costumes so that people could not see who they were. Then they went on a ship loaded with tea, and they dumped the tea into the harbor. It was called the Boston Tea Party.

These are examples of colonial playing cards. Cards were very popular, so they were taxed by the Stamp Act. The British hoped to make money from the taxes on playing cards.

Blooming on the Vine

Understand the Stamp Act

1. What was the Stamp Act?
2. How did the colonists fight the Stamp Act?
3. Imagine there is a stamp tax on paper today. Make a list of all the things you would have to pay taxes on.
4. If there was a tax on e-mail, how would you feel? How could you fight against it?

This drawing shows men from Boston dumping tea into the harbor. People in Charles Town did not like the Tea Act, either. They dumped a load of tea into the Cooper River!

The Intolerable Acts

The Boston Tea Party made the British very upset. They punished Boston by closing Boston Harbor. They stopped all ships from bringing in goods or taking them out. The British also took power away from leaders in Massachusetts. These two actions were part of what the colonists called the Intolerable Acts. *Intolerable* means something is unfair and should not be allowed.

The British thought punishing Boston would send a strong message to the other colonies. They hoped the colonies would follow England's laws. Instead, more and more people became upset with England. The colonists decided it was time to do something more.

The Colonies Come Together

The colonists decided to work together. They wrote letters back and forth to each other. They shared what was happening in their colonies.

Leaders from all the colonies met in Philadelphia to talk about their problems with England. The meeting was called the First Continental Congress. A *congress* is a group of representatives who meet to work out a problem. The leaders wrote down their problems with England in a letter and sent it to the king of England. The leaders said they would meet again and take stronger action if England did not treat the colonies better.

Patriots and Loyalists

Some of the colonists wanted to break away from England and rule themselves as a new country. They wanted **independence.** They were called **Patriots.**

No one wanted to think that all this might lead to war, but the Patriots started to say they would do whatever it took to be free.

Other colonists just wanted the British to stop the taxes. They were called **Loyalists** because they stayed loyal to England. They did not want to go to war.

After the British closed Boston's port, people in Charles Town sent money and 200 barrels of rice to Boston to feed the people.

Many backcountry settlers were not rich. They had to work hard to survive.

Problems in the Backcountry

The Tea Act did not upset everyone living in South Carolina. Settlers in the backcountry thought it was foolish to worry so much about a silly little tax. They didn't share the same concerns as the wealthy lowcountry leaders. They had other problems.

Trouble Over Land

Most settlers lived on farms smaller than plantations. The land they were settling was home to the Cherokee and Catawba. This caused problems. The Native Americans wanted to protect their land, and there were many fights between them and the settlers. People on both sides were killed. The settlers wanted the leaders of the colony to help protect their homes.

Thieves

There were also many thieves in the backcountry. They stole cattle and horses, burned down homes, and hurt people. No one was there to stop them. There were no courts or jails.

No Leaders

The leaders of the Commons House of Assembly were almost all from the lowcountry. They did not think it was very important to help the backcountry settlers. This made the settlers in the backcountry very upset.

Leaders in the backcountry worked together to protect their settlements. They wanted things like roads and schools to be built. They shared their concerns with the Commons House. It was many years before the government hired sheriffs, built jails, and opened schools in the backcountry.

Memory Master

Lesson 1

1. What is a revolution?
2. Why were the colonists upset about the taxes?
3. What were the Intolerable Acts?
4. List two problems backcountry settlers faced.

A State Constitution

Things were not getting better between the colonists and England. Battles had already broken out in Massachusetts. The colonies began to call themselves states. South Carolina's leaders decided to make a statement. In March of 1776, they wrote a state constitution. A *constitution* is a set of written laws. South Carolina was the first southern colony to write its own constitution. The document set up a new government. It said England had no right to choose leaders for South Carolina.

England Responds

The British were not happy that South Carolina's leaders had written a state constitution. They decided to attack Charles Town. British ships with hundreds of soldiers sailed to Charles Town. The soldiers saw the colonists were building a fort on Sullivan's Island. They wanted to bring down the fort.

The Palmetto Fort

Black slaves and white soldiers were working fast to build a fort on Sullivan's Island. Men cut down palmetto trees and used them for the walls. They placed the palmetto logs in the soft sand.

Soldiers brought cannons to the fort. *Cannons* are big guns that can shoot large shells and balls across long distances. The soldiers needed these guns to fire at the British ships.

A man named William Moultrie commanded the fort. His men had not fought before, but they believed in what they were fighting for. They wanted freedom from the British. Because of their bravery, this fort became known as Fort Moultrie.

Attack!

The British thought they had a good plan. After they landed on a nearby island, the soldiers were ordered to wade across the water to Sullivan's Island. This way, they could sneak up to the back of the palmetto fort.

At low tide, the British soldiers began crossing the water. Soon the water was so deep, they were not able to keep going.

The British ships started firing cannonballs at the fort, but the fort did not fall. The cannonballs either landed on the soft sand or bounced off the palmetto wood. The British plans had not worked.

Saving the Flag

In one corner of the palmetto fort, there was a special flag. It was blue with a crescent shape. It had the word "Liberty" written inside the crescent. The flag flew from a large pole. Suddenly, a cannonball hit the pole, and the flag fell outside the fort.

The flag was important. If the flag flew, it meant the men at the fort were still fighting. If the flag was taken down, it meant the fort was *surrendering.* The men at the fort were not going to give up!

A soldier named William Jasper jumped down. He made his way to the flag. He cut it from the pole. With the flag in his hands, he went back over the wall. Someone gave him a rammer from a cannon. A *rammer* is a long rod used to push cannonballs into a cannon. Jasper tied the flag to the rammer and up it went over the fort. Both the British and the people watching from Charles Town knew that the men at the palmetto fort were still fighting.

After a while, the British had no choice but to give up. They sailed away. Charles Town had been saved.

Fort Moultrie ●

William Jasper sent a clear message when he saved the flag. The palmetto fort would not give up!

Linking the Past to the Present

Do you remember reading about our state symbols? One of our symbols came from the fight at Fort Moultrie. It is the palmetto tree. What is its meaning?

The Declaration of Independence

More and more colonists wanted independence. Leaders met again at the Second Continental Congress in Philadelphia. They agreed to break away from England and start their own country. They decided to send a letter to the whole world. They called the letter a declaration. A *declaration* is an announcement. This announcement was called the Declaration of Independence. It explained the reasons why the colonists wanted to be free:

- People have rights that cannot be taken away, "among these are Life, Liberty, and the pursuit of Happiness."

- A government should protect these rights.

- If the government does not protect them, the people can start a new government.

- Governments get their power from the people.

- The colonists had a right to go to war. They had the right because the British had hurt them instead of protecting them.

This is a painting of the Second Continental Congress. It shows leaders like Thomas Jefferson and Benjamin Franklin talking about the Declaration of Independence.

Spreading the News

On July 4, 1776, the Declaration of Independence was approved. Congress printed copies of it, and riders carried the copies to all the states.

About one month later, the Declaration was ready to be signed. It was copied onto special paper. One by one, the leaders signed it. Four men from South Carolina were among them. They were Edward Rutledge, Thomas Lynch Jr., Thomas Heyward, and Arthur Middleton.

When the people in Charles Town learned about the Declaration, they held a big celebration. Leaders read the Declaration out loud at the Exchange Building (today's Old Exchange and Provost Dungeon). Patriots paraded through the town. The states were on their way to being a new country. It was not going to be easy, though. They still had to fight a long war.

People in Boston gathered to hear leaders read the Declaration of Independence. They heard the news soon after the declaration was signed. It took just over one month for people in Charles Town to learn about the Declaration of Independence.

Linking the Past to the Present

When something important happens in the world today, how do we hear about it? We watch the news, read newspapers, or check the Internet. We hear about things as soon as they happen. Long ago, it took a while for news to travel. Riders on horseback had to carry messages from place to place.

Memory Master

Lesson 2

1. When did South Carolina write its first state constitution?

2. Who built Fort Moultrie?

3. What did William Jasper do at the battle of Fort Moultrie?

4. List two ideas from the Declaration of Independence.

Lesson 3

PEOPLE TO KNOW

Kate Barry
Abraham Buford
Emily Geiger
Isaac Hayne
Andrew Jackson
Francis Marion
Daniel Morgan
Rebecca Motte
Andrew Pickens
Thomas Sumter

PLACES TO LOCATE

Georgetown
Pennsylvania
Stateburg
Yorktown, Virginia

WORDS TO UNDERSTAND

blockade
heroic
militia
oath
peninsula
quarter
threaten
traitor

The War Continues

For a while after the colonists declared war on England, things were mostly peaceful in South Carolina. That would not last.

The Fall of Charles Town

British ships circled Charles Town and blockaded the city. The *blockade* kept ships from sailing in or out. British soldiers also surrounded the land around Charles Town. No supplies could get in by sea, and nothing could get in or out by land.

Things were not going well in Charles Town. Food was running out, and people were hungry. They were worried. After 42 days, the city of Charles Town surrendered to the British.

Patriots Sign Oaths

At first, the surrender was not too bad. The British made the men in the city sign an oath of loyalty to England. An *oath* is an agreement. The people thought that with the fall of their city, the war was over. It made sense to say they would stop fighting and be loyal to the British. Then things got worse.

There was a second oath to sign. This oath said that the men would fight for the British against other Americans. This oath meant they would have to fight their own people. This they would not do.

Isaac Hayne Fights Back

Many men who had signed the first oath left their homes and went to fight with the Patriots. Isaac Hayne did this, and he was captured during a fight with the British. They knew he had signed the first oath, and they decided to make an example of him. They said he was a traitor to the British. A *traitor* is someone who acts against his country. Of course, his country was now America not England, but that did not matter to the British. They hanged him as a traitor.

Some who had signed the first oath were frightened, and they quit fighting. Others grew more willing to continue fighting.

British ships set up a blockade around Charles Town. This made it hard to get supplies in and out of the city.

Thomas Sumter
1734-1832

"No Quarter"

After the fall of Charles Town, something happened that made the Patriots mad. British soldiers attacked a group of Patriots led by Abraham Buford. Buford's men were quickly overpowered. They asked for *"quarter."* This meant they wanted to surrender. The British didn't stop fighting. Many Patriots were killed or wounded. People all over our state knew they could not surrender now. They had no choice but to fight.

Things Get Worse

Soon, the British army moved into the backcountry. As the soldiers marched through the state, they treated people poorly. They burned homes. They destroyed crops. They killed anyone they thought was disloyal. This only made the colonists fight more.

The Gamecock Fights Back

Thomas Sumter's home was burned by British soldiers. This made him so upset that he started his own militia. A *militia* is a group of men who fight together. Sumter's militia was made up of men from the backcountry.

Sumter's militia moved quickly through the woods and swamps. They surprised the British with sudden attacks. Sometimes they attacked supply wagons and small camps. As quickly as they attacked, they disappeared back into the woods. This kept the British on guard. Thomas Sumter had a nickname. People called him "the Gamecock." A gamecock is a fighting rooster.

Thomas Sumter was born in Virginia. His family was very poor. As a young man, he moved to South Carolina.

Sumter was a very proud man. He was not shy at all. When Charles Town fell to the British, Sumter knew he had to fight back. He led the only group of men who were willing to fight against the British at that time. Sumter never gave up the fight. He inspired other Patriots to keep fighting. A British leader disliked him and called him his "greatest pest."

When the American Revolution ended, Sumter founded the town of Stateburg. The town and county of Sumter are named for him.

Francis Marion
1732-1795

The Swamp Fox

Francis Marion grew up in the lowcountry, where there were a lot of swamps and rivers. Marion knew this land very well.

Even though he was a small man, Marion was a very brave Patriot. He was one of the soldiers at the palmetto fort at the Battle of Fort Moultrie. He helped aim the cannons toward the British.

Later, Francis Marion led a militia of Patriots. His militia was made up of both black and white men. They lived off the land and traveled through the swamps. He made his men drink vinegar to keep away bugs and mosquitoes.

Marion and his men attacked the British by surprise, usually at night. Then they disappeared into the swamps. Because of this, Marion became known as the Swamp Fox. The British were never able to catch the Swamp Fox!

Later, a poem was written about Marion. Part of it said:

> Our band is few but true and tried,
> Our leader frank and bold;
> The British soldier trembles
> When Marion's Name is told.

The South Carolina Adventure

Two Blows to the British

There were many battles fought in South Carolina—more than in any other state. Many of the battles were fought in the backcountry. Two of the most important were the Battle of Kings Mountain and the Battle of Cowpens.

Battle of Kings Mountain

The Battle of Kings Mountain

As the war continued, the British army marched farther into the backcountry. It *threatened* anyone who was not loyal to the British. The Patriots were not scared. Men from our state joined men from North Carolina and Tennessee. They surrounded the British at Kings Mountain and a great battle started.

The Patriots were winning the fight, when the British leader asked for "quarter." The Patriots remembered when Buford's men were not allowed to surrender. They shouted that they would not let them surrender. They fought on. It was a bad defeat for the British.

Patriots fought bravely at the Battle of Kings Mountain. It is thought of as one of the important battles of the war. Long after the battle, 150 years later, President Herbert Hoover visited the site of the battle. He said, "It was a little army and a little battle, but it was of mighty [importance]."

The Battle of Cowpens

After the Battle of Kings Mountain, British soldiers chased Patriots in the backcountry. But the Patriots set a trap. Daniel Morgan and Andrew Pickens led a group of men. Some of them faced the British, and the rest of the Patriots hid behind them.

When the British soldiers attacked, the Patriots in front ran away. They wanted the British to think they were scared. This made the British come at them even faster. Then the hidden Patriots attacked the British. Soon the British soldiers were surrounded. It was another bad loss for the British. It was called the Battle of Cowpens because it was fought near a place where cows were kept.

Battle of Cowpens

The Battle of Cowpens lasted for about one hour. Morgan's militia dealt a big blow to the British. Over 110 British died, 200 were wounded, and 500 were captured. Morgan lost only 12 men.

Linking the Past to the Present

Kings Mountain and Cowpens were very important battles. They made the British army much weaker. Today, they are both national battlefields. Thousands of people visit the battlefields every year. They want to see how the Patriots helped win the American Revolution.

Andrew Pickens

1739-1817

Andrew Pickens was born in Pennsylvania. When he was about 13 years old, the Pickens family moved to the backcountry.

Andrew Pickens was a quiet and serious person. Some say he hardly ever smiled. People had a lot of respect for him. He was wise like an owl. People called him "The Wizard Owl."

When the American Revolution began, Pickens was a farmer. After fighting in an early battle, Pickens decided he didn't want to fight anymore, but his Patriot friends wanted him to fight again. After a group of Loyalists attacked his family and destroyed part of his farm, Pickens decided to fight again.

He joined the Patriot army fighting under Daniel Morgan. Morgan was a general. He was very glad to have Pickens on his side. He needed Pickens to help fight a very important battle. Pickens and Morgan led the Patriots to victory at the Battle of Cowpens.

Today, at Drayton Hall, people gather together to remember the American Revolution. These women are dressed like women from the 1700s.

Women in the War Effort

Women did many things to help during the war. They raised money to buy supplies for the soldiers. Some women worked as nurses and traveled around with the soldiers.

Many poor women went with their husbands to the army camps. They did the cooking, washing, and sewing. Other women stayed home. They kept the family farms and shops running.

Kate Barry

Several women were spies for the Patriots. They learned things about the British. They gave warnings to the Patriots. Women also warned families when battles were about to happen.

Kate Barry lived in the backcountry. She was the mother of five sons and six daughters. During the war, she was a guide for Patriot armies. She wanted to protect her family and other families. When she learned that a fight was going to happen at a cow pasture nearby, she spread the news. She hopped on her horse named Dolly and warned all her neighbors. Because of this, she was called "The Heroine of the Battle of Cowpens."

Emily Geiger

Emily Geiger was a young girl during the American Revolution. She wanted to help the Patriots. She said she would deliver an important message to Thomas Sumter. Before she left, she memorized the written message. She had to travel through unsafe land. She knew her job was risky, but she was brave.

On the second day of her trip, a group of Loyalists captured Emily. They believed she was a spy carrying an important message. They took her to a farmhouse and searched for her note. Emily had hidden the note in her dress. When the Loyalists were not looking, Emily tore the paper into bits and swallowed them. It was a good thing she had memorized the message. The Loyalists had no proof she was a spy, so they let her go. Emily kept traveling and got the message to Thomas Sumter.

Rebecca Motte

Rebecca Motte lived in Charles Town when the war began. Because she had no sons to serve the Patriots, she sent her slaves to fight. Rebecca's husband was very sick, and she cared for him until he died. When the British took over the city, soldiers moved into her house.

After her husband died, Rebecca moved to her summer home. Later, British soldiers also took over that home. Rebecca and her daughters moved to live in a farmhouse nearby.

Francis Marion learned that the British were using the Motte home. He knew it needed to be burned down to make the British leave. When he told Rebecca this, she did a very **heroic** thing. She offered Marion the bows and arrows needed to do the job. Marion's troops lit the arrows on fire and shot them onto the roof of the house. The British soldiers fled the burning home, and the Patriots were there to catch them.

That evening, the Patriots put out the fire. Rebecca Motte served dinner to both the Patriots and their British prisoners.

This drawing shows Rebecca Motte's brave act.

What do you think?

Why do you think Rebecca Motte served dinner to the British prisoners?

Everyday Heroes

Many South Carolinians were heroes of the American Revolution. Some of them were well-known, like Thomas Sumter, Andrew Pickens, and Francis Marion, but there were many other men and women who did great things. Many farmers and settlers gave their lives to fight in Patriot militias. Catawba men fought with the Patriots. They were also at the Battle of Fort Moultrie.

Black men fought with Francis Marion. They were also very important in building the palmetto fort. Most of the black men who fought were slaves, but some of them were free. Black men also served as messengers and spies. Some black men fought with the British because England said it would give freedom to enslaved people after the war was over.

SOUTH CAROLINA PORTRAIT

Andrew Jackson
1767-1845

During the American Revolution, a young boy named Andrew Jackson lived in the South Carolina backcountry. When he was an adult, Jackson became president of the United States. He is the only U.S. president who was born in South Carolina.

Andrew's parents moved to the colonies from Ireland. They settled near Lancaster. His father died before Andrew was born, so Andrew and his two brothers had to help keep the family home going. He was able to go to school, and he liked to read.

Andrew was only 13 years old when he became a messenger for a Patriot militia. His brothers helped out, too. One time, Andrew and his brother, Robert, were captured. A British officer told Andrew to clean the officer's boots. Andrew refused, and the British man struck his face with a sword. It left a lasting scar on Andrew's face.

By the time the war ended, Andrew's two brothers and mother had died. Andrew was 14 years old, and he had to learn how to make it on his own. He spent time in Charleston. Later, he studied law in North Carolina. He went on to become the seventh president of the United States.

The South Carolina Adventure

The British Move Out

The British had not done well in our state. Their army was tired. They needed supplies. They began to march to Virginia. There they hoped to find rest and supplies.

The army moved to a place called Yorktown. This was a terrible mistake. Yorktown is on a peninsula. A *peninsula* is a piece of land surrounded by water on three sides. By land, there is only one way in and one way out of a peninsula.

The tired British army hoped to get new supplies at Yorktown from the sea. That is not what happened. The Americans blocked the land side of the peninsula. Then they got help from the French. French ships surrounded the British ships. The British army was trapped!

Why did the British army allow itself to be trapped? One reason is what happened right here in South Carolina. The fighting at Kings Mountain and Cowpens had made them too weak.

Chesapeake Bay

Yorktown

America Wins the War

The British general surrendered at Yorktown. America had won! We were now a free country. The fighting in our state played a big part in this victory.

It would be a while before all the British ships left Charles Town, but soon the city and the state were on their own. Charles Town officially changed its name to Charleston.

Whose Freedom Was It?

Freedom and independence was the battle cry for the American Revolution, but whose freedom was it? Most African Americans were still enslaved. Those who were free were not given the same rights as white people. Native Americans did not have the same rights either. They were being forced off their native lands.

While the American Revolution brought freedom to the colonies, it would be a long time before true freedom was granted to all people living in the United States of America.

Memory Master

Lesson 3

1. What did the British blockade do to Charles Town?
2. What was Thomas Sumter's nickname?
3. Why was Francis Marion called the Swamp Fox?
4. Name two important battles in South Carolina that the British lost.
5. List one way women helped in the war.

Palmetto Detectives in
A VISIT TO FORT MOULTRIE

It was a field trip day! Ms. Izard's class had visited Fort Moultrie. They had enjoyed looking through the fort's tunnels.

After the visit, the class got back on the bus. "We're going to see something you read about in your history book," Ms. Izard said. The bus stopped at a parking lot on Sullivan's Island that overlooked the Isle of Palms. The class got out and walked toward the water. Ms. Izard said, "That's where the British were when they tried to cross the water to get to Sullivan's Island."

Carter asked Kevin for the telescope. Then he put it up to his eye.

"Wow!" he said.

"What do you see?" Grant asked.

"Wow!" Carter said again. "You won't believe this. I can see soldiers."

"Do you see the British soldiers in the red coats crossing the water?" Grant asked.

"Look, the water is getting too deep for them to keep going," Kevin shouted.

"What's that noise?" Carter asked. "It's the British ships firing cannonballs at the fort," Grant said.

"There's the flag on top of the fort," Carter said. "See how the cannonballs bounce off the palmetto walls."

"Oh no! The flag has fallen down. And there's Sergeant Jasper making his way to it," shouted Kevin.

"Sergeant Jasper has put the flag back up. Now everyone will know the fort is still fighting," said Carter.

What's Next...

Look at the timeline at the beginning of the chapter to find the date for the Battle of Fort Moultrie. Choose an event on the timeline that took place after this battle. Answer the following questions:

1. What event did you choose?
2. How long after the Battle of Fort Moultrie did the event take place?
3. Write three sentences to explain how the event was part of the American Revolution.

Chapter 5 Review

Blooming on the Vine

Read a Political Cartoon

One of the Founding Fathers, Ben Franklin, drew this political cartoon. A political cartoon uses a picture to make a point. Look at the cartoon. It was made just as the colonies were starting to break away from England. What do you think it means? Answer the questions to help you.

1. How many pieces is the snake cut into?
2. Which letters stand for South Carolina?
3. What do you think the snake stands for?
4. Why do you think the snake is cut into pieces?
5. What do you think the words, "Unite or Die" mean?

Now you get to draw your own political cartoon. England was often called the "Mother Country." The colonies were her "children." Use this idea to draw a political cartoon of your own. How do you think the British would draw it? How would the Americans draw it?

Geography Tie-In

Spreading the Word From Far Away

1. On a map of the world, locate London, England. That is where the British government met to pass new taxes for the 13 colonies. Now locate Philadelphia, Pennsylvania. That is where the colonists met to talk about their problems. Use the map's scale to figure out how many miles separate London and Philadelphia.

2. Locate Charleston, South Carolina. How many miles did the men from our state have to travel to get to the meetings in Philadelphia?

3. If you wanted to travel to Philadelphia today, how would you get there? What options do you have? How is the way we travel today different from the way colonists had to travel?

Blooming on the Vine

A Letter From the Revolution

When you want to send a message to someone, what do you do? You can call them or write an e-mail. Long ago, people did not have telephones or computers. They still needed to send messages to others, though. How do you think militia leaders in the American Revolution communicated with people? They often wrote letters.

Francis Marion carried a wooden case with him. He kept paper and ink inside. The case was like a laptop computer because it could be moved easily from place to place. Look at part of a letter Francis Marion wrote to his leader. After you have read it, answer these questions:

1. What is the purpose of Marion's letter?
2. What supplies is he asking for?
3. How does he say to send the supplies?
4. Why would a message like this be important when fighting a war?

> January 26, 1780
>
> Dear Sir,
>
> . . . We find it Cold here. I don't know how it may be where you are. . . . Our men are in Great want of shoes & Shirts & Blankets . . . many of the men is without a shirt & shoes. I wish you would try to get them & send by two waggon's now to town."

Genuine Genius!

Class Debate: Loyalist or Patriot?

If you were one of the colonists, do you think you would choose to be a Loyalist or a Patriot? Divide your class into two groups. One group will be Loyalists. The other group will be Patriots. Each side must defend its position by giving reasons for its decision. You might want to think about these things:

- Were you born in England or in America?
- Do you still have relatives in England?
- How have England's rules and taxes affected you?
- How has trade with England helped your business?
- Are you afraid of what will happen if England wins the war?
- Are you afraid of what will happen if America wins the war?
- Do you believe that people should have the right to choose their own leaders?
- Do you believe that America is so far away from England that it should be a separate country?

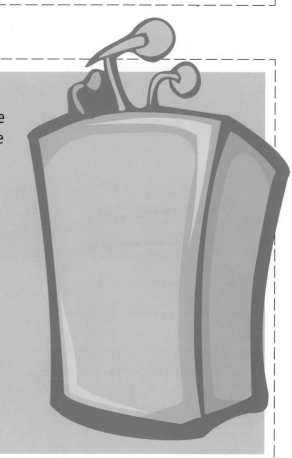

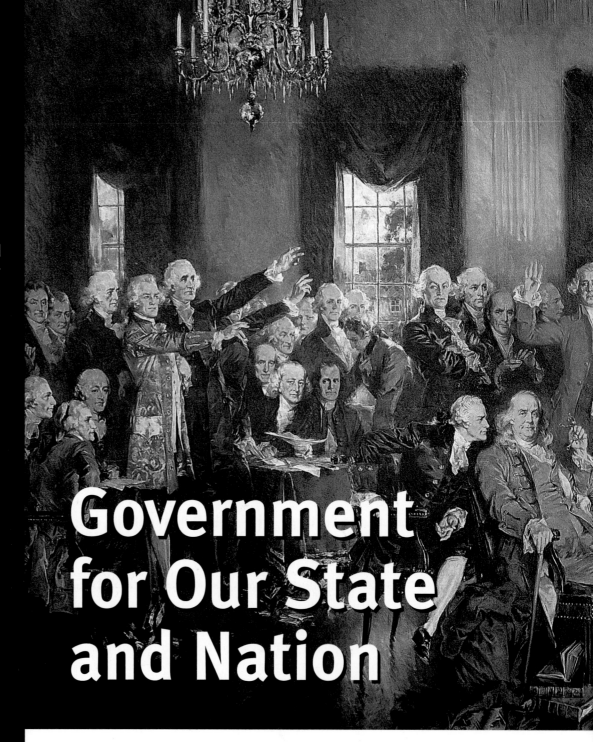

"*The wounds of our country will be healed, [and] the sources of our differences forever dried up.*"

—Charleston Herald
October 29, 1795

Government for Our State and Nation

Timeline of Events

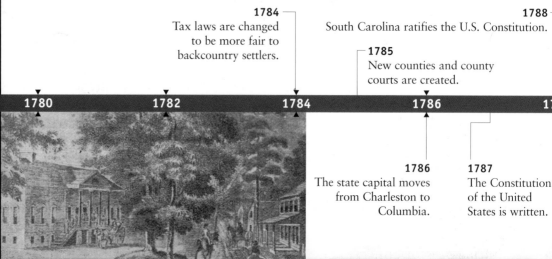

1784
Tax laws are changed to be more fair to backcountry settlers.

1788
South Carolina ratifies the U.S. Constitution.

1785
New counties and county courts are created.

| 1780 | 1782 | 1784 | 1786 | 1788 |

1786
The state capital moves from Charleston to Columbia.

1787
The Constitution of the United States is written.

Chapter 6

Do you recognize the man standing up at the front of this meeting? He is George Washington. He was a great leader. He led Patriot soldiers against England during the American Revolution. In this painting, he is helping to write the U.S. Constitution. Men from South Carolina were also at this meeting. They shared their ideas and helped build a new country.

1791
The Bill of Rights is adopted.

1790   1792   1794   1796   1798   1800

Lesson 1

PLACES TO LOCATE
the backcountry
Charleston
Columbia

Problems in Our State

After the American Revolution ended, South Carolina faced some big problems. Our economy was in bad shape. The British were no longer buying a lot of our rice, indigo, and other goods. Homes had been burned, and crops had been ruined. British soldiers had stolen things from people. Many people were having a hard time making a living.

Keeping a Promise

Our state did not have enough money to pay soldiers who had fought in the war. To show the soldiers they would be paid, the state gave them a special document that promised payment.

Look at the document here. Can you see how it is cut in a special pattern? The soldier kept one part, and the state kept the other. When the state was ready to pay the soldier, he had to show his part of the document. When the two parts of the document matched up, the soldier was given his money. It was a way to keep a promise.

This document shows a promise to pay Thomas Sumter. What do you remember about him? It is interesting to see that the state could not pay one of its most important soldiers.

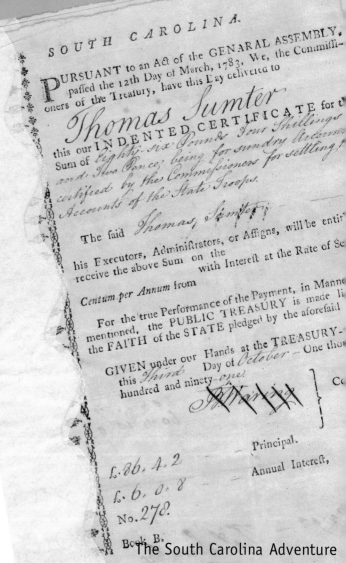

The Backcountry

Most of the fighting in the war had happened in the backcountry. Life for settlers there was not easy. They needed to rebuild their farms and homes.

Still, new settlers kept moving into the backcountry. Some of them were thieves. Things were so bad that one settler wrote, "No man has security for even a worthless plow horse." The settlers needed their government to help make things better.

Three Changes Help the Backcountry

After many years of asking for more help, the backcountry settlers finally saw some changes. The General Assembly (once called the Commons House of Assembly) made three big changes.

Taxes

A new rule said that land would be taxed based on its value. Before, settlers in the backcountry had to pay the same tax for their land as rich planters paid for theirs. This was not fair because the settlers did not make as much money off their land as planters made growing rice or indigo. This new tax rule meant settlers would pay less tax money.

Linking the Past to the Present

Today, if someone broke the law in your community, there are police officers and courts who take care of things. The backcountry settlers did not have that kind of protection, and they wanted it. Protecting people and keeping peace is one responsibility of government.

Genuine Genius!

You Do the Math!

Pretend you are a backcountry farmer. You own a large piece of land where you grow crops of corn, beans, and squash to sell. Each year you make about $400 off your land, but you have to pay $100 in taxes. A planter in Georgetown owns a large piece of land where he grows rice. Each year he makes about $1,000 off his land, and he also pays $100 in taxes.

1. After you pay taxes, how much money do you make off your land each year?
2. After taxes, how much does the rice planter make each year?
3. Do you think the tax on land is fair? Why or why not?

A new law says taxes on land will be based on the value of the land. This helps backcountry farmers like you. Now you only have to pay $40 in taxes when you make $400. The rice planter will have to pay $300 when he makes $1,000.

1. Under the new law, how much money will you make after taxes?
2. How much will the planter make?
3. How did the new law help backcountry farmers?

People built a capital city called Columbia. They built a new capitol building there.

Columbia ●

Counties

New counties and county courts were created. This helped the backcountry settlers have more representatives, and more say, in their government. Having courts closer to the settlers helped things be more peaceful. Thieves and other lawbreakers could be caught and punished more easily.

A New Capital

The biggest change was moving the state's capital city. Charleston had been the capital. It was far away from the backcountry. People did not have cars or paved roads to travel to Charleston like we have today. If they wanted to visit the capital to get help from the government, they had to travel a long way. A capital city in the middle of the state would better serve all the people. A new town was created to be the capital. It was called Columbia.

Lesson 1

Memory Master

1. Name two problems our state faced after the American Revolution.
2. What changes did the General Assembly make to help the backcountry?
3. Why was the capital moved to Columbia?

A National Government

After the American Revolution, other states were having problems, too. The new country needed a strong **national government.** It would help all of the states. There were many ideas on how to set up a better government for the nation. All the states sent representatives, or **delegates,** to a meeting in Philadelphia, Pennsylvania. It was called the Constitutional Convention.

The Constitutional Convention

It was a hot, sticky summer in Philadelphia. Inside a building, the delegates were hard at work. Even in the hot weather, they kept the windows closed. They did not want people outside to hear what they were saying. Why was everything such a secret? The men believed that by keeping their talks private, they could speak more freely.

They had come to write a constitution. It would set up a new government for the United States of America. It would be based on the will of the people. It would not be easy to get each state to agree on everything. Each state wanted what was best for itself. At the same time, each state knew it needed the others to survive.

PEOPLE TO KNOW
Pierce Butler
Charles Cotesworth Pinckney
Charles Pinckney
John Rutledge

PLACES TO LOCATE
Charleston
Philadelphia, Pennsylvania

WORDS TO UNDERSTAND
amendment
delegate
national government
privacy
ratify

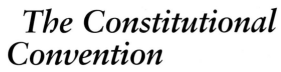

Philadelphia

Charleston

John Rutledge

Pierce Butler

Charles Cotesworth Pinckney

Charles Pinckney

South Carolina's Delegates

Four delegates from our state were at the meeting. All of them were from the lowcountry. Pierce Butler, Charles Pinckney, Charles Cotesworth Pinckney, and John Rutledge were all rich planters.

The men had ideas about the new government. When they spoke, the others listened. Charles Pinckney spoke more than 100 times at the meeting. One of his ideas was that there would be no official church in the new country.

Pierce Butler said that 9 of the 13 states had to agree with the new government in order for it to be approved. This meant the new government would not have to wait until all the states agreed before it got started.

The Question of Slavery

South Carolina's delegates wanted what they thought was best for our state. They wanted to keep slavery. Why? Because they, and others like them, had become rich from crops grown by enslaved people.

Members from some other states wanted to end the slave trade. They did not want white people to bring new slaves to the country. Other leaders wanted to totally end slavery. In the end, the delegates agreed that the slave trade would end in 1808. After that year, no new slaves could be brought into the country. But slaves who already lived in the country were not freed, and they could still be bought and sold.

What do you think?

How do you think people in the backcountry felt about the Constitutional Convention?
Did they think it was fair that all the state's delegates were from the lowcountry?

What do you think?

How would things have been different if slavery was made illegal when the Constitution was written?

The South Carolina Adventure

The U.S. Constitution

The leaders wrote a constitution that outlined how the national government would be set up. Here are its main points:

- The people run the government. They vote for their leaders.
- Power is divided among the president, the Congress, and the courts.
- The Constitution is the highest law of the land.
- The Constitution can be changed.

"The happy union of these states is a wonder: their constitution [is] a miracle: their example [is] the hope of liberty throughout the world."

— James Madison

South Carolina Approves

Once the Constitution was written, it had to be approved, or *ratified,* by nine states. This meant that each state had to have its own meeting to decide if it would ratify the Constitution or not. In our state, the meeting was held in Charleston.

Most leaders from South Carolina liked the new Constitution. They wanted a strong government to protect them and keep peace. They believed the new Constitution would do this.

Linking the Past to the Present

In the early days of our government, people talked to their representatives in person or wrote them letters. They told them what they liked and didn't like. We still do the same thing today, but we can use telephones and e-mail as well.

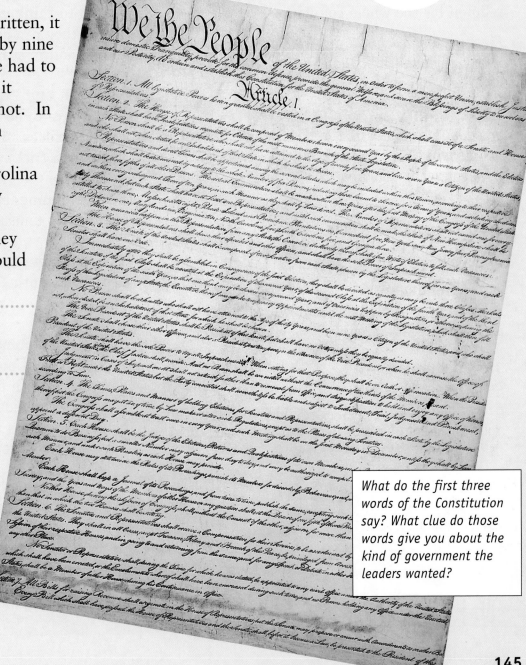

What do the first three words of the Constitution say? What clue do those words give you about the kind of government the leaders wanted?

The Bill of Rights

Our nation had set up a new government. But some people worried that the Constitution might not protect important rights. They wanted a document that listed the basic rights of the people.

A few years after the Constitution was signed, 10 **amendments,** or additions, were added. They protect people's freedom. They are called the Bill of Rights.

1st Amendment:

Freedom of religion: You can worship as you wish, or not at all. The government cannot choose one religion for the whole country.

Freedom of speech: You can express your opinion about any subject without being arrested. But what you say cannot cause danger or harm to others.

Freedom of the press: The government cannot tell people what they can or cannot print in newspapers or books.

Freedom of assembly: You have the right to join and meet with any group. However, you cannot commit crimes with the group.

2nd Amendment:

Right to bear arms: You can own guns for hunting and other legal activities.

3rd Amendment:

Right to not have soldiers in your home during peacetime: In the past, kings made people feed and house soldiers not only during wars, but in times of peace.

4th Amendment:

Freedom from improper search and seizure: You have a right to **privacy.** But if the police have a reason to think you have something illegal in your home, they can get a paper that gives them permission to search your home.

5th, 6th, and 7th Amendments:

These have to do with rights people have if they commit crimes. They include the right to a speedy trial and a trial by a jury.

8th Amendment:

No cruel or unusual punishment is allowed.

9th Amendment:

People have other rights not named in the Bill of Rights.

10th Amendment:

A great deal of power will remain with the states, so the federal government does not have all the power.

Memory Master

1. Why was the Constitutional Convention held?

2. Why did South Carolina's delegates want to keep slavery?

3. Name two points of the Constitution.

Government Today

You have just read about how our national government got started. Today, our government still works to meet people's needs.

Have you ever thought about what it takes to keep things going in your town, city, or state? We need water and power for our homes and farms. We need sidewalks, streets, and streetlights. We need parks, schools, libraries, police officers, and all sorts of things. What makes these things possible? People do—especially people who work for our government.

Government is all around us, and people run it. You are an important part of government, too. Let's learn more about how government works in our state.

WORDS TO UNDERSTAND
executive
judicial
legislative
volunteer

Government helps take care of our cities and towns. The city of Greenville used tax money to pay for a new bridge at Falls Park.

The Branches of Government

If our government looked like a tree, you would see three large branches. Each branch has a name. It also has certain responsibilities.

Each of the three branches helps balance the tree. For example, the legislative branch cannot make a law unless the executive branch approves it.

Legislative Branch

The *legislative* branch makes laws. It also decides how the state's money is spent. Our state legislature is called the **General Assembly**. It is made of the **Senate** and the **House of Representatives**. Our senators and representatives meet at the capitol building in Columbia.

Executive Branch

The *executive* branch carries out the laws. The governor is the head of our state's executive branch. He works with people who help run schools, law enforcement, state parks, and other important things.

148

Judicial Branch

The *judicial* branch decides what laws mean. It also chooses punishments for people who break the law. We have a state supreme court and many other courts.

Activity

Chart the Branches of Government

Show what you know by making a chart of how our state government is set up. Draw your own tree. How many branches should it have? Write the name of each part of the government on the three branches. Write the name for our legislature and its two parts.

Below your drawing, write a paragraph about what each branch does.

Local Government

Did you know that your county, city, or town also has a government? It is local government. That means it is close to home.

Different Needs

Different places have different needs. In some parts of our state, there are many buildings, and the streets are crowded with cars. In other parts, farms or beaches spread over the land. Local governments make rules and laws that fit the people in the community.

Providing Services

Local governments provide many services. Some of them are:

- Public schools
- Public parks, beaches, and swimming pools
- Police departments
- Community welfare

- Fire departments
- Libraries
- New roads and road repairs
- Garbage pick-up
- Recycling

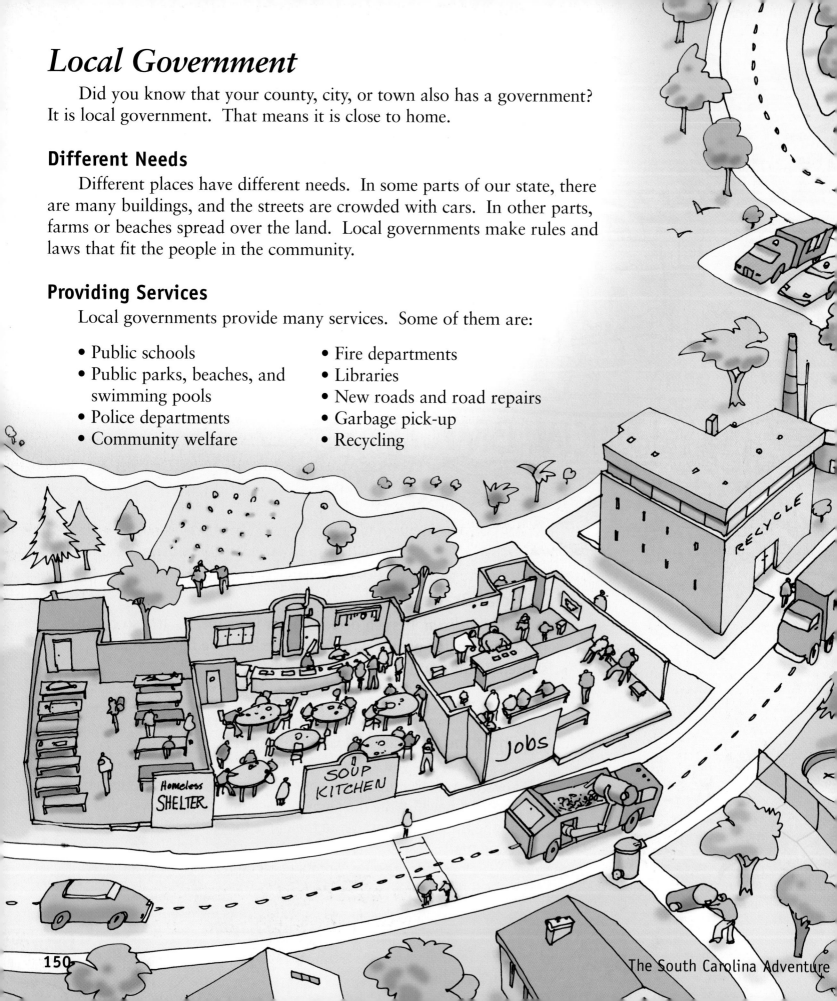

POLICE

School

SCHOOL

HEALTH CARE

LIBRARY

WATER

How many public services can
you find in this drawing?

Citizenship

Our government does a lot to make life good for citizens. We have rights, like freedom of speech and freedom of the press. Laws help protect our homes and businesses, but it is not just up to the government to make life good. Citizens have responsibilities, too.

It is part of good citizenship to respect rules. What rules do you follow at your school? What rules does your family have? Good citizenship also means obeying the laws made by leaders of our town, state, and nation.

Adults have a responsibility to take part in government. This is what "government by the people" means. Voting is one way adults take part in government. They can also go to town meetings and let their representatives know how they feel about things.

Some people help their communities by being volunteers. *Volunteers* help others without being paid for their time. They help raise money for good causes, they help older people take care of their homes, and they help people learn to read. Have you ever volunteered in your community or school? Do you know anyone who volunteers?

Today, citizens of the United States include anyone who was born here and immigrants who pass a special test to become citizens.

Linking the Past to the Present

When the U.S. Constitution was written, not every adult in the state had the right to vote. Women could not vote. African Americans could not vote. Native Americans could not vote. Not all white men could vote, either. For a while, only white men who owned land could vote.

Today, people who are 18 years and older and are citizens of our country can vote. Citizens of any race or religion can vote. Both men and women can vote. You no longer have to own land to be able to vote.

You Can Make a Difference

People can make a difference in their schools, communities, states, and nations. They can:

Go to town meetings

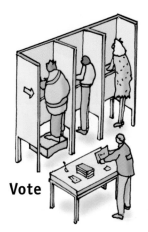
Vote

Run for office

Activity

Being a Good Citizen

Being a good citizen means helping make sure your school, community, state, and nation are good places for people to learn and live. Look at the list below for some ways you can be a good citizen. What other ways can you think of? Discuss these ideas as a class and make a list on the board.

- Obey all of your family rules.
- Obey all of your school rules.
- Tell the truth.
- Be polite and helpful.
- Help keep your own home and yard clean.
- Write a letter to the editor of your town's newspaper (Letters from kids often get printed).
- Talk with adults about what is going on in your town.

Respect everyone

Memory Master

Lesson 3

1. Name the three branches of government.
2. Name three services local governments provide.
3. Describe two things people can do to be good citizens.

Palmetto Detectives in MAKING A DIFFERENCE

"Ms. Izard! There was almost an accident this morning!" Christina blurted out as she came into the classroom.

"Where?" Kevin said.

"It was at the place where all the cars turn into the school," Christina explained.

"There needs to be a stoplight there. My dad complains about that place every morning," Ben joined in.

"Mine, too," Carter added.

"Maybe we can do something about that," Ms. Izard finally spoke. "Do you remember reading about citizenship and government? We have the right to take part in our government. I have an idea. Next week we are having the school open house. We could start a petition and have all the parents sign it that night."

"What's a petition, Ms. Izard?" Erin asked.

"A petition is a written request that people sign to show they want something changed," Ms. Izard answered. "Let's write one today."

The class talked about what they wanted to change. With Ms. Izard's help, they wrote a petition. It said:

Ms. Izard's third grade class believes the corner near our school is dangerous. Each morning all the cars and buses have to turn at this corner to get to the school. A stoplight would make this corner much safer. Please sign this petition if you agree that there should be a stoplight.

The students typed the petition on the class computer. They hoped a lot of parents would sign it.

At the open house, more than 300 parents signed the petition. The next morning in class, the students were excited to see that so many people had signed.

"What do we do next?" Grant asked.

"We take the petition to the city council meeting," Ms. Izard told the class. "The council meets two weeks from tonight. I have prepared letters for all of you to take home. The letter asks your parents to bring you to the council meeting. As a class, we will present our petition to the council."

Almost the whole class came to the meeting. The students weren't sure the council would be happy about the petition. It would cost tax money to put up the stoplight.

The council members read the petition very carefully. Then one of the council members spoke up.

"This corner is in the part of the city that I represent. My children went to this school when they were young. It was not a very safe corner back then. Now there are even more children who go to this school. I am proud of these young citizens for showing their concern. I will work to get a stoplight for this corner."

Ms. Izard's class felt good about the meeting. Three months later, city workers hung a new stoplight.

Ms. Izard's class learned an important lesson about citizenship.

QUESTION

Now it's your turn to think of ways you can help your community.

1. Write a list of problems you see in your community.
2. As a class, choose one problem, and write down your ideas about how to solve it.

Activity

Chart the South Carolina Constitution

The South Carolina constitution outlines the rights and responsibilities of everyone in our state. It groups the rights and responsibilities into parts called articles. Look at the chart below. There are four articles: Voting, Local Government, Public Education, and Declaration of Rights.

On a piece of paper, write each item below under the correct article.

- All elections must use a secret ballot.
- There will be a State Board of Education with members elected from counties around the state.
- The General Assembly must register all voters.
- The powers, functions, and responsibilities of cities will be decided by general law.
- The General Assembly will provide counties with the power to tax different areas.
- Citizens have the right to a speedy trial.

- The General Assembly will provide free public school open to all children in the state.
- All U.S. citizens 18 years old or older can vote.
- No state money will be used for private or religious schools.
- Citizens have the right to speak freely and belong to any religion.
- Citizens have the right to own guns.
- The boundaries of counties will remain the same.

Voting	Local Government	Public Education	Declaration of Rights

Make a Book About Government

Why is government important? Make a book about some of the things you have learned in this chapter.

1. Choose the topics you would like to include in your book, and make a page for each one.
2. At the top of each page, write the name of the topic. Draw a picture and write some things about it so others can learn about it.

Here are some examples:

- **Taxes**
  Backcountry farmers were unhappy about the taxes on land. They had to pay the same taxes on their land as wealthy rice planters had to pay on theirs. This was not fair because rice planters made more money off their land than backcountry farmers made.

- **Services**
  The government provides services our towns need. It provides public schools, parks, beaches, a police department, new roads, and garbage pick-up.

Geography Tie-In

A Closer Capital

Many people had to travel far distances to get to Charleston. When the capital was moved to Columbia, people from all over the state could travel there more easily. Look at the map to answer the questions.

1. What is the distance between Charleston and Columbia?
2. What is the distance between Greenville and Charleston? Between Greenville and Columbia?
3. Is Georgetown closer to Charleston or Columbia?
4. Is Darlington closer to Charleston or Columbia?
5. Is your town closer to Charleston or Columbia?

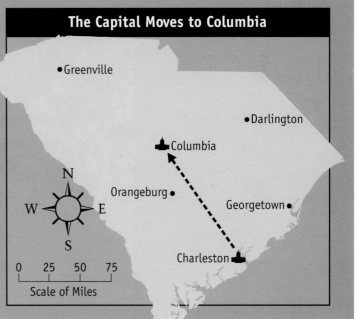

The Capital Moves to Columbia

Greenville
Darlington
Columbia
Orangeburg
Georgetown
Charleston

N W E S

0 25 50 75
Scale of Miles

Cotton Is King

"*S ince the discovery that cotton would mature in South Carolina, she has reaped a golden harvest; but it is feared it has proved a curse rather than a blessing.*"

—*William Gregg, 1845*

Timeline of Events

1790   **1795**   **1800**   **1805**   **1810**

1793
Eli Whitney invents a new cotton gin.

1799
The Santee Canal is completed.

1810
Cotton and slavery spread to every part of our state.

Chapter **7**

Our state had grown rich from rice and indigo. After the American Revolution, another cash crop made people even richer. It was cotton, and it was so important that people said, "Cotton is King!"

Not everyone grew rich from cotton. Many enslaved blacks worked long hours without pay to plant and harvest the cotton.

1824
The Columbia Canal is completed.

1830
The Best Friend train takes its first ride in Charleston.

1842
A railroad connects Charleston and Columbia for the first time.

1845
William Gregg starts Graniteville, a textile town.

1815   1820   1825   1830   1835   1840   1845

1822
Denmark Vesey is arrested and killed when suspected of planning a slave rebellion.

159

PEOPLE TO KNOW
John Bratton
Eli Whitney

PLACES TO LOCATE
Connecticut
Historic Brattonsville

WORDS TO UNDERSTAND
antebellum
cotton gin
invention
overseer

This woman is telling people about daily life for slaves at Historic Brattonsville.

Welcome to Historic Brattonsville

The smell of fried bread fills the air, and you can hear a woman singing as she works. There are people all around you dressed in clothes that don't look like what people wear today. They are telling others about life in the past.

Do you remember reading about Brattonsville in Chapter 4? A Scots-Irish settler started the farm. By 1840, Brattonsville was a busy plantation. About 200 people lived there. There was a store, post office, sawmill, blacksmith shop, and a school. There was also a brickyard and a cotton press.

Dr. John Bratton managed the cotton plantation. He lived in a beautiful, large house with his wife and 14 children. Over 100 slaves lived in small slave cabins on the plantation. Some of them worked in the Bratton's house. They cooked, cleaned, and made clothes. Other slaves worked in the cotton fields.

In some ways, life was the same for all the people who lived in Brattonsville. For example, no one had electricity. People used candles for light when it was dark. In other ways, their lives were very different. The planter's family had freedom and wealth. The enslaved people did not.

A Time Called Antebellum

Today, people use the word "antebellum" for this time in our history. *Antebellum* describes the time before a war. In this case, it was the time before the Civil War. We will read about that war in the next chapter.

A New Cash Crop

In colonial times, many people grew rich from planting rice and indigo. After the American Revolution, people looked for another cash crop. They wanted something that was easier to grow. Cotton was the answer. It was in demand. Many people wanted to buy it. They wanted to make textiles, or fabrics, from it. There was a lot of money to be made from cotton.

Picking Prickly Cotton

Enslaved people worked hard to grow and harvest cotton. They were supposed to pick a certain amount of cotton each day. A child might pick 50 pounds of cotton a day. A strong man or woman could pick 300-400 pounds of cotton a day.

Plantation owners and **overseers** kept track of how much cotton each slave picked. At the end of each day, they weighed the cotton. One planter had 36 slaves picking cotton on his plantation. He wrote that a woman named Mary picked 596 pounds in one day. A young boy named Adam picked 51 pounds. In one week, the slaves picked over 10,000 pounds of cotton.

Overseers weighed the cotton each slave picked.

People needed cotton to make cloth. They spun the fluffy, white fibers into thread.

The Cotton Gin

Before cotton could be made into fabric, it had to be cleaned. All the seeds had to be removed from the cotton fiber. Slaves worked long hours cleaning cotton by hand.

Two types of cotton grew in our state. One type grew well along the coast, and the other type grew well in the upcountry. It was very hard to clean the cotton grown in the upcountry. Its seeds were sharp and hard to remove.

Since so many people wanted to buy cotton, plantation owners wanted to find a quicker way to clean it. Their wishes came true when a young man from Connecticut, Eli Whitney, *invented* a new type of *cotton gin.* The machine was good at removing seeds from cotton—especially the type of cotton grown in the upcountry. Before the new cotton gin, a slave could only clean about 5 pounds of cotton per week. With the new cotton gin, a slave could clean 50 pounds per day.

Expansion of Slavery

The new cotton gin expanded slavery in South Carolina. Once cotton was easier to clean, upcountry planters started more cotton plantations. Many slaves were moved to the upcountry to work in the fields. The number of slaves coming into our state also grew. It took many more slaves to grow and harvest all the cotton.

Almost overnight, cotton became an important cash crop. Planters were paid a lot of money for their crops. People said that cotton was king.

Eli Whitney sent this notice of his invention to the government. His cotton gin used sharp metal teeth to grab cotton fibers. There were slits between the teeth. The cotton seeds were too large to pass through the slits. When the cotton came out of the gin, it was clean.

1793 Cotton Gin Invented	
Before	**After**
Slaves were needed to separate seeds from the cotton fiber.	It took less time to clean cotton, so more slaves were needed to plant and harvest cotton.

More and more upcountry plantations grew after Eli Whitney invented a new cotton gin.

Activity

Interpret a Cotton Production Chart

Study the cotton production chart. Then use it to answer these questions:

1. How much did one bale of cotton weigh?
2. How many cotton bales did the United States produce in 1790?
3. How many more cotton bales were produced in 1800 than in 1790?
4. Look at the timeline at the beginning of this chapter. What happened in 1793 that explains the growth of cotton?
5. Slaves planted, harvested, and cleaned cotton. If the amount of cotton went up, what do you think happened to the demand for slaves?

U.S. Cotton Production, 1790-1820	
Year	**Number of Cotton Bales***
1790	3,000
1795	17,000
1800	73,000
1805	146,000
1810	178,000
1815	209,000
1820	334,000

*each cotton bale weighed 500 pounds

Memory Master

Lesson 1

1. What does antebellum mean?
2. What was our state's new cash crop?
3. Why did planters want a better way to clean cotton?
4. List one change the cotton gin brought to South Carolina.

Cotton Is King

PEOPLE TO KNOW
William Gregg

PLACES TO LOCATE
Alabama
England
France
Graniteville
Mississippi
Texas

WORDS TO UNDERSTAND
canal
textile mill
transportation

Getting Cotton to Market

Farmers and plantation owners sometimes sold their crops in towns nearest to them. However, most crops went to Charleston.

Charleston was a good place for people to sell cotton. It had a large port. Most farmers traveled on rivers to the city. People used rivers like we use highways today. Farmers sent their crops down the rivers to the city. In the city, they sold their crops to a merchant. Then the merchant sold the crops to someone else.

People in the North bought our cotton. People in England and other countries also bought it. Our state depended on selling products to these places.

People wanted better ways to get cotton and other goods to Charleston and other places. *Transportation,* or the ways people or goods travel, needed to be improved.

Boats traveled along the Santee Canal, carrying cotton and other goods.

Canals

Moving heavy goods by water was easier than moving them across land, but the rivers didn't always flow where the people wanted to go. To help improve transportation, people built canals. *Canals* are waterways made by people. The people built canals to connect one river to another. They then had an all-water route. Building canals was very hard work. All the work was done by hand.

Our state's first canal was the Santee Canal. It joined the Santee River with the Cooper River. It helped people send their trade goods to Charleston faster than they could before. Soon, workers were building more canals.

Railroads

Railroads were a new type of transportation. Trains traveled on railroad tracks. The trains could carry a lot of cotton. People were very excited to hear about the railroad. It was a new invention.

The first train in our state was called *The Best Friend of Charleston*. It carried passengers for the first time on Christmas Day in 1830. It went only six miles. One person wrote about riding *The Best Friend*:

> We flew in the wings of the wind at the varied speed of 15 to 25 miles an hour . . . leaving all the world behind . . . like a live rocket, scattering sparks and flames on either side.
>
> —*Charleston Courier*, 29 December 1830

Soon, railroads went to Columbia, North Augusta, and Florence. Tracks were also laid to Cheraw, Spartanburg, and Greenville. The railroad helped people move their goods faster and more easily.

What do you see in this drawing of The Best Friend?

William Gregg started a whole new town with his textile mill. You can still visit Graniteville today.

People Leave South Carolina

The railroad helped our state, but we still had problems. Many people were leaving to look for better land where they could plant cotton. They moved to Alabama, Mississippi, and Texas.

Growing cotton on the same land year after year hurts the soil. Some farmers rotated their crops. This means they grew cotton one year. Then they grew another crop, like corn, in the same field the next year. Many farmers did not rotate crops. They just grew cotton over and over again. This wore out the soil.

Since land did not cost too much, farmers could afford to move around. Farmers might farm a field of cotton for a few years until the land was worn out. Then the farmer would move on to new land. Many people moved to other states where there was better land.

Graniteville

One man had an idea to help keep people in our state. His name was William Gregg. He wanted people to do other things

The South Carolina Adventure

Workers used cotton at the Graniteville mill to make fabric.

● Graniteville

besides grow cotton. He wanted to build a textile mill. *Textile mills* turned cleaned cotton into fabric. South Carolina had only a few small textile mills. There were lots of textile mills in England, France, and in the northern states.

William Gregg traveled to northern states to study how the mills worked. He came back to South Carolina and got permission from the General Assembly to start the Graniteville Manufacturing Company.

Workers

William Gregg hired local people to build the mill. They cut hard rock called granite from a place nearby. They used the granite to build the mill. That is why it was named Graniteville. Gregg also hired local people to work in the mill.

Gregg built good homes for his workers. He also built a church and a library. There was even a doctor for the mill workers. He built a school for the mill workers' children. If the children did not go to school, their parents had to pay a nickel a day. That was a lot of money back then.

Linking the Past to the Present

People were leaving South Carolina because of changes in natural resources and jobs. Today, people still move because of jobs. They need to make a living, and they go to places where they have good opportunities.

Lesson 2 Memory Master

1. What is a canal?

2. How did railroads help South Carolina?

3. What did textile mills make from cotton?

PEOPLE TO KNOW

Dave the Potter
William Ellison
Robert Wilson Gibbes
Celia Mann
Denmark Vesey

PLACES TO LOCATE

Beaufort
Edgefield
Edisto Island
Georgetown
Pawley's Island
Pendleton
Sullivan's Island

WORDS TO UNDERSTAND

gang system
leisure
manual
ration

Ways of Living

In antebellum South Carolina, there were some very rich people and some very poor people. There were people who made enough to get by. Sometimes we call these groups "classes." People in a class share a certain lifestyle. The classes of people living in antebellum South Carolina were:

- The elite
- The middle class
- The lower class
- Independent farmers
- Enslaved African Americans
- Free African Americans

The Elite

People who were part of the elite owned at least 20 slaves and at least 500 acres of land. Some people who were part of the elite class were born into wealthy families. Others worked hard to be wealthy. They started out by clearing trees off the land. They lived in log cabins. As they made more money, they bought more land and more slaves. After a while, they became part of the elite.

Activity

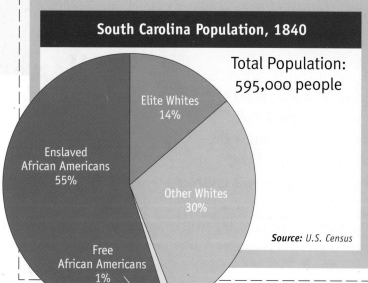

South Carolina Population, 1840

Total Population: 595,000 people

Elite Whites 14%

Enslaved African Americans 55%

Other Whites 30%

Free African Americans 1%

Source: U.S. Census

Antebellum Population

Look at this graph to learn more about antebellum population. Answer these questions:

1. What year's population is shown on the graph?
2. What group had the largest population?
3. What group had the smallest population?
4. Were most white people part of the elite?

What does this painting tell you about the life of the elite?

Free Time

Running a plantation could be hard work, but the elite also had time for *leisure.* They could relax and enjoy social events. They read books, went to plays, and hosted big parties. Men enjoyed hunting, fishing, and horse racing. The elite had the finest things of the time. They had nice furniture and fancy clothes. They also had the finest foods.

Many of the elite had more than one home. They had a plantation home, a home in town, and a summer home. They had summer homes on Edisto Island, Pawley's Island, Sullivan's Island, or in Beaufort or Pendleton. They relaxed at their summer homes with friends and family. They took some of their slaves with them to cook meals and clean the house. One woman wrote about moving to her family's summer home in Georgetown. She said:

> All of our belongings, servants, horses, cows, furniture were loaded [and shipped] seven miles through broad rivers and winding creeks . . . [then they were taken] four miles by land.

—Elizabeth Waties Allston Pringle

Wade Hampton I was an upcountry plantation owner. He had fought in the American Revolution. Later, he set up a cotton plantation. His plantation was near Columbia. His first cotton crop made him $75,000. He became a rich man very quickly.

Cotton Is King

Robert Wilson Gibbes
1809-1866

Robert Gibbes was born in Charleston. His father was a lawyer. Robert went to South Carolina College, where he studied science. He liked to learn about animals, rocks, and minerals. He also liked to study fossils, especially fossil shark teeth.

Robert also liked the arts. He collected paintings. He gave money to artists, so they could paint.

Robert wanted to help his community. He served as Columbia's mayor. He was also an editor of a newspaper.

Leadership and Education

Most of the government leaders in our state were part of the elite. They were governors or senators. They worked to make laws that served their interests. They wanted laws that protected slavery and helped them sell cotton to other places.

The elite were also well-educated. They had money to send their children to the best schools. Children learned other languages, like Latin and French. They took music and drawing classes. Young elite men were able to go to college. Sometimes they went to universities in Europe.

The elite spent time in Charleston doing business.

These firemen worked in Charleston. The elite people were in charge of the fire department, and they paid middle-class white men to run it and fight fires.

William J. Snider was a merchant in Charleston during the 1850s. He was also a minister. Later in his life, he started a new town in Orangeburg County.

The Middle Class

Some people made a good living, but they were not rich like the elite. They were part of the middle class. Middle-class men worked as teachers, nurses, clerks, store owners, railroad developers, and merchants. Some worked as college professors and lawyers. They had enough money to live in comfort. They had nice homes and enough food to eat. Some middle-class people owned slaves to do household chores.

With the spread of cotton, many new towns were built. Middle-class people ran stores in the new towns. As new towns grew, the middle class grew. Some of them worked at the county courthouse.

The Lower Class

People who were part of the lower class had very little. If they owned land, it was a small amount. They were sometimes called poor whites. Most poor whites lived on poor land that was not suited for cotton or rice.

People in the lower class did *manual* work. That means they worked with their hands. Some helped build canals and railroads. Some of them worked in factories or textile mills.

Some poor whites did work usually given to slaves. For example, a group of poor white women made clothes for the slaves of James Henry Hammond. Hammond was an elite planter. He owned slaves who could do this work, but he chose to pay these white women to do it since they needed the money.

Lower-class people helped build canals. Horses helped haul away the dirt the men dug out of the canal.

Independent Farmers

Many white people in South Carolina were independent farmers. They worked the land themselves. They planted crops to feed their families. Sometimes they sold part of their crops. Independent farmers were not rich. Their days were full of hard work.

Most independent farmers did not own slaves. Those farmers who did own slaves worked side by side with them. Everyone had to help with the farm work.

Some independent farmers also worked as overseers for the elite. They were paid to manage slaves on a plantation. Many overseers hoped to become part of the elite themselves.

Children

Most white children were not able to go to school. There were few public schools, and most parents did not have money to send their children to private schools.

Children spent most of their time helping at home. They did chores on the farm. Young boys learned how to plant and harvest crops. Young girls learned how to sew, cook, and clean. They planted small gardens. They helped their mothers make soap, butter, and candles.

Linking the Past to the Present

Do you like summer vacation? Do you know why you don't go to school in the summer? One reason has to do with farming. Long ago, children were needed to help out on the farm during the summer and early fall.

Independent farmers worked hard to clear land. They grew enough food to feed their families. Sometimes they sold part of their crops.

Slaves were often sold at auctions, like this one in Charleston. Many slaves were sold away from their families. This was their worst fear. Like all people, they wanted to be near their families.

Enslaved African Americans

Most black people living in our state were enslaved. Most of them lived on plantations. On large plantations, slaves and masters did not work closely together.

Long Days of Work

Some planters used the task system for their slaves. They had used this system for growing rice. Slaves were given a task to complete each day. When they were done, they were free to do other things.

Many planters used another system of work to grow cotton called the **gang system.** Slaves worked as a group. They worked in the cotton fields all day, from sunup to sundown. Some used plows to turn the soil. Some planted the cotton. Some kept weeds out of the fields. Some picked the cotton.

An overseer watched over the slaves in the field. His job was to make sure slaves did their work. The overseer worked for the planter. Overseers were white. Sometimes the overseer was mean to slaves. Most slaves did not like their overseer. Some black slaves worked as drivers. Drivers also watched over slaves in the field.

There were forty of us Africans in all and it took all of us to keep the plantation going. Most Africans worked in the fields. They went to work as soon as it got light enough to see how to get around; when twelve o'clock came, they all stopped for dinner and didn't go back to work 'til two. They worked on 'til it got almost dark."

—Former slave Victoria Adams, Columbia, South Carolina

These workers are returning from picking cotton all day near Mt. Pleasant.

Planters gave rations of food to their slaves.

Food and Clothing

Most planters gave clothes to their slaves twice a year—once in the spring and once in the fall. Adults were given shoes with their clothes once a year in the fall. Slave children did not wear shoes. Young children usually only wore a long shirt.

Slaves got a ration of basic foods from their masters. A *ration* is a set amount of food. One former slave wrote: "Master put out a side of meat and a barrel of meal and all of us would go and get our rations for the week." Slaves usually ate cornmeal, salt pork, molasses, potatoes, and beans. Some slaves had their own vegetable gardens and livestock. Those who did had better food to eat. They also hunted and fished if they had free time.

Homes

Slaves lived in small cabins made of wood or stone. Some lived in brick cabins. Many of the cabins had only one room for an entire family. Sometimes two or more families lived together in a cabin. Slave cabins on large plantations were grouped together in rows. They were called slave rows or slave quarters. These slave rows formed a neighborhood.

Slaves who lived in Charleston did not live in cabins. They lived in kitchens or carriage houses that were next to their masters' houses.

The South Carolina Adventure

Cruel Treatment

Sometimes slaves were treated very badly. They were given difficult tasks to complete, and they were beaten if they didn't finish the tasks. Slaves lived a hard life.

Slaves did not always choose to follow a master's rules. Some chose to rebel. Slaves who broke the rules were often punished. They were whipped or sold away.

Enslaved people were not allowed to leave their masters' plantations without a special pass. If a slave was caught without a pass, he was punished. White men formed slave patrols to watch for slaves who were away from the plantations where they lived. If slave patrols caught a slave without a pass, they put him in jail.

In Charleston, and on some large plantations, slaves wore tags. The tags had a number and a description of what jobs the slaves did. The tag was a way to identify a slave. If a slave did not wear a tag, he could be punished.

Running Away

Some slaves ran away. They wanted freedom. Often, slaves would run away if they learned they were going to be sold. When a slave ran away, his owner placed a notice in the newspaper.

PETER ran away.
TWENTY DOLLARS REWARD

Will be paid for the delivery of the Subscriber's Cook, PETER, at the Work-House in this city. Peter is about five feet 5 inches high, of a black complexion, thin visage and small eyes, he is a plausible Fellow and has some hesitation in his speech. He has been seen several times lately about the wharves, and is supposed to be working on board some vessel. The law will be rigidly enforced against any person harboring or employing said Fellow.

HUGH ROSE, Bull-street.

June 7   wfm6

This is a notice in a newspaper about a slave named Peter. What does the notice say?

Dave Drake

Some slaves were skilled craftsmen. In Edgefield, there were many skilled potters.

A slave named Dave made pottery. His pottery can be seen in museums today. This pottery was used to store foods, like cane syrup, lard, pork, and bacon. Dave made pots in many different sizes. He even made pots that could hold 40 gallons.

It was against the law for slaves to learn to read and write. But some slaves like Dave learned anyway. He worked at a newspaper when he was young. Dave wrote poems on his pottery. Here are some of Dave's poems:

Dave belongs to Mr. Miles where the oven bakes & the pot biles.

I wonder where is all my relations Friendship to all-and every nation.

A very large jar which has four handles pack it full of fresh meat-then light candles.

Celia Mann
1799-1867

Celia Mann was born a slave in Charleston. Later, she bought her freedom. Legend has it that Celia walked all the way from Charleston to Columbia.

Celia earned her living as a midwife. A midwife is a nurse who helps women give birth. Midwives were very important to the community. Celia helped deliver both white and black babies.

Celia and her family lived in a house in Columbia for many years. The house is a museum today.

Free African Americans

A small number of black people in South Carolina were free. Some masters freed their slaves. Some slaves were allowed to buy their freedom. They saved and saved until they had enough money.

Free African Americans were better off than slaves, but they were not as free as whites. Most free blacks simply tried to fit in with their communities. Some were independent farmers. Some were poor. Some were part of the middle class. A few were even rich and owned slaves.

William Ellison was born a slave. When he was 26 years old, he bought his freedom. William learned how to make cotton gins. He moved to Stateburg and became a cotton gin maker. He also started a cotton plantation. In time, he owned over 900 acres of land and 63 slaves. His plantation home had even belonged to a former governor.

Most free blacks lived in either Charleston or Columbia. They worked as mechanics or craftsmen. Some of them owned small stores or started schools. They also started churches. Yet, no matter how well off they were, free blacks did not have complete freedom.

Special Tax

Free African Americans had to pay a special tax each year to remain free. If they didn't pay the tax, they could be taken back into slavery. They had to carry special papers to show they were free. They could get in trouble if they did not have their papers with them.

Free blacks always lived in fear of being made slaves again. Because of this, many free blacks left our state.

Even some free African Americans had to wear tags.

The Denmark Vesey Plot

In 1822, white people in Charleston were in a panic. They had heard that a group of 117 black people was going to revolt against slavery. This group was made of both free and enslaved blacks. They were prepared to fight, kill, and die for their freedom.

The panic started when a slave told his master about the plan. He said the leader of the plan was Denmark Vesey. Denmark Vesey was a free black carpenter who was respected in the black community. He was also a leader in the African Methodist Episcopal Church.

The revolt never happened. The group of blacks, both free and enslaved, was arrested. Vesey and 34 other people were hanged.

The Denmark Vesey story changed life for slaves and free blacks. As bad as life had been for blacks, it got even worse. Our state passed new laws about slaves and free blacks. Free blacks who left our state were not allowed to return. It also became more difficult for slaves to get freedom.

A NARRATIVE

OF THE

Conspiracy and Intended Insurrection,

AMONGST A PORTION

OF THE

Negroes in the State of South-Carolina,

In the Year 1822.

AT the head of this conspiracy stood Denmark Vesey, a free negro; with him the idea undoubtedly originated. For several years before he disclosed his intentions to any one, he appears to have been constantly and assiduously engaged in endeavoring to embitter the minds of the colored population against the white. He rendered himself perfectly familiar with all those parts of the Scriptures, which he thought he could pervert to his purpose; and would readily quote them to prove that slavery was contrary to the laws of God; that slaves were bound to attempt their rescue, however shocking and bloody might be the consequences, and that such efforts would not only be pleasing to the Almighty, but absolutely enjoined, and their success predicted

Memory Master

Lesson 3

1. Name three classes of people who lived in antebellum South Carolina.
2. What type of work did most lower-class people do?
3. What was the gang system?
4. Why did slaves in Charleston have to wear tags?

Palmetto Detectives in

A VIRTUAL VISIT

It was Ben's first day at a new school. He had moved to South Carolina from Kansas. Ms. Izard introduced him to the class. Everyone welcomed him, and Ben took his seat next to Grant.

The class started the day by reading about antebellum times. When they finished the chapter, Ms. Izard asked the students to name one thing they had learned.

Erin raised her hand. "I didn't know that most whites were not plantation owners. I always thought all whites in the South were rich."

Grant added, "I liked learning about the free African Americans. It was neat to read about how Celia Mann walked from Charleston to Columbia."

"Ben, what did you learn?" Miss Izard asked.

"I had never heard the word 'antebellum' before, but now I know what it means," Ben said.

"That's great!" Ms. Izard replied. "We're going

to be palmetto detectives this afternoon. We'll look for clues on a virtual visit to Historic Brattonsville. During antebellum times, it was a busy cotton plantation." After lunch, the class went to the computer lab. Ms. Izard wrote an Internet address on the board, and the students pulled up the web page.

"Let's start by looking at the backwoods cabin," Ms. Izard told the class. "This cabin was built long before antebellum times. Does anyone remember reading about Brattonsville in Chapter 4? What did we learn?"

"I remember!" Kevin said. "Brattonsville was started by a Scots-Irish settler."

"That's right, Kevin." Ms. Izard asked the class to explore inside the cabin. Then they were off to the next place.

"This house was built during the American Revolution. By this time, the Bratton family was richer. They were able to build a better home.

Can you see how much larger it is? The furniture is nicer, too. But, let's not stay here too long. We've got to see the antebellum home."

The class clicked on the antebellum home. Then Ms. Izard gave an assignment. "I want each of you to explore this home and the slave cabin on your own. Look for clues that tell you about daily life of people living on this cotton plantation."

Ben thought this virtual tour was cool, but what did Ms. Izard mean by clues? Then he noticed a candle in the bedroom. *Wow*, he thought. *Does that mean they didn't have electricity? Maybe that is what Ms. Izard means by clues.*

After a while, Ms. Izard asked the students to share the clues they had found.

Carter raised his hand. "I noticed something that looked like a piano. That means the Brattons were rich enough to buy things like that. There was not a piano in the slave cabin."

"Yeah," Erin added. "The table in the slave cabin looked like it was made from scraps of wood. But the table in the Bratton's house looked really nice."

"Did anyone read how many slaves the Bratton family owned?" Ms. Izard asked. "They owned over 100 slaves. They were part of the elite class. Carter and Erin, your clues show some differences between the lives of the elite and the lives of slaves. What other clues did you see?"

"I read that Mr. Bratton was also a doctor. In his study, he had medicine and needles," said Grant.

"That meant he had time and money to go to school," added Ms. Izard.

"I explored the warming kitchen," said Christina. "I read that the slaves worked in the kitchen. It must have taken a lot of work because they didn't have any stoves or microwaves like we have."

Ms. Izard asked, "Did you also notice that almost every room in the planter's house had a fireplace? That is how the family kept warm."

"I saw that," Ben spoke up. "I also saw a candle in the bedroom. That must be how they got light when it was dark."

"That's true, Ben. There was no electricity back then," said Ms. Izard.

Ben was glad he had seen such a good clue.

"It's time to end our virtual visit. I can tell that everyone learned a lot. Each of you had some great clues about life in antebellum times. You were great palmetto detectives. Next week, we'll learn how life began to change for everyone in our state," Ms. Izard said.

ACTIVITY

Find Your Own Clue

It's your turn to be a detective! Use the Internet and search for antebellum plantations in our state. Look for at least three clues that tell about life for the people living there. Write a sentence about each clue.

Chapter 7 Review

Slavery Spreads

These two maps show the slave population in South Carolina. After you have studied the maps, complete the multiple choice questions. Write down the letter that best answers each question.

1. In 1790, most slaves in South Carolina lived in the _____.
   a. lowcountry
   b. upcountry
   c. Sea Islands
   d. none of the above

2. Compared to 1790, in 1840 there were _____ slaves living in the upcountry.
   a. less
   b. more
   c. the same number of
   d. no

3. Most slaves worked on cotton plantations. What is one reason that cotton plantations spread to the upcountry?
   a. People were tired of working near the ocean.
   b. Slaves wanted to move.
   c. Eli Whitney's cotton gin made it easier to clean cotton grown in the upcountry.
   d. The U.S. president said to move the plantations.

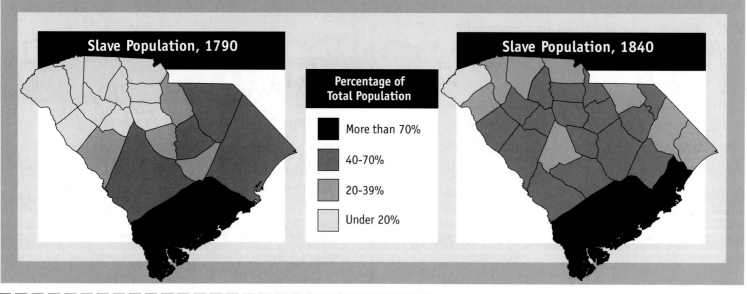

Slave Population, 1790

Slave Population, 1840

Percentage of Total Population

- More than 70%
- 40-70%
- 20-39%
- Under 20%

Blooming on the Vine

Comparing Daily Life

You have read a lot about different classes of people during antebellum times. Make a chart to help organize the information you learned.

Copy the chart onto a piece of paper or a bulletin board in your classroom. For each class of people, fill in as much information as you can. Use what you learned in this chapter. You can also look for more information in books at the library or from sources on the Internet.

Once you have filled in your chart, choose two groups. Then write a paragraph, comparing their daily lives. What is the same? What is different?

	Work	Homes	Food	Clothing	Education
Elite					
Middle Class					
Lower Class					
Independent Farmers					
Enslaved African Americans					
Free African Americans					

Genuine Genius!

Picking Cotton

Picking cotton was very hard work. The cotton plant has sharp parts that cut people's hands. It was hard to bend over all day and pick the cotton. Some people picked on their knees.

Cotton is not very heavy, so slaves had to pick a lot of it to make one pound. To get an idea of what cotton-picking was like, take a few packages of cotton balls and spread the cotton out in a long line on the floor. The longer you make the line the better. Get a plastic grocery bag. Now pick the cotton and put it in the bag. Have someone time how long it takes to pick up all the cotton. Now weigh the bag of cotton on a scale. Does it even weigh a pound? Now imagine that you actually have to pick each piece of cotton from a sharp plant that cuts your hand.

Describe what you think it was like to pick cotton all day long. You can:

- Write a poem or story
- Draw a picture
- Write a song
- Prepare a speech

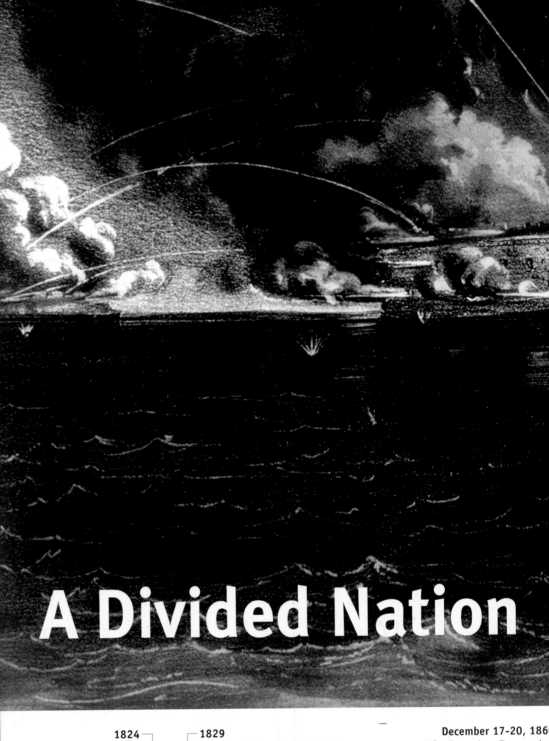

> " **I** have . . . believed from the first that the agitation of the subject of slavery will, if not prevented by some timely and effective measure, end in disunion."
>
> —John C. Calhoun, 1850

A Divided Nation

Timeline of Events

1824
The U.S. government creates new taxes on imports. This upsets South Carolina's leaders.

1829
Sarah and Angelina Grimké move to the North to work for the abolition of slavery.

1848
Telegraph lines are built between Columbia and Charleston.

December 17-20, 186
The Secession Conventio

| 1820 | 1830 | 1840 | 1860 |

November 18
Abraham Lincoln
elected president
the United Stat

Chapter 8

In time, differences between the North and South led to the Civil War. The first battle of the war was fought at Fort Sumter, near Charleston. The South wanted control of the fort. The battle lasted for over 30 hours, until the U.S. soldiers gave up and left.

1861-1865
The Civil War

February 9, 1861
The Confederate States of America is formed.

1862
Penn School begins on St. Helena Island.

July 1863
The South loses the Battle of Gettysburg.

1864
The *Hunley* submarine sinks in Charleston Harbor.

1861   1862   1863   1864   1865

April 12, 1861
First shots of the Civil War are fired at Fort Sumter.

April 19, 1861
Lincoln orders the blockade of Charleston Harbor.

1862
Robert Smalls sails the *Planter* out of Charleston Harbor. The Battle of Secessionville.

January 1, 1863
Abraham Lincoln issues the Emancipation Proclamation.

1865
Sherman's troops march through our state. They destroy many buildings and homes in Columbia.

December 20, 1860
South Carolina becomes the first state to secede.

185

PEOPLE TO KNOW
John C. Calhoun
Jefferson Davis
Angelina Grimké
Sarah Grimké
Abraham Lincoln
James Louis Petigru
Robert Barnwell Rhett

PLACES TO LOCATE
Charleston
Clemson
Columbia

WORDS TO UNDERSTAND
abolitionist
import
secede
tariff

North and South

Life was not the same in all parts of the United States. In the North, industry and business were very important. There were many large factories. Towns grew into big cities. Many people owned farms, but most of the powerful people worked in other businesses. Some of them made cloth from cotton grown in the South.

In most parts of the South, farming was still the most important part of the economy. Cotton, tobacco, sugar, and rice were the most important crops. Powerful people owned large plantations. They depended on enslaved people to do the hard work on the plantations.

Because of these things, the North and the South wanted different things from the government. The North wanted the government to help business and industry. The South did not like being taxed to help businesses.

A State's Right

The U.S. government issued a special tax called a *tariff*. People in the North were happy about it, but people in the South were upset. The tax raised the cost of *imports*, or goods coming into the country from other places. Factories in the North made some of the same products that were being imported. With the new tax, northern factories could sell their products at a lower cost than the imports. This would help them sell more and make more money.

People in the South felt the tariff was unfair. They needed to buy imports, and they didn't want to pay more for them. Leaders from South Carolina spoke out against the new tariff. A leader named John C. Calhoun wrote letters and gave speeches against the tariff.

When the tariff was approved, Calhoun said that South Carolina did not have to follow the new law. He said it was the state's right to disagree with the U.S. government. Other leaders agreed. People in South Carolina began to feel that the U.S. government did not care about their needs.

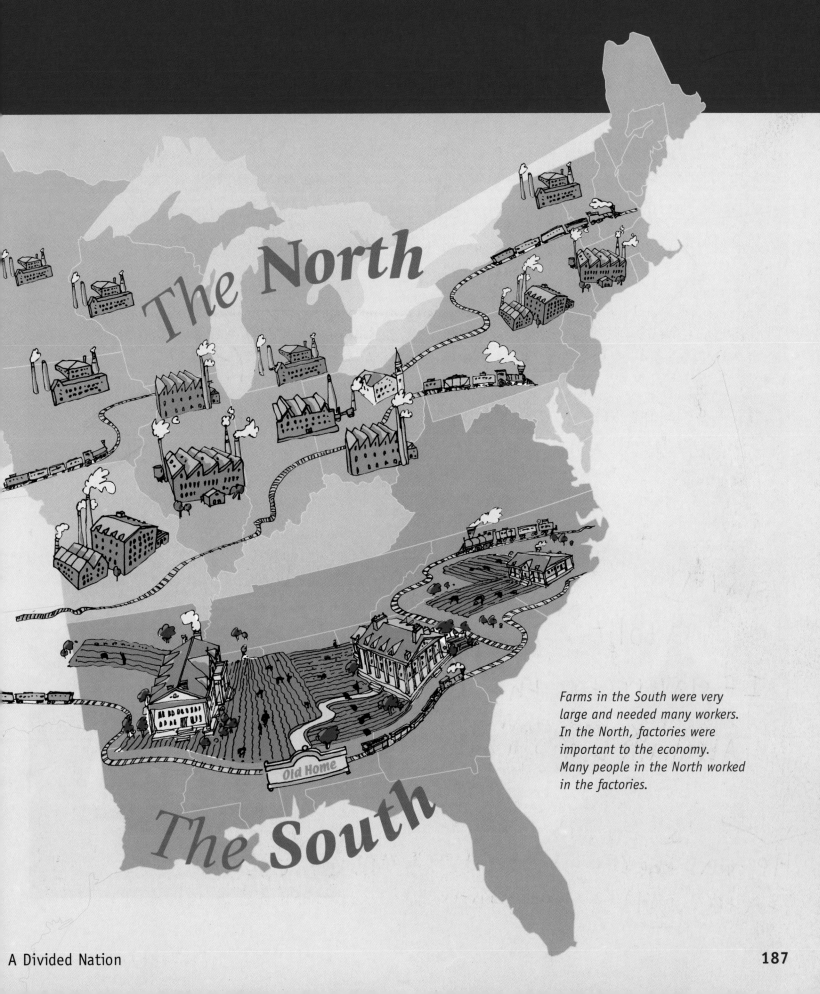

The North

The South

Old Home

Farms in the South were very large and needed many workers. In the North, factories were important to the economy. Many people in the North worked in the factories.

A Divided Nation

John C. Calhoun
1782-1850

I do not wish to destroy the Union! I only wish to make it honest!
—John C. Calhoun, 1831

John C. Calhoun was born in the backcountry near Abbeville. His parents were Scottish. After his father died, Calhoun ran the family's plantation until he went away to school. He graduated from Yale College and later studied law.

When he was 26 years old, he was elected to the state legislature. He later served in the U.S. Congress, where he was a member of the "Warhawks." This group of men convinced U.S. leaders to fight a war against England. After the war, Calhoun spent the next several years serving as secretary of war, vice president, and secretary of state.

Calhoun owned a large plantation called Fort Hill. It was in what is now the city of Clemson. He spent his political career trying to preserve states' rights. He believed the U.S. government should protect slavery because slavery was a "positive good." That meant he thought slavery was good for the slaves, and it was good for slaveowners because it helped the South's economy.

Calhoun spent his career trying to preserve the Union. He believed it was a mistake for South Carolina to leave the United States. He wanted the northern and southern states to work together to have a strong economy.

Calhoun died in Washington, D.C., as a U.S. senator. He is buried in St. Phillips Churchyard in Charleston.

Calhoun lived at this house on his plantation. Fort Hill later became part of Clemson University.

No Expansion of Slavery

At this time, people across the country were divided over the issue of slavery. More and more people in the North wanted slavery to end.

Rich southerners depended on slaves to grow and harvest crops. Cotton and other crops brought wealth to southern states. The leaders of the South knew slavery could not end without hurting the economy.

Our country was growing, too. New states and territories were being added. The U.S. government decided that each new place could decide whether or not to allow slavery. Leaders in the South hoped the new places would want slavery. They wanted to have more states on their side.

People felt very deeply about the issue of slavery. People in the North and South were becoming more divided over slavery and other important issues.

Activity

Compare Maps

Use this map and a modern map of the United States to answer the questions.

1. How many slave states are shown on the 1854 map?
2. How many free states and territories are shown on the map?
3. Which of today's states were open to slavery in 1854?

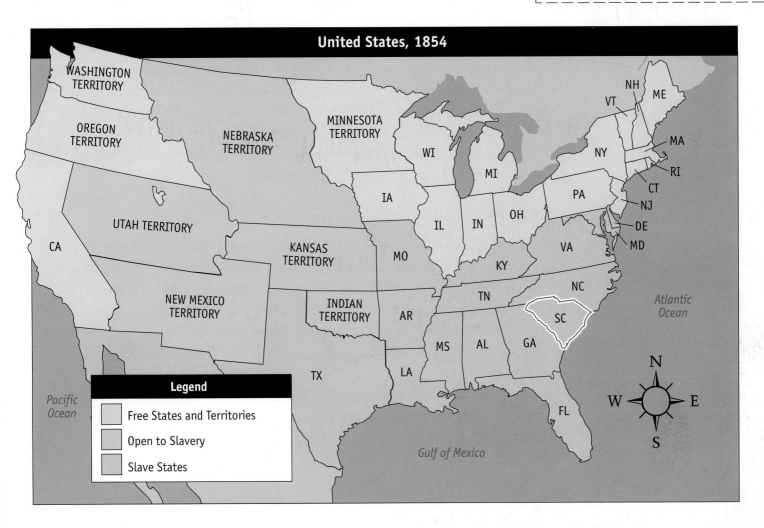

United States, 1854

Legend
- Free States and Territories
- Open to Slavery
- Slave States

Working to End Slavery

People across the country worked to end slavery. They were called *abolitionists*. They were men and women, black and white, young and old. Some abolitionists were freed slaves. All of them wanted others to know about the way enslaved people lived. They gave speeches and wrote in newspapers and books.

The Grimké Sisters

Two well-known abolitionists were from our state. They were sisters. Sarah and Angelina Grimké were born into a rich planter family. They grew up in Charleston. As children, they saw how slaves were treated. Sarah wanted to help the slaves. It was against the law to teach slaves how to read, but Sarah did so anyway.

When Sarah and Angelina grew older, they felt more strongly that slavery was wrong. Their father did not agree. The sisters chose to move to the North to join other abolitionists. They wrote about the evils of slavery in newspapers and booklets.

South Carolina's Concerns

In South Carolina, many white people felt abolitionists were a threat. Some abolitionists had asked slaves to fight against slavery. This terrified many whites. They were afraid that there would be a war between masters and slaves. They tried to stop the abolitionist movement. One time, a group of white men broke into the post office in Charleston. They destroyed many letters written by abolitionists.

John C. Calhoun said that abolitionists were dangerous and wrong. He knew if slavery ended, our economy would suffer. The state depended on slavery to keep the cotton industry going.

Angelina Grimké

Sarah Grimké

People gathered to discuss whether or not South Carolina should leave the Union.

Defending a Way of Life

People in South Carolina had talked about leaving the United States for many years. Sometimes they felt strongly about doing so, and other times they felt that things would work out. That all changed when Abraham Lincoln was elected president of the United States. He was against the spread of slavery. He said he would not end slavery in the South, but he would not let it spread into new parts of the country.

If none of the new states allowed slavery, then the slave states would have fewer representatives in the government. They would begin to lose more and more votes. In time, there might be a vote to end slavery.

Since none of the southern states had voted for Lincoln, southerners were worried that the South would be treated unfairly by a president they had not supported. Many white southerners saw this as a threat to end their way of life. Leaders in South Carolina called for a special meeting to decide what to do. They were prepared to act quickly.

The Fire-Eaters

Dislike for the North made some people feel very strongly about leaving the Union. They were tired of trying to make things work. They did not want to be part of the United States anymore. They wanted to create their own country. These people were called fire-eaters.

A well-known fire-eater in our state was Robert Barnwell Rhett.

The Secession Convention

Leaders met in Columbia. Their meeting was called the Secession Convention. They talked about whether or not South Carolina should secede from the United States. To *secede* means to break away from a country.

Almost everyone at the meeting wanted our state to secede. Only a few men were against South Carolina leaving the nation. One man against secession was James Louis Petigru. He knew our state was too small to be a country on its own. If we did secede, would we be alone? Would any other states join us?

South Carolina Secedes

During the meeting, there was talk that an illness called smallpox was breaking out in Columbia. The leaders moved the meeting to Charleston. Soon, the men wrote the Ordinance of Secession. All the members of the convention signed it. The document said that South Carolina was no longer part of the United States. It had left the Union. The signers hoped other states would join the state.

States' Rights

Do you remember reading about the U.S. Constitution? The Constitution gives power to the national and state governments. South Carolina felt its state government should have more power to decide what was best for its people. It did not want the national government to make all its laws, especially laws about slavery.

The Ordinance of Secession said that South Carolina was leaving the Union. Another document said South Carolina was leaving the Union because our state's rights were being denied. It said that each state had a right to make its own decisions. The state leaders especially wanted to make decisions about slavery. Even southerners who disagreed with slavery believed it was up to the state government to control it.

After the Secession Convention, people celebrated across the state.

There were celebrations all over South Carolina. Many people felt the North could no longer control the state. They were excited about the future.

Not all South Carolinians were happy. Some people did not want to be a separate country. James Petigru was very sad. He said, "I have seen the last happy day of my life."

The Confederate States of America

South Carolina was the first state to leave the Union. Soon, other southern states followed. Together they formed a new country. They called it the Confederate States of America. One of the first things they did was to write a new constitution. They also chose a president, Jefferson Davis. The leaders hoped to set up a peaceful new country.

This banner hung at the Secession Convention. What symbols do you see on the banner?

SOUTHERN REPUBLIC

BUILT FROM THE RUINS.

Lesson 1

Memory Master

1. Name one difference between the North and the South.
2. Why did the South want new states to allow slavery?
3. What did abolitionists want?
4. What was the result of the Secession Convention?

Lesson 2

PEOPLE TO KNOW
Jefferson Davis
Ulysses S. Grant
Robert E. Lee
Abraham Lincoln

PLACES TO LOCATE
Beaufort
Charleston Harbor
Europe
Fort Sumter
Port Royal
Sea Islands

After Confederates took over Fort Sumter, they flew this flag. What tree is shown on the flag?

Things Heat Up

President Lincoln refused to allow the southern states to leave the Union. He believed it would destroy the nation. He chose to keep U.S. troops at forts near Charleston. One of the forts was Fort Sumter. Because South Carolina was no longer part of the United States, Confederates felt the United States should have no control over the forts.

The First Shots at Fort Sumter

For over three months after South Carolina seceded, the U.S. flag flew over Fort Sumter. This made the Confederates more and more upset. They could not claim to be in charge of Charleston if they did not control the fort. They knew that Fort Sumter would soon run out of supplies. When that happened, the U.S. soldiers would have to leave. But that didn't happen. Instead, Lincoln ordered supplies to be sent to Fort Sumter. Confederates decided it was time to act.

Confederate soldiers planned to attack Fort Sumter before the supply ships arrived. They pointed cannons at the fort and waited for the order to fire. During the early morning of April 12, 1861, shots began to fall on Fort Sumter.

For over 30 hours, the cannons blasted away. Finally, the U.S. soldiers surrendered. The flag of the United States came down. Fort Sumter was now under Confederate control.

Charleston

Fort Sumter

Atlantic Ocean

What do you think?

South Carolinians watched the fight at Fort Sumter from their rooftops in Charleston. How do you think they felt?

A Nation Divided—the Civil War

North	South
Name: Union	**Name:** Confederacy
Nickname: Yankees	**Nickname:** Rebels
Color: Blue	**Color:** Gray
Number of States: 23	**Number of States:** 11
President: Abraham Lincoln	President: Jefferson Davis
General: Ulysses S. Grant	General: Robert E. Lee

The Civil War Begins

The shots fired at Fort Sumter were the first shots of a terrible war. Many people in our state died during the war. Over time, it came to be known as the Civil War. It would change our state and country forever.

Preparing for War

With the fall of Fort Sumter, four more states joined the Confederacy. Eleven states had left the Union. Lincoln wanted to defend the United States. He formed an army to invade the southern states. People in the South began forming armies to defend their new country. Over the next four years, many battles would take place. Most of them happened outside of South Carolina, but many South Carolinians fought in them.

Asking for Help

The South was a land of farms and plantations. It did not have many factories to make guns and bullets. The Confederate armies had to get these things from somewhere else. They hoped to buy supplies from countries in Europe. South Carolina planned to send ships loaded with cotton across the ocean to Europe. The cotton would be used to buy guns, bullets, and other supplies.

Lincoln Orders the Blockade

Lincoln knew of the South's plan to get supplies. He wanted to stop the supply ships, so he ordered a blockade of Charleston and the entire South. The Union placed its ships in the Atlantic Ocean outside Charleston Harbor and fired at any ship trying to get in or out.

Over time, the blockade made things very hard for people living in the South. Without supplies coming in, they ran out of things like cloth, thread, needles, and medicine. People tried to get by with what they had.

Port Royal

To make the blockade work, the Union needed a base in the South. The base was a place where they could keep soldiers and ships. The Union decided to attack Port Royal, near Beaufort.

Only three riverboats and a tugboat protected Port Royal. The four little boats were no match for the Union's ships. After a short fight, Port Royal was lost.

As Union troops took over Port Royal, they also took over Beaufort and some of the Sea Islands. Many whites left the islands, but many slaves stayed. The slaves hoped to gain their freedom from the war.

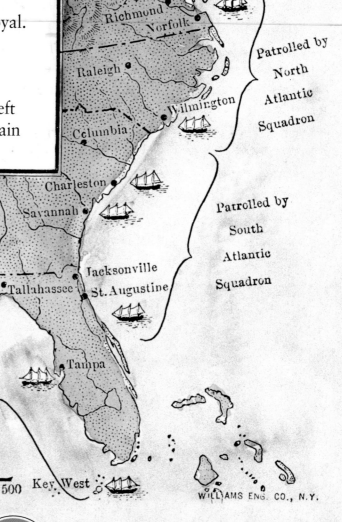

The Union Blockade

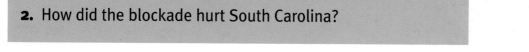

Memory Master

Lesson 2

1. Where were the first shots of the Civil War fired?

2. How did the blockade hurt South Carolina?

PEOPLE TO KNOW
Alexander Campbell
James Campbell
Richard Kirkland

PLACES TO LOCATE
Fredericksburg, Virginia

WORDS TO UNDERSTAND
cartridge
draft
technology

A Soldier's Life

Almost every able white man in South Carolina fought in the war. More than 60,000 men from our state joined the cause of the Confederates. Some of them volunteered to fight. Others were drafted by the government. *Drafted* soldiers were forced to join the war.

Fighting in battles was hard, but soldiers did not fight all the time. They marched from place to place. They set up camp in one place for a time. Then they moved on and set up another camp.

Life in Camp

Soldiers spent most of their time in camp. They did drills and learned how to march. Some soldiers played cards in their spare time. Others played games like baseball. Many soldiers played musical instruments, like fiddles or flutes. Soldiers missed home. They wrote letters to their families and friends.

Soldiers found ways to entertain themselves in camp. They hunted, read books, and played cards. These soldiers are chasing after a rabbit.

Soldiers marched for many hours.

Carrying Everything

Since the soldiers marched so much, they could not carry many things with them. They usually carried their rifles and cartridges. *Cartridges* were made of paper and had bullets and gunpowder in them. Soldiers also carried food, water, and a bedroll or tent. Some soldiers carried books, paper, and playing cards.

Hot and Cold

Being a soldier could be miserable. Can you imagine walking through sticky mud carrying a heavy pack on your back? Imagine the bugs and mosquitoes buzzing around you as you sleep. It got very hot in the summer, and soldiers wore heavy uniforms. Winters were very cold, rainy, and sometimes snowy. Sometimes two soldiers tied their tents together and slept next to each other. This kept them warmer during chilly nights. Many soldiers got sick and died. More soldiers died from sickness than from wounds on the battlefield.

Genuine Genius!

Hardly Worth Eating

Many soldiers ate hardtack during the Civil War. It was a hard cracker that would not spoil or go bad. It was called hardtack because it was very hard. A soldier once wrote home that he bit into his hardtack and found something soft. It was a nail! Of course, that was just a joke, but the story hints that hardtack was very hard to bite and chew.

With the help of an adult, you can make your own hardtack. Here is the recipe:

Mix 2 cups of flour, 1 cup of water, and a pinch of salt into a dough. Spread dough out on a cookie sheet. Divide the dough into 3-inch squares with a butter knife. Then use a fork, or a big nail, to poke three rows of three holes in the dough. Be sure not to leave the nail in the dough! Bake at 375 degrees for one hour. You've got hardtack!

Why Did the Soldiers Fight?

Soldiers fought in the war for many reasons. Many men joined the Confederate cause to protect their homes and way of life. Some wanted to keep the right to own slaves. Many simply thought the South should not take orders from the North. Another reason men fought in the war was for adventure. Some men thought the war would be exciting. They wanted to be part of history.

Brothers Against Brothers

Not every person in the South disliked every person in the North. They had lived side by side for many years. People had friends on both sides.

In some cases, brothers actually fought each other. Sometimes one brother joined the North and the other joined the South. This happened with two brothers named James and Alexander Campbell. James fought for the South. Alexander fought for the North. The brothers even fought each other in a battle called the Battle of Secessionville. One brother said, "It's rather too bad to think that we should be fighting." They hoped they would not see each other in battle again. Luckily, both brothers survived the war.

James Campbell fought for the South during the war. His brother fought for the North.

A Message Through Wire

Many people call the Civil War the first modern war because there was a lot of new **technology** used in the war. The telegraph was a new technology that helped communication.

Telegraphs were the fastest way to send a message. A letter could take weeks to arrive, but a message from a telegraph arrived in a couple of hours. Armies could communicate faster. Newspaper reporters could send their stories to their printers more quickly.

Telegraph machines sent messages over an electric wire. Telegraph wires were strung for many miles between towns. Messages were tapped into the telegraph machine by using a system of dots and dashes. It was called the Morse code. An operator touched a key quickly for a dot and held it down longer for a dash.

Linking the Past to the Present

Today, people can communicate quickly. They use phones, the Internet, and e-mail. Can you think of other technology we use that makes communication easier?

Why do you think Richard Kirkland helped the Union soldiers?

The Angel of Marye Heights

A big battle happened in Fredericksburg, Virginia. It was very bloody, and many soldiers died or were wounded. The North, especially, had many dead and wounded soldiers.

During the battle, the two sides stopped fighting for awhile. A man named Richard Kirkland was there. He was a Confederate soldier from Camden, South Carolina. He saw many wounded northern soldiers calling for help. They were in the middle of the battlefield, between the two armies. Richard wanted to help these soldiers. He took water to them and risked being killed. Because of his courage, Richard Kirkland became a hero. He became known as "The Angel of Marye Heights."

Memory Master

Lesson 3

1. Name one thing soldiers carried with them as they marched from camp to camp.
2. List one reason soldiers from the South fought in the Civil War.
3. How did telegraphs help communication?

Lesson 4

PEOPLE TO KNOW

Mary Boykin Chesnut
Malvina Gist
Abraham Lincoln
Ellen Murray
Sarah Kenziah Rowe
Robert Smalls
Laura Towne

PLACES TO LOCATE

Orangeburg
Penn Center
St. Helena Island

WORDS TO UNDERSTAND

Emancipation Proclamation
missionary
sacrifice
wayside hospital

Life on the Homefront

Even though most of the battles were fought outside South Carolina, things were hard for people in the state. Men left their homes to fight. Wives and mothers were left behind to run the farms and plantations. Women had to do the work the men had done. They still had to take care of the children, make clothes, and cook meals.

Many people struggled to get enough food. Confederate leaders asked farmers to plant less cotton and more wheat, beans, and corn. They wanted farmers to be able to feed themselves and help feed the armies. People started saying, "Plant corn and be free, or plant cotton and be whipped."

Struggles for Plantation Families

Because of the war and the blockade, everything was in short supply, even for wealthy plantation owners. Most of the clothing and food was given to the armies. People in the state did without many things. Things people used everyday could not be found anywhere. Families did without sugar, salt, and flour. There were no clothes in the stores to buy. As clothes wore out, they had to be mended. Mending was not easy because cloth, thread, and needles were in short supply, too.

While the war was going on, many slaves left the plantations. Plantation women had to learn how to do the chores their slaves used to do. They learned how to do laundry and care for the sick.

Family Photographs

Photographs were a new invention at the time of the Civil War. Many families traveled to Columbia and other cities to have a photographer take their photo. Before George Wilson left to fight, he and his family had their photographs taken. The photos were small, only about three inches on all sides. George carried the photo of his wife, Catherine, and their daughter, Tabitha, with him into battle. Catherine kept the photo of George with her at home.

Mary Boykin Chesnut
1823-1886

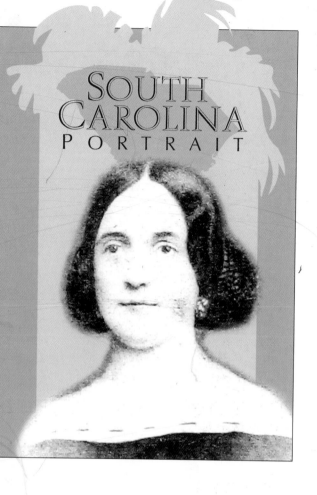

SOUTH CAROLINA PORTRAIT

Mary Boykin Chesnut had a lot to say about the Civil War. She was the wife of a wealthy plantation owner. Their plantation was near Camden. Her husband, James Chesnut had signed the Ordinance of Secession. He had been at the Battle of Fort Sumter. Both Mary and James knew Jefferson Davis, the president of the Confederacy.

Mary supported the Confederacy and owned slaves, but she felt bad about slavery. She recorded her feelings about the war in a journal. Today, historians read her journal to learn what life was really like for people during the war. Here are samples of what Mary wrote in her journal:

"February 18, 1861. The Southern Confederacy must be supported now by calm determination and cool brains. We have risked all, and we must play our best, for the stake is life or death."

"March 18, 1861. I wonder if it be a sin to think slavery a curse to any land. . . God forgive us, but ours is a monstrous system and wrong."

Struggles for Poor Farmers

Do you remember why the Civil War started? Slavery and states' rights were two reasons. Many farmers in South Carolina did not own slaves or care very much about government, but they still had to make sacrifices for the war. To *sacrifice* means to give up something. They had given up their way of life and were far from their homes and families.

The war hurt the poor farmers. They were expected to raise crops to feed the soldiers. Because food and supplies were low, prices went up. This meant that only wealthy people could buy the supplies. Without their own crops and money to buy food, many poor families went hungry.

Poor farmers also fought in the Confederate army. Many were proud to be soldiers. They believed they were fighting for a good cause. Some poor farmers thought the war was unfair to them. They called the war "a rich man's war, and a poor man's fight."

"The prices of everything are very high. Corn seven dollars a bushel, calico [cotton cloth] ten dollars a yard, salt sixty dollars a hundred, [and] cotton from sixty to eighty cents a pound."

—Dolly Sumner Lunt

Women Help the War Effort

All over the state, women's groups helped the war effort. They collected food and clothing. They set up hospitals. They raised money for the war. Many women used cotton from their farms and turned it into cloth to make uniforms.

Sarah Kenziah Rowe of Orangeburg helped soldiers on both sides of the war. Many wounded soldiers remembered her for her warm smile and baskets of food. One hungry southern soldier remembered eating until he was full. A northern soldier said that he would have starved if it hadn't been for Sarah Kenziah Rowe. After the war, Sarah raised money to help take care of the many men wounded in the war.

Wayside Hospitals

Women set up *wayside hospitals.* The hospitals were close to the railroad lines. Women cared for wounded soldiers who came off the trains. If a soldier was well enough, he waited for another train to take him home. The Young Ladies Hospital Association started a

Malvina Gist

Signing Money

During the Civil War, the Confederate States of America printed money. Malvina Gist was one of many young war widows who found work signing bills, or money, for the Confederate Treasury Department. She was 21 years old when her husband died in battle. They had only been married for 11 months, and most of that time he was away at war.

Malvina worked at the treasury in Columbia. Her job was to sign her name on each bill. Her signature made the money official. She worked with many other women, too. They did the same thing. Some workers could sign over 3,000 bills each day. Malvina wrote in her journal,

While I cannot sign the bills as rapidly as Nanny Giles can, today I finished up four packages of the denomination of fifty dollars. Mr. Tellifiere says I am a treasury girl worth having, and that I did a big day's work.

Malvina Gist signed this 50 dollar bill.

wayside hospital in Columbia. Mary Boykin Chesnut volunteered at this hospital. She wrote about her experiences in her journal:

August 19, 1864

Today we gave wounded men (as they stopped for an hour at the station) their breakfast. Those who are able to come to the table do so. The badly wounded remain in wards prepared for them, where wounds are dressed by nurses and surgeons, and we take bread and butter, beef, ham, and hot coffee to them there.

One man had hair as long as a woman's. A vow, he said. He had pledged himself not to cut his hair until war was over, and our Southern country free. Four of them had made this vow. All were dead but himself. This poor creature had [lost an arm].

Losing Loved Ones

When great battles were fought, the names of those who died were sent home by telegraph. The people of a town gathered to see if the name of someone they knew was on the list. Sometimes a person read the names out loud for everyone to hear. Sometimes the lists were posted on a wall for those who could read.

Over 20,000 soldiers from South Carolina died during the war. This was about one out of every three men who served. Almost every white family was affected. Women lost their sons and husbands. Children lost their brothers and fathers.

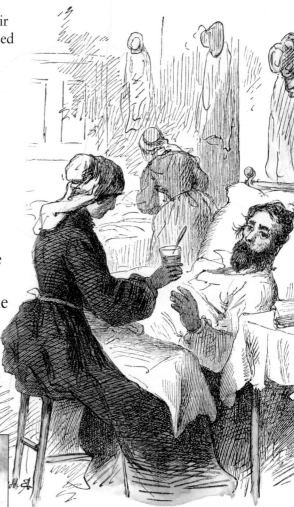

Sometimes soldiers were hurt so badly that nothing could be done for them. They were taken to hospitals and cared for until they died.

Many families had to bury loved ones who died in the war.

These slaves worked on a plantation on Hilton Head Island. When Union soldiers came to the Sea Islands, many plantation owners fled and left their slaves behind.

Struggles for African Americans

Many blacks still worked on plantations. Others fled to the Union lines, and some joined the Union army. Some plantation owners were paid to send their slaves to build forts or drive wagons in the Confederate army.

Slaves on Plantations

During the war, many slaves stayed on plantations. Some of them were afraid to leave while the war was happening. Some decided to watch and wait to see what the course of the war would bring. Others stayed and worked because they were faithful to their masters. Some even followed their masters to war and joined the Confederate army.

The South Carolina Adventure

Slaves who stayed on plantations tried to keep up with the war news. Since most of them could not read newspapers, they had to get news other ways. One enslaved man would hide under his master's house and listen to him read the newspaper to his wife. Then the man would tell others what he had heard.

Fighting for the Union

Many freed slaves left the South to fight for the North. They were formed into groups of black soldiers and fought against the South. Although they were no longer slaves, they were still separated from the white soldiers. Black soldiers were given worn-out uniforms. They were paid little or no money for being in the army. They were free, but they were not yet equal.

Many white men from the North did not believe black men could fight. But they were proven wrong. Black men were very good soldiers. They fought bravely. One white officer believed black soldiers fought better than white soldiers because they had a stronger purpose—they were fighting for their own freedom.

Robert Smalls Sails to Freedom

Robert Smalls was the pilot for a gunboat called the *Planter*. His owner rented him to the ship's captain. The captain taught Smalls important things about sailing ships. One night when the captain was away, Smalls sailed the *Planter* away from land. He planned to sail out of Charleston Harbor and on to freedom. On board were his wife, children, and the black crewmembers.

Smalls' escape was not easy. He had to pass by the guns at Confederate forts. He tricked the guards into thinking he was the real captain. In the dark of the night, he put on the captain's straw hat. When he was near a fort, he gave a call on his whistle. The guards called back that it was all right to sail on.

Once he was past Fort Sumter, Smalls directed the *Planter* toward the Union ships in the blockade. As he sailed to the edge of the harbor, he lowered the Confederate flag and raised a white flag. This meant he was surrendering the gunboat to the Union. People in the North called Robert Smalls a hero for leading his family and crew to freedom.

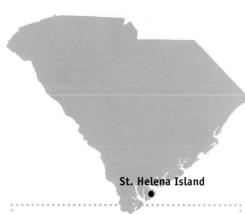

St. Helena Island

The Penn School

Most African Americans had never been allowed to go to school. Many could not read or write. They wanted an education. Some missionaries came from the North to start schools for African Americans. *Missionaries* are people who are sent by a church to help people.

Laura Towne and Ellen Murray started the Penn School on St. Helena Island. It started as a single room. The school quickly outgrew this small room because so many of the newly freed people wanted to attend. Soon, a larger school was built.

Students at the Penn School learned to read and write. They also learned other skills that would help them get jobs. Many of them learned more about taking care of a farm. Women learned medical skills and worked as nurses.

Students helped keep the school running. Girls prepared the meals for the students and teachers. They also did everyone's laundry. Boys grew crops and raised cows, which provided the school's vegetables and milk. Students sold baskets, milk, clothing, and vegetables to people on the island to earn money for the school.

These men are making sweet grass baskets at the Penn School.

African Americans celebrated Emancipation Day on January 1, 1863.

The Emancipation Proclamation

On January 1, 1863, Abraham Lincoln issued the *Emancipation Proclamation*. It said that all slaves in southern states were free. Blacks in Port Royal gathered to hear this news. Confederate leaders from South Carolina ignored the proclamation. Since South Carolina was no longer part of the Union, the proclamation did not really free the slaves here. But African Americans in the South didn't lose hope. They looked forward to being free someday.

Memory Master

1. Name two ways women helped in the war effort.
2. How did Robert Smalls get his family to freedom?
3. Who started the Penn School?
4. Why didn't the Emancipation Proclamation free the slaves in the South?

Lesson 4

PEOPLE TO KNOW
Wade Hampton III
William T. Sherman

PLACES TO LOCATE
Atlanta, Georgia
Columbia
Earhardt
Gettysburg, Pennsylvania
North Carolina
Savannah, Georgia
Sullivan's Island
Vicksburg, Mississippi

WORDS TO UNDERSTAND
submarine

Linking the Past to the Present

In 1995, scientists used special equipment to find the *Hunley* on the bottom of the ocean. It was a few miles away from Sullivan's Island. On August 8, 2000, the *Hunley* was brought up out of the ocean.

An Underwater Weapon

The Union blockade of Charleston had gone on for almost four years. The South looked for ways to end it. People hoped a secret weapon would help.

One day, a strange-looking ship arrived in Charleston. The ship was a long thin tube with room inside for nine men. It was a submarine called the *H. L. Hunley*. A **submarine** is a boat that travels under water. People hoped the *Hunley* could help end the blockade.

To make it work, one man guided the ship and others turned a crank. The *Hunley* sank in the Charleston Harbor twice during trial runs. Both times, all of the men inside died, and the *Hunley* had to be raised from the water.

Explosion!

Soon, it was time for the *Hunley* to battle the blockade. With a bomb attached, the submarine sneaked close to a Union ship. After the sailors pushed the bomb into the enemy ship, the men quickly steered the submarine away. Then the bomb exploded. The *Hunley* became the first submarine in history to sink a ship.

Not everything turned out well, though. After sinking the Union ship, the *Hunley* sank. The crew was trapped inside, and all of them died. Because the *Hunley* sank in deep water, it could not be raised up again.

This drawing shows how men inside the Hunley *worked to move it through the water.*

The Tide Turns

For the first two years of the war, the South won the big battles. But then things began to change. The South lost battles at Gettysburg, Pennsylvania, and Vicksburg, Mississippi. After Gettysburg and Vicksburg, things began to go badly for the South.

Sherman's March

People began to hear the bad news of the South losing battles. They heard stories of one of the North's armies. General William T. Sherman led this army, and his men had taken over Atlanta, Georgia.

After General Sherman took over Atlanta, he ordered his men to march to Savannah. He told them to take what they needed from Georgia's farmers. They did that, and more. They killed farm animals, burned crops, and destroyed homes and railroads.

Sherman's men destroyed cotton presses.

Too Close for Comfort

Everyone wondered where Sherman's men would go after they reached Savannah. Most people thought they would head to Charleston. People living there sent their important things to Columbia. They didn't want their family treasures stolen or destroyed. Some families in Charleston headed to Columbia as well.

Sherman led over 60,000 men. The South had less than 20,000 soldiers to protect our state. Many of them were young teenagers. Others were too old to fight.

Many people thought Columbia was the safest place in the South. They were in for a surprise. When Sherman's men crossed into South Carolina, can you guess where they headed? It was not Charleston. They headed for Columbia!

William Tecumseh Sherman

Confederates Fight Back

The Confederate army tried to stop Sherman's men. The soldiers fought hard, but Sherman's army was too powerful. Sherman continued to march toward Columbia.

Sherman's men did what they had done in Georgia. They took what they wanted and destroyed the rest. Homes and barns were burned. Towns were not safe. Courthouses were destroyed.

Sherman Arrives in Columbia

It took Sherman's men two weeks to get to Columbia. As they got closer, there was panic in the capital city. Remember, many had come to Columbia for safety, but they were not safe. Every building was full of people. Most were women, children, and older people.

The Confederate soldiers decided to leave Columbia. They hoped they could stop Sherman's men before they reached Columbia, but that didn't happen.

Before the Confederate soldiers left the city, their leader told them to burn cotton stored in warehouses. He did not want the North to get it. Another Confederate general, Wade Hampton III, thought this was a bad idea. He told the men not to burn the cotton.

No one could defend the city. The mayor of Columbia rode out to meet Sherman. To save the city, he surrendered it to Sherman.

Rivers Bridge

Have you heard of a place called Rivers Bridge State Historic Site? This is where Confederate soldiers held off Sherman's men for two days. Rivers Bridge is located along the Salkehatchie River near the town of Earhardt. This was the last major fight Sherman faced before he marched through the state.

Sherman's men crossed the Saluda River on their way into Columbia.

The South Carolina Adventure

Columbia Burns

Even though Columbia had surrendered, things got out of control. Sherman's men drank lots of alcohol and became drunk. They were mad at South Carolina. They blamed the state for starting the war, so they began stealing people's things, destroying buildings, and starting fires.

It was a windy day when Sherman came to Columbia. Fires spread all over the city. The fires burned through the night. The horrors of war were felt the night Columbia burned. By the next morning, the city was in ruins.

In a few days, Sherman's men moved north. As they headed toward North Carolina, they destroyed other cities and farms.

The War Ends

For nearly two months after Sherman's march, the South fought hard against the North, but the South finally surrendered. The Civil War was over. South Carolina would never be the same. Much of the state had been destroyed. How could it be rebuilt? There was much work to be done.

SOUTH CAROLINA
P O R T R A I T

Wade Hampton III
1818-1902

Wade Hampton III was one of our state's leading figures during the Civil War. His grandfather, Wade Hampton I, had become a wealthy planter. The Hamptons were among the state's richest families at the time of secession.

Wade Hampton III was not anxious to secede. But when the Civil War began, Hampton supported his state. He bought all of the weapons and gear for a unit of soldiers and led them into war.

Wade Hampton III was a brave and fierce fighter. He led his soldiers through many battles.

When the war was over, many people still looked to Hampton. He helped to rebuild the state and served as governor and senator. He worked to help improve life for blacks. Before he died, Hampton said, "God bless all my people, black and white."

Memory Master

Lesson 5

1. What was the Confederate army's underwater weapon?
2. What major city in South Carolina did Sherman's men destroy?

Palmetto Detectives in
READING MARY CHESNUT'S JOURNAL

After recess, Ms. Izard's class went to the school library. Erin stopped by the classroom to get a book she needed to return. She looked through her cubby for the book. Kevin's cubby was right next to hers.

There's that silly telescope he carries around with him, she said to herself. *All the boys think it's so neat.*

Erin found her book. She was about ready to leave when she looked at the telescope again. She knew she shouldn't touch other people's things, but something made her want to look through the telescope. Those boys were always looking through it and saying the oddest things like, "Have you seen anymore history in there?" or "Let me know when you see something else."

Erin put her book down and pulled the telescope from Kevin's cubby. She put it up to her eye and looked through it.

"What is the big deal about this thing? I don't see . . . Oh my goodness! Who's that? It is Mary Boykin Chesnut. She's writing in her journal. I wonder what she's writing about."

April 12, 1861

"At half-past four, the heavy booming of a cannon. I sprang out of bed. And on my knees. . . I prayed as I never prayed before. There was a sound of stirring all over the house. . . all seemed to be hurrying one way. I put on my double gown and shawl and went . . . to the housetop. The shells were bursting. . . I knew my husband was rowing about in a boat somewhere in that dark bay. And that the shells were . . . bursting toward the fort."

November 16, 1861

"Our life here would be very pleasant if there were no Yankees. My husband's [library] a beautiful room in the third story, overlooking this beautiful lawn and grand old oaks up here—all is my very own. Here I sit and make shirts for soldiers, knit, or read or write [in my] journal."

June 1, 1865

"We came down, for three days' travel, on a road laid bare by Sherman's torches. There were nothing but smoking ruins left in Sherman's track. That I saw with my own eyes—no living thing left, no house for man or beast."

It's Your Turn...

Mary Boykin Chesnut wrote about important events in the Civil War and about her daily life. Her journal helps us understand what life was like during that time. Choose an event happening in your school, town, state, or country. Write a short journal entry, telling your thoughts or feelings about the event.

Geography Tie-In

An Ocean Advantage

Look at the map of the blockade on page 197. How many ships does the map show? What do you think the ships stand for? The blockade ships did not guard the entire coast. They guarded the ports because that was where supply ships came in and went out.

Now, imagine that all of the South is completely surrounded by land. Write down ways this would have affected the war. Could the North have used ships? Would the South have needed the *Hunley*? How would people in the South have received supplies from overseas?

Blooming on the Vine

Comparing Political Cartoons

During the war, the South used this political cartoon as a symbol. Do you remember seeing a similar cartoon on page 136 in Chapter 5? Ben Franklin drew that cartoon just as the colonies began to break away from England. Compare the two cartoons, and answer the questions.

1. Both cartoons say, "Unite or die." Who is Franklin's cartoon calling on to unite? Who is this cartoon calling on?
2. What do you think the pieces of the snake stand for in this cartoon?
3. In what ways are the cartoons alike?
4. In what ways are the cartoons different?
5. In this cartoon, why do you think the head of the snake stands for South Carolina?
6. Why do you think the South used the same political cartoon the colonists used when they were fighting for freedom from England?

Activity

Cause and Effect

Whenever we do something there is an effect, or result. For example, when we enter a dark room and flip on the light switch, the room is filled with light. This is called cause and effect. The cause is flipping on the light switch. The effect is that the room is filled with light. Events in history also have causes and effects.

CAUSE: Something that happened first and caused something else to happen
EFFECT: What happened as a result of the cause

Look at each pair of sentences below. On a separate piece of paper, write "C" for the cause and "E" for the effect.

EXAMPLE:
C Abraham Lincoln became president.
E South Carolina seceded from the Union.

1. _____ Planters needed many slaves to work in the cotton fields.
   _____ Southern planters wanted to make money from huge crops of cotton.

2. _____ The South wanted to defend states' rights and its way of life.
   _____ Southern states seceded.

3. _____ Lincoln ordered the blockade of Charleston Harbor.
   _____ The South wanted to get supplies from Europe.

4. _____ People thought Sherman would attack Charleston.
   _____ Many people went to Columbia.

Genuine Genius!

A Country Torn in Half

Work with a partner to complete this activity. You will get a sense for what happened to the Union when the southern states broke away.

Stand opposite your partner, holding a piece of cloth between you. Pull on the cloth in opposite directions. Can you feel the strength of the cloth? Now cut a small tear in the cloth, and pull again. Does your cloth rip apart more easily?

What does this mean? The cloth stands for the United States of America. The tear stands for the southern states seceding from the Union. You and your partner stand for the North and South. Each of you pulled on the cloth just like the North and South pulled away from each other to protect their own interests.

Make a drawing or write a paragraph to show what you learned from this activity.

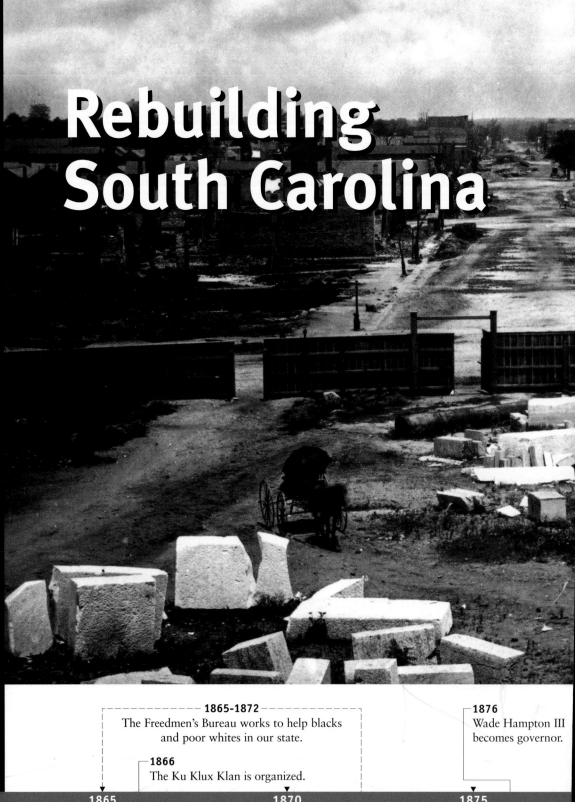

"*The slaves in South Carolina have been emancipated by the action of the United States authorities, neither slavery no involuntary servitude . . . shall ever be re-established in this state.*"

—*South Carolina State Constitution, 1865*

Rebuilding South Carolina

Timeline of Events

1865-1872
The Freedmen's Bureau works to help blacks and poor whites in our state.

1876
Wade Hampton III becomes governor.

1866
The Ku Klux Klan is organized.

| 1865 | 1870 | 1875 |

1865
Abraham Lincoln is killed.

1865
The Constitution of 1865 is written. The Black Codes are adopted.

1868
South Carolina ratifies the Fourteenth Amendment.

1868
A new state constitution is written. It focuses on equal rights.

1868
Francis Cardozo becomes the state's first black secretary of state.

Chapter 9

If you have been to downtown Columbia, you may have noticed that there are not many old buildings there. That is because over 400 buildings were ruined during the Civil War. This photograph was taken at the end of the Civil War. The photographer was standing near the Capitol. Today, you can stand on the Capitol's steps and see a rebuilt city.

1890
Ben Tillman becomes governor.

1898
A new state law requires separate railroad cars for blacks and whites.

1880   1885   1890   1895   1900

1895
A new state constitution creates segregation in schools. It also creates other laws that separate blacks from whites. They are called Jim Crow laws.

219

Lesson 1

PEOPLE TO KNOW
William T. Sherman

PLACES TO LOCATE
Charleston
Cheraw
Columbia
Lexington
Orangeburg
Winnsboro

WORDS TO UNDERSTAND
contract
debt
poverty
sharecropper
unstable

A Ruined Economy

After the Civil War ended, the South was in bad shape. Many of South Carolina's farms, towns, businesses, and railroads had been destroyed. Our economy was *unstable.* It was not strong and could have easily fallen apart.

Destroyed Plantations and Towns

When the Civil War began, many plantation owners started planting food crops instead of cotton. They grew food so they could feed their own families as well as the soldiers. Since plantation owners made money by selling cotton, they did not earn much money during the war.

When Sherman's troops came through, they destroyed many plantations and small farms. They burned cotton fields and stole livestock. With their fields burned and their animals gone, farmers had a hard time making a living.

Many towns were also hurt. In Charleston, much of the city was burned in a great fire in 1861. Union cannons destroyed many churches. Since church steeples were tall, they were good targets. Banks, hospitals, and government buildings were also hit. Columbia was badly hurt by Sherman's men. Orangeburg, Lexington, Cheraw, and Winnsboro were also hurt.

These young boys are sitting outside the ruins of a church in Charleston.

Many homes and mansions in Charleston were ruined during the Civil War.

"[Charleston is a city] of ruins, of desolation, of vacant houses, of widowed women . . . of deserted warehouses, of weed-wild gardens, [and of] miles of grass-grown streets."

Factories

The Civil War brought hard times to factories in our state. Before the war, factories made cloth and paper. During the war, factories produced only those things needed by southern armies. The Confederate government did not pay very much money for those things. So, factories lost a lot of money during the war.

Factories had also been destroyed during the war. The Saluda River Factory was burned. Sherman's troops burned the factory to the ground on their way to Columbia.

Transportation Systems

Roads, bridges, and railroads were ruined during the war. Both Confederate and Union armies tore down bridges and blocked roads to keep their enemies from traveling. On the Saluda River, Confederates burned down the old State Road Bridge. They were trying to keep Sherman's army from coming into Columbia.

Sherman's army destroyed railroad tracks. The soldiers wanted to make sure Confederates could not use the railroads to move their troops or supplies. They ripped up the rails and threw them into big fires. When the rails were hot, the men bent them around tree trunks. These became known as "Sherman's Bowties." The rails were so twisted they could not be fixed.

Sherman's men destroyed railroads so Confederate soldiers couldn't use them.

After the war, railroads needed to be repaired. New tracks to new places also needed to be built. Our roads and bridges needed to be fixed or rebuilt. People needed good transportation systems so they could ship their products to markets. They also needed a way to bring supplies to their towns.

Trying to Make a Living

Since our economy was in such bad shape, many people took whatever jobs they could find. Some people left South Carolina to find work in other states. Others stayed here and worked on farms. Many people lived in *poverty.* They didn't have enough money to provide the basic things they needed to live.

Sharecropping

Owning land was important to people. You could make money if you owned your own farm. You could grow cotton and other crops.

Landowners needed people to work on their land. Many people who didn't own land needed a way to make a living. These groups started working together. Many people became sharecroppers. A *sharecropper* was a farmer who worked land owned by someone else. Sharecroppers signed contracts with landowners. A *contract* is a written agreement. A sharecropper agreed to work the land. In return, a landowner agreed to give the sharecropper a house, tools, and some of the crop.

If a sharecropper owned a mule and farm tools, the landowner did not have to provide these things. Then the sharecropper got a bigger share of the crop. Some sharecroppers sold the crops for money and paid rent to the landowner.

Being a sharecropper was hard. Many sharecroppers went into debt. To be in *debt* means to owe money to someone else. A sharecropper had to buy things like food and clothing. He traded his share of the crop for these things, but this was not enough. He had to borrow money to get the rest of the things he needed. Each year sharecroppers went deeper and deeper into debt.

After the war, many South Carolinians lived in poverty. They had to work hard to get the things they needed.

Freed slaves faced new challenges. They had to find ways to make a living. They had to start new lives. This photo shows a family who had been slaves near Beaufort.

What do you think?

Look closely at the photograph. If you could talk with someone in the photo, how do you think he or she would describe what it was like to become free?

On the Edge of Freedom

Even though slaves had been freed, their lives were still difficult. Before the war, they had not been given the chance for an education. Most people who had been slaves did not know how to read or write. They had a hard time finding a way to make a living. One person who visited Charleston wrote about seeing a group of black people who had nowhere to live. He wrote:

> Families were cooking and eating their breakfasts around smoky fires. On all sides were their humble household goods—tubs, pails, pots and kettles, sacks, beds, barrels tied up in blankets, boxes, baskets, bundles.

> —John T. Trowbridge, 1866

The Freedmen's Bureau

The U.S. government set up a special organization in South Carolina and other states. It was called the Freedmen's Bureau. It helped people who had been slaves. It also helped poor white people. The Freedmen's Bureau gave food, shelter, and medicine to people in need. Workers built schools where former slaves could learn to read and write.

Many people felt that owning land was the best symbol of freedom. Many former slaves wanted their own land. The Freedmen's Bureau helped black people get land where they could build a home and farm.

What I Like Best Is Freedom

It was not an easy time for most people in South Carolina, especially for former slaves. Still, black people were glad for their freedom. One former slave said:

> What I likes best, to be slave or free? Well, it's this way. In slavery I owns nothing . . . In freedom I's own the home and raise the family. All that cause me worriment, and in slavery I has no worriment, but I takes the freedom.

Memory Master

Lesson 1

1. Name two ways the Civil War hurt South Carolina.
2. Describe how sharecropping worked.
3. In what ways did the Freedmen's Bureau help freed slaves?

SOUTH CAROLINA PORTRAIT

Mary McLeod Bethune
1875-1955

Mary was born in Maysville after the Civil War ended. Her parents had been slaves. She and her 16 brothers and sisters worked with their parents to pick cotton. Mary's mother also made money washing clothes for white people in the town. One time, Mary went with her mother to deliver laundry. She saw a young white girl reading a book. Mary could not read, and this experience made her want to learn how.

Mary spent most of her life helping others learn how to read. When she was 29, she set up a small school for African Americans in Daytona, Florida. Mary faced tough times at the school, but she worked hard to keep it going. The small school grew larger, and today it is Bethune-Cookman College.

Mary also worked for four U.S. presidents, where she led efforts to help bring equality for African Americans. She also helped the government in many other ways.

I had no furniture. I begged dry goods boxes and made benches and stools; begged a basin and other things needed and in 1904 five little girls here started school.

—Mary McLeod Bethune

Lesson 2

PEOPLE TO KNOW

Francis Cardozo
Andrew Johnson
Abraham Lincoln
William Beverly Nash
Joseph H. Rainey
Jonathan Wright

PLACES TO LOCATE

Bermuda
Charleston
Georgetown
Scotland
Virginia

WORDS TO UNDERSTAND

convention
federal
Reconstruction

A Plan to Rebuild

The Civil War hurt our state. Who could help rebuild it? The U.S. government, also called the *federal* government, wanted to bring the country back together. The southern states needed to rejoin the northern states.

Abraham Lincoln had a plan to help the country. His plan was called **Reconstruction.** To reconstruct means to rebuild. Lincoln never had a chance to rebuild the nation. Just after the war ended, he was shot. Lincoln and his wife were watching a play when a man fired a gun at him. Early the next morning, he died.

When Lincoln died, Andrew Johnson became president. He was from the South. He also had a plan to rebuild the South. He wanted to change our state government. He wanted the South to agree that slavery was over.

The Black Codes

Many of the white leaders who had wanted to secede from the Union were still in charge. They wrote a new state constitution in 1865. It said slavery was against the law, but it did not give blacks equal rights. The leaders still wanted blacks to live like slaves. These leaders passed the Black Codes.

The Black Codes were special rules for African Americans. They were meant to make blacks more like slaves than like free men. African Americans did not have the right to vote. They could not travel freely. They had to have special permits to have a business.

The U.S. Congress did not like the Black Codes. Its members knew the codes were really meant to take away black people's rights. They wanted African Americans to enjoy these rights.

The Fourteenth Amendment

Congress wrote the Fourteenth Amendment to the U.S. Constitution. It said that anyone born in America was a citizen. This meant that if a person had been born into slavery, he was now a citizen. It also said that every citizen was equal under the laws of the land.

The federal government said that southern states could not rejoin the Union until they ratified the Fourteenth Amendment. The white leaders in South Carolina were not happy about this. They said they would not ratify the Fourteenth Amendment.

The Federal Government Takes Over

The federal government was getting upset with South Carolina's leaders. Congress decided to throw out our government leaders. They sent an army into the state. Instead of a governor, the U.S. government put a general in charge. He was in charge of Reconstruction in South Carolina.

Blooming on the Vine

A Reconstruction Political Cartoon

This cartoon was drawn after the end of the Civil War. Look at it closely to answer these questions:

1. What is the title of the cartoon?
2. What does the kettle stand for?
3. The kettle is leaking. What do you think that means?
4. The woman is a symbol for the United States. Her name is Columbia. The baby stands for the Fourteenth Amendment. Why do you think the woman is holding the baby?
5. The man is President Andrew Johnson. What do you think the cartoon says about him?

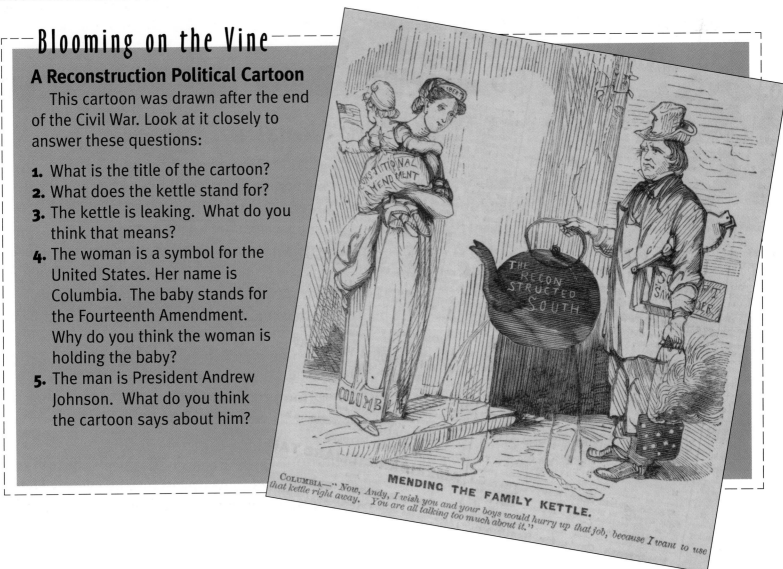

MENDING THE FAMILY KETTLE.

COLUMBIA—"Now, Andy, I wish you and your boys would hurry up that job, because I want to use that kettle right away. You are all talking too much about it."

African American men were able to vote for the first time.

A New State Constitution

In 1868, the federal government ordered South Carolina to write a new state constitution. It had to say that all men were equal. It had to give every man the right to vote.

The first thing people did was call for a ***convention,*** or meeting. The people at this meeting would write the new constitution. South Carolinians voted for people to go to the convention. More than half of the men at the meeting were black. For the first time, black people played a big role in making decisions about state government.

The Right to Vote

The new state constitution promised equal rights for everyone. It promised every man the right to vote. It also made public education available to every child.

After the new constitution was written, there was an election for new government leaders. Many white people refused to vote. They did not agree with the new freedoms black people were given under the constitution. They did not want African Americans to be elected into government.

Black Leaders

After the votes were counted, there was a whole new group of leaders. Francis Cardozo became the first black man elected to office in South Carolina. He was the secretary of state.

In the General Assembly, over half of the people elected were black. Many of them had been free before the war. Others had been enslaved. These leaders wanted equality. They voted to ratify the Fourteenth Amendment to the U.S. Constitution. They also wanted to improve education for black people. They said education was the key to bringing equality to blacks. Jonathan Wright was one of the black leaders. He said, "Where there is no education, people sink deeper and deeper into misery."

This is a painting of South Carolina's legislature in 1874. This was the first time in our state's history that black men were allowed to be part of government.

Joseph H. Rainey
1832-1887

Joseph Rainey was born a slave in Georgetown. When Joseph was young, his father bought the family's freedom. They moved to Charleston. Later, Joseph worked as a barber in a Charleston hotel.

During the Civil War, Joseph was forced to help the Confederate army build defenses for Charleston. He and his wife later escaped to Bermuda. There he worked as a barber. He also learned to read.

After the Civil War, Joseph came back to South Carolina. The people in Georgetown elected him to help write the new state constitution. Later, he became the first African American to hold a seat in the U.S. House of Representatives. Today, there is a park in Georgetown named after Joseph Rainey.

SOUTH CAROLINA PORTRAIT

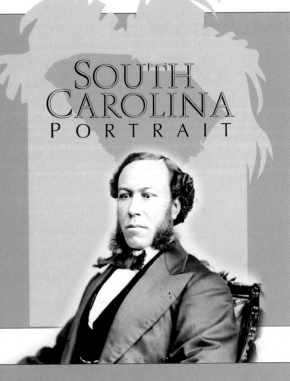

William Beverly Nash
1822-1888

SOUTH CAROLINA PORTRAIT

William Nash was born a slave in Virginia. He was brought to South Carolina when he was 13 years old. Later, he worked in a hotel in Columbia. He helped people with their bags, and he shined shoes. Legislators and other leaders visited the hotel. William listened to people talk about what was happening in the state.

William never went to school. He taught himself how to read and write. He became known as a powerful leader. He helped write the new state constitution. At one meeting, he said:

We are not prepared for this [freedom]. But we can learn. Give a man tools and let him commence to use them and in time he will learn a trade. So, it is with voting. We may not understand at the start, but in time we shall learn to do our duty.

Lesson 2

Memory Master

1. The plan to rebuild the South after the Civil War was called

_____.

2. What does the Fourteenth Amendment say?
3. Name two things the 1868 state constitution promised.
4. Why did black leaders believe education was important?

This was a one-room school for black children near Summerville.

PEOPLE TO KNOW
Wade Hampton
Ben Tillman

WORDS TO UNDERSTAND

integrate
Jim Crow laws
monument
segregate
tension
violent

Racial Tension in Public Schools

As time went on, there was growing *tension,* or uneasiness, between white and black people. This tension showed up in schools.

The new state government set up public schools. Before this time, there were many private schools. But few people could afford to send their children to them. A few poor whites went to school with aid from the state.

The new public schools created a big problem between white and black people. Whites did not want schools to be integrated. To *integrate* means to bring together. Integrated schools meant blacks would be socially equal with whites. Whites wanted schools to be *segregated.* This means they wanted blacks and whites to go to separate schools.

White people fought hard for segregated schools, and they got their way. Schools were supposed to be separate but equal, but they were not. White schools were usually nice buildings, and the students had books and supplies. Many blacks went to one-room schools. Some had dirt floors. Students usually did not have very many supplies. They often got old books that white schools would not use any longer.

Rebuilding South Carolina

Choosing to Be Separate

Although the laws said blacks and whites were equal, black and white people continued to live apart. Whites chose to not ride in streetcars or eat at restaurants with blacks. They were afraid that African Americans were taking over the state.

In many ways, African Americans chose to be separate from whites, too. They began to start their own churches. They celebrated the day that slavery ended. They formed communities where they celebrated their African traditions and culture.

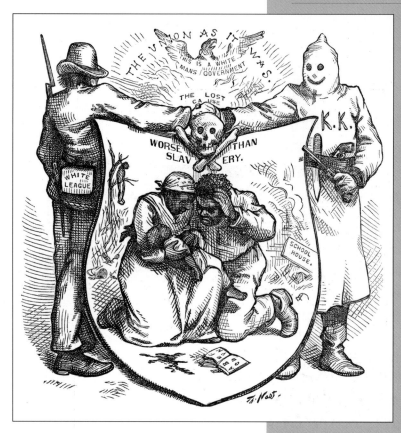

Ku Klux Klan members wore sheets and masks so people wouldn't know who they were.

The Rise of the Ku Klux Klan

The Ku Klux Klan, or KKK, was started in Tennessee after the Civil War. It was organized by old Confederate soldiers as a social club, but it soon turned violent. **Violence** is using force to hurt someone.

The KKK did not like blacks. The members were angry that blacks had been given the same rights as whites. They did not want blacks to vote or be government leaders. KKK members broke into blacks' homes and attacked them. They set fire to homes, schools, and churches. Sometimes they killed black people. They also hurt whites who stood up for blacks.

The KKK first came to South Carolina not too long after the Civil War ended. It was mostly active in the upcountry. A group of black Carolinians organized to protect people from the KKK, but the Klan continued to spread violence in towns and homes.

Finally, the U.S. government sent in soldiers to control the KKK. But there were many more Klan members than U.S. soldiers. Then Congress passed a law against the KKK. Many Klan members were put on trial for their actions. This did not stop the Klan, either. The Klan attacked other people for many more years.

The South Carolina Adventure

The "Lost Cause"

Many white southerners remembered the cause of the Confederate States. They called it the "Lost Cause." They were upset that they lost the war. They wanted to return to their old ways of life they had before the war.

People wanted to remember the men who had died in the Civil War. They built *monuments* in honor of the soldiers. People build monuments to remember important things. They often put these in parks or by government buildings. Our state has many Confederate monuments.

The End of Reconstruction

As more black men were elected to government offices, white South Carolinians became more upset. They did not want African American leaders. They did not want blacks to be allowed to go to school with white children or be allowed to own land. White southerners wanted a segregated society. They wanted blacks to be separate from whites in every way possible.

In time, Reconstruction ended. This meant that military leaders from the North no longer had control over the South. Leaders from South Carolina could now control the state.

People throughout the South gathered at Confederate cemeteries to honor soldiers who fought in the Civil War. This was one way they remembered the "Lost Cause."

Linking the Past to the Present

Does your community have any monuments? If so, what kind? Have you ever visited one?

A New Governor

South Carolinians elected a new governor. His name was Wade Hampton III. Do you remember reading about him in Chapter 8? Hampton was well-liked by most people, but some whites thought he gave too many rights to blacks.

For some people, life got better with Wade Hampton III as governor. But for farmers, things seemed to get worse. Farming had changed. New machines had been invented to help farmers grow more crops, but farmers could not afford the new machines. They also did not know the best way to farm the land. They wore out the land. Unlike the planters who moved on when their land wore out, most farmers could not afford to move on. When the land wore out, they couldn't produce very good crops.

Farmers started to complain about the leaders who controlled the state. They wanted new leaders who would help them.

The Rise of Ben Tillman

Ben Tillman spoke out for the white farmers. People called him "Pitchfork Ben." He said that people like Wade Hampton III did not care about the common farmer.

Tillman wanted to be a new kind of leader. He wanted to help white farmers. He also wanted whites to have total control of government. Blacks had no place in his plans. Tillman wanted to take rights away from blacks. He promised that if he was elected governor, he would help poor white farmers. In 1890, he won the election for governor.

Tillman created an agricultural college. It was a place where farmers could learn how to grow better crops without hurting the land. This new school was called Clemson Agricultural College. Today, it is Clemson University.

The Constitution of 1895

Tillman helped write a new state constitution. It took away the rights of blacks. Tillman wanted to take away their right to vote. This wasn't easy. The Fourteenth Amendment to the Constitution said voting rights could not be taken away based on skin color.

Ben Tillman said he would help South Carolina's farmers.

Tillman helped pass a new law about voting. In order to vote, a man had to prove he could read and write. Tillman used this new law to keep black men from voting. To prove he could read, a man had to explain part of the state constitution. Blacks who could read were told they were not able to explain the state constitution well enough to vote.

Jim Crow Laws

Once African Americans were kept from voting, they lost more and more rights. New state and local laws were passed that segregated them from whites. These new laws were called *Jim Crow laws.* They set up two different worlds. One world was for whites. The other world was for blacks. For example, one law said blacks and whites had to ride in separate railroad cars. There were different schools for whites and blacks. There were different stores and restaurants. There were different water fountains and restrooms. If a black person tried to use a white water fountain or eat at a white restaurant, he or she could be arrested.

With the Jim Crow laws, whites had more rights than blacks. Blacks were not given all the rights of American citizens. For over the next 50 years, the people of South Carolina lived under the Jim Crow laws.

Linking the Past to the Present

We still use the 1895 constitution today, but it has been changed. The laws that kept people from voting are no longer part of it. Other laws have also been changed.

Memory Master

1. Name two places where blacks and whites were segregated.
2. What was the "Lost Cause"?
3. What group of people did Ben Tillman speak for?
4. What were Jim Crow laws?

Lesson 3

Palmetto Detectives in TALKING ABOUT EQUALITY

"Ms. Izard, I thought America was the land of the free. It seems that a lot of people were not free in our history." Kevin said

"What do you mean?" Ms. Izard asked.

"You know, there were Black Codes. Then the Jim Crow laws made it hard for blacks to vote. That's not being free. I thought in America, all people were equal."

"Class, how do you feel about what Kevin has to say?" Ms. Izard asked.

Everybody agreed with Kevin.

"Well, you do know how things work out in this story of South Carolina, don't you?"

They shook their heads.

"Well, this class is part of the end of the story. Look around you. You are all different in many ways and yet you are still part of my class. You

are all equal in my eyes. You see, the story does have a good ending."

They all agreed to that.

"But why was there so much fighting? Why didn't people see that they were all equal back then? The Declaration of Independence said all men are created equal, but they didn't believe it." Kevin said.

"When the leaders who wrote the Declaration of Independence said all men are created equal, that was kind of a dream—a goal. Have you ever made a goal?" Ms. Izard asked.

"Yes, I'm in Cub Scouts. My goal is to get my Bear badge." Kevin said.

"Were you a Bear as soon as you joined Cub Scouts?"

"No, I am working hard to become a Bear."

"Well, when our leaders wrote that all men are created equal, it was something America had to work for. In fact, America is still working at it. As a country, we work at it every day." Ms. Izard explained.

"Yeah," Ben spoke up. "If we don't work on it all the time, then we might forget about it. We might start treating people badly, thinking that we are better than other people."

"Exactly! If we don't protect our rights," Ms. Izard continued, "then we might lose our rights. Part of protecting our rights is protecting the rights of others."

Grant jumped in. "My mother says to treat people how I would want to be treated."

"That's right, Grant. It's a thing we must never stop working for. It's something that is never completely finished. If we want to live in a country that believes that all people are created equal, then we must always think about other people and not just ourselves."

QUESTION

The belief that all men are created equal is stated in the Declaration of Independence. Show what this statement means to you by making a poster. You can include pictures, quotes, or your own writing.

Chapter 9 Review

Activity

Understanding Reconstruction

After the Civil War, the U.S. government had a plan to reconstruct the South. Answer the questions below about the plan for Reconstruction.

1. President Johnson wanted the South to:

A. continue slavery
B. help make new laws for the country
C. agree that slavery was over
D. grow corn instead of cotton

2. Congress passed the Fourteenth Amendment that said:

A. anyone born in America was a citizen
B. only African Americans could vote
C. only whites were citizens
D. only farmers had to pay taxes

3. Southern states could not rejoin the Union until:

A. they repaired their economy
B. South Carolina grew more cotton
C. they ratified the Fourteenth Amendment
D. they agreed to obey Jim Crow laws

4. The U.S. government took over South Carolina:

A. because it was upset with our state's leaders
B. to help our economy
C. to help farmers
D. to help African Americans find jobs

Genuine Genius!

Point of View

Write a newspaper article on the Constitution of 1868 from either a white farmer's point of view or a former slave's point of view. Give reasons why you like or dislike the Constitution of 1868. Then write a title for your article. The title should tell your opinion of the topic. Draw a picture to go along with your article.

Geography Tie-In

Rebuilding Transportation

During the Civil War, many of South Carolina's transportation systems had been destroyed. Railroads were ruined, bridges were burned, and roads were torn up. How did this affect our state? Make a list of ways South Carolina was hurt by the destroyed transportation systems.

Now imagine what would happen if the roads and highways in your area were destroyed. How do you think that would affect our state?

A Sharecropper Contract

Landowners and sharecroppers signed contracts that described their working arrangements. Most often, the contracts favored the landowners and kept the sharecroppers in debt.

To understand what a contract was like, you get to fill one out with a partner. Choose who will be the landowner and who will be the sharecropper. Write the following contract on a piece of paper, and fill in the blanks. Then answer these questions:

1. What does the landowner agree to provide?
2. Does the sharecropper get all of the cotton crop? If not, how much does he or she get?
3. What are some of the chores the sharecropper agrees to do?

This contract is made on _____ _____, _____
(month)   (date)   (year)

between _____ and _____. _____
(landowner)   (sharecropper)   (landowner)
agrees to provide land, a horse, plow, and other farming

tools. _____ must provide his or her own cart.
(sharecropper)

_____ will be given money made from one half of
(sharecropper)

the cotton crop. _____ is not allowed to have any
(sharecropper)

of the cotton seed raised from the cotton crop he or she

plants. _____ agrees to harvest all cotton by
(sharecropper)

September _____, _____.
(date)   (year)

_____ also agrees to repair fences, keep the land
(sharecropper)

free from weeds, take care of farm animals, and do any

other chores given by _____. If _____ fails
(landowner)   (sharecropper)

to do these things, he or she will only receive money

from one quarter of the cotton crop.

Signed: _____
(landowner)

_____
(sharecropper)

" *Between you and me and the graveyard, the farmer can sit by his fire all day when it freezes, rains or snows, but we got to go to the mill every day, just the same.* "

—Edward Fulmer, Newberry Cotton Mill Worker

Into a New Century

Timeline of Events

1879
The first telephones in Charleston are used.

1895
A textile boom begins. Construction begins on Olympia Mill in Columbia. It was the world's largest textile mill under one roof.

1903
The state's first child labor law is passed. It says that children cannot work until they are 12 years old.

1904
People begin to buy automobiles in South Carolina.

1912
Woodrow Wilson is elected U.S. president.

1880   1895   1900   1905   1

Chapter **10**

Sadie Pfeifer worked at Lancaster Cotton Mills. Many children had to work in mills to earn money for their families.

1914-1918
World War I

1917
The United States enters the war.

1920s
Many people migrate to other states. Our state's cotton and textile industries face tough times.

1930s
The Great Depression
The New Deal creates jobs.

1915

1920

1925

1930

1935

1940

1915
A new state law requires all children to attend school.

1919
Boll weevils destroy the state's cotton crop.

1920
The 19th Amendment is ratified, giving women the right to vote.

1921
Wil Lou Gray starts the Opportunity School.

1930
The Ocean Forest Hotel opens in Myrtle Beach.

1939
Workers begin to build dams along the Santee and Cooper Rivers. The dams help create electric power.

PEOPLE TO KNOW
Wil Lou Gray
"Shoeless" Joe Jackson
Daniel Jenkins

PLACES TO LOCATE
Atlanta
Baltimore
Charlotte
New York
Philadelphia

WORDS TO UNDERSTAND
illiteracy
loom
migration
orphan
prejudice
promote
reformer
scrip
spindle

A New Century Brings Change

At the end of the 1800s, many changes were taking place. Life had been hard since the Civil War. Many people lived in poverty. Wages were low. New roads were needed. Schools didn't have enough money to buy books and pay teachers.

The 1900s brought hope. They also brought new inventions in technology like telephones, electric power, and automobiles.

Electricity

In 1880, if you wanted to cook food or heat your house, you had to fill a stove with wood or coal and light a fire. Today, you only have to turn a knob to get gas or electric heat. To get light in 1880, you filled a lamp with oil and trimmed the wick every day. You had to clean the lamp once a week. Today, you flip a switch.

Electric power was one of the great inventions of the early 1900s. It changed the way people worked, played, and lived. Streets and homes were lighted with electric lights for the first time. There were electric washing machines, irons, stoves, refrigerators, and vacuum cleaners. In our state, many people did not have electricity. It took a long time for people in small towns and on farms to get electric power.

The Telephone

In 1880, if you wanted to talk to people across town, you had to write a letter or visit them. A new invention—the telephone—made communication easier. In South Carolina, telephones first came to Charleston and Columbia. It would be many years until most people had telephones in their homes. They had to wait for telephone lines to be built.

New Ways to Get Around

Towns and cities were growing. Soon, it was no longer easy to walk from one end of town to the other. In large towns, streetcars and buses carried people from place to place. People also rode bikes around town.

The first streetcars were pulled by horses or mules. Then some streetcars got steam engines. Later, electric streetcars were invented. They got their power from electric wires. Charleston and Columbia had streetcars.

Automobiles

The first automobiles were built in the late 1800s. Wealthy people began to buy them. Doctors were some of the first people to buy cars. They needed them so they could visit their patients.

Other people used cars mainly for fun. They were not very dependable. In most areas, the roads were not paved. If the weather was bad, the roads got muddy. It was hard to drive a car in the mud.

The first automobiles were small and had no roofs or windshields. In some parts of Columbia, the speed limit was 12 miles an hour. Drivers had to watch for horses, as many people still traveled in horse-drawn carriages.

In time, people were able to travel easier and faster with automobiles. Government leaders paid for better roads to be built.

A century is a period of 100 years. The 19th century was from 1801-1900. Can you guess what years the 20th century included?

Century		Years
18th	→	1700s
19th	→	1800s
20th	→	1900s
21st	→	2000s

Hint: To know the century, go up one number.

For example, 1600s = 17th century.

Before new roads were built, people traveled on old wagon roads. Crossing rivers and swamps in the lowcountry was tricky.

New Businesses

People in South Carolina wanted new businesses to come to our state. This would give more people jobs. If people had good jobs, they would not need to leave.

To attract new businesses, towns began to *promote* themselves. People called town boosters told others around the country how nice their town was. If people in other states thought our cities and towns were new and modern, they might move here. This would bring new business and new jobs. People called Greenville the "Pearl of the Piedmont." Town boosters in Spartanburg said their town was the "City of Smokestacks and Education." Anderson was called "The Electric City."

Expanding the Railroad

Another way to help our state grow was to expand the railroads. Railroads helped people ship their goods to market. In the late 19th century, more rail lines were built across the state. Many of the new lines were in the upcountry.

Upcountry towns, like Glen Springs, grew when the railroad came through.

Railroads helped many industries. Peach farmers in Edgefield and Lexington Counties needed a fast way to send their peaches to buyers. If the peaches were not shipped soon after being picked, they would spoil. Special refrigerated trains shipped peaches to many places. This helped the peach industry grow.

Trains carried passengers and goods to and from other cities like Charlotte and Atlanta. The railroad connected South Carolina to faraway cities like Baltimore, Philadelphia, and New York. With railroads, goods could be made here and sold to markets far away.

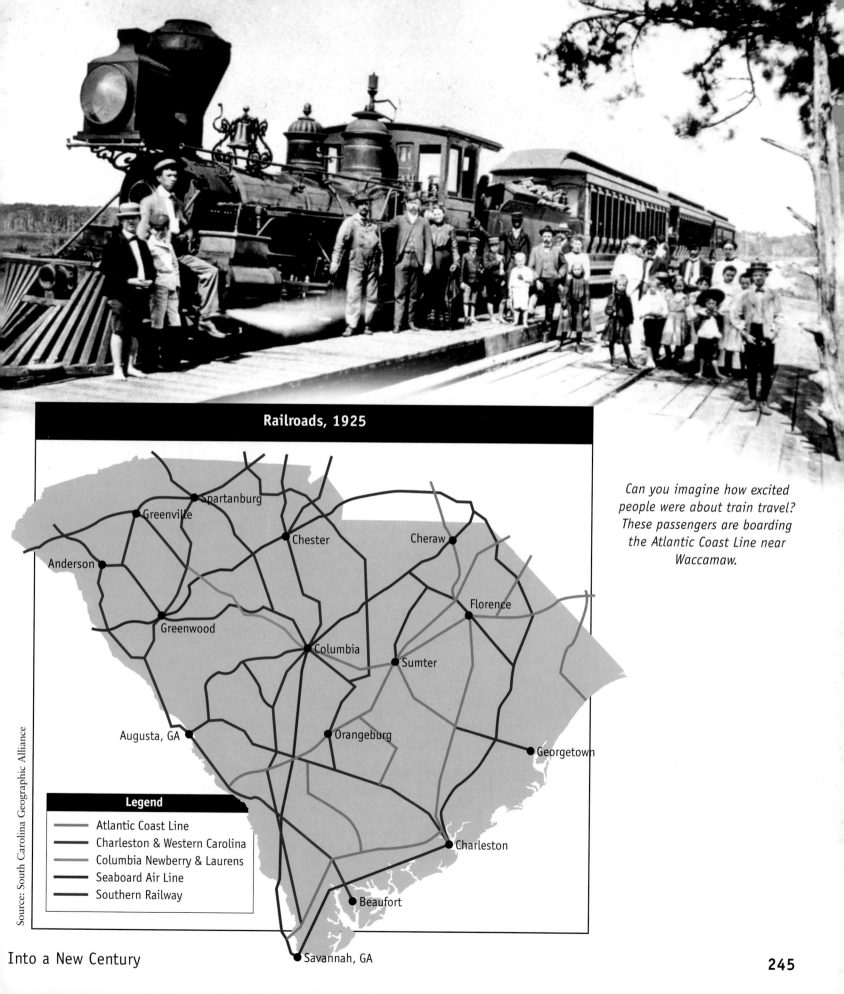

Railroads, 1925

Can you imagine how excited people were about train travel? These passengers are boarding the Atlantic Coast Line near Waccamaw.

Spartanburg
Greenville
Chester
Cheraw
Anderson
Florence
Greenwood
Columbia
Sumter
Augusta, GA
Orangeburg
Georgetown
Charleston
Beaufort
Savannah, GA

Legend
— Atlantic Coast Line
— Charleston & Western Carolina
— Columbia Newberry & Laurens
— Seaboard Air Line
— Southern Railway

Source: South Carolina Geographic Alliance

Into a New Century

The Rise of the Textile Industry

New railroads also helped the textile industry. Trains began carrying thread and fabric to places across the country. In the late 19th century, the textile industry was on the rise. Town boosters worked to get textile mills to come to their town. Having a textile mill meant that people would move to the town. Most people who owned textile mills made a lot of money.

Many workers were needed to run a mill. They worked long hours, from sunup to sundown. Entire families worked in the mills. Many of the workers were children as young as eight years old. If children were working all day, they could not go to school. People worked to pass laws that would protect children. In 1903, a new law said that children could not work in the mills until they were 12 years old.

A Great Migration

The larger textile mills hired as many as 1,000 people. Many people left their farms and other jobs to work in the mills. When many people move to a new place at the same time it is called *migration.* Farmers who faced hard times moved to work in a mill. White sharecroppers, who had never owned land, saw a new way to make a living at a mill. So many people moved to work in mills that some people called it "a great migration."

Not everyone was welcome at the mills. There was still a lot of racial tension. Mills usually did not hire blacks. African Americans who did work at mills had to load and unload cotton and cloth outside.

Hard Work

In time, more textile mills were built across our state. Most of them were in the upcountry and the midlands. The new mills were large brick buildings. Inside the buildings, thousands of *spindles* of cotton thread fed the looms. The *looms* wove the thread into fabric.

Working in a mill was dangerous, hot, damp, and noisy. The spindles moved very quickly. When they ran out of thread, the spools had to be changed. Some people were hurt by the spinning spindles.

These boys worked at Olympia Cotton Mills in Columbia. The room held 104,000 spindles of thread. What else do you see in this photograph?

The South Carolina Adventure

This young girl worked long days
at Lancaster Cotton Mills.

All three boys in this photo worked in a textile mill. Pamento Benson is the one standing next to the cow. His father said, "Just as soon as the boys get old enough to handle a plow, we go straight back to the farm. A factory is no place for boys."

This doll was made by a five-year-old girl. She made the doll with scraps of cloth from the mill where her mother worked.

Life in a Mill Village

When a new worker arrived at a mill, he found there was a whole town just for him and the other workers. It was called a mill village. The workers and their families lived in the mill village. Almost everyone in the family worked at the mill. They awoke to a loud bell at 6:00 a.m. It was time to get ready for work.

Families bought their food and clothes from the mill's stores. They went to church at one of the mill's churches. Their children went to the mill's school from age 5 until 12. When they turned 12, children were sent to work in the mill.

The workers were not paid much money, but they were paid regularly. They were a little better off than they had been as sharecroppers. Many mills paid their workers with *scrip*. This was paper money printed by the mill. It could only be spent at the mill's stores. To pay the rent for their small home and keep the family fed and clothed, almost everyone in a family had to work in the mill.

Mills were usually built near towns, but train tracks separated the town from the mill villages. The mill workers were looked down upon by the other people of the town. They were said to be from the "wrong side of the tracks." The mill workers faced prejudice from the townspeople, much like blacks faced prejudice from whites. *Prejudice* is making judgments about people because of their race, religion, or social class.

Fun Times

People living in mill villages made the most of their lives. For fun, they got together to play baseball. Each mill village formed a baseball team. The teams traveled to other villages to play their teams. Many of these players were able to leave the mills by signing big-league contracts.

What do you think?

Do you think people today are judged on how they look or where they come from?

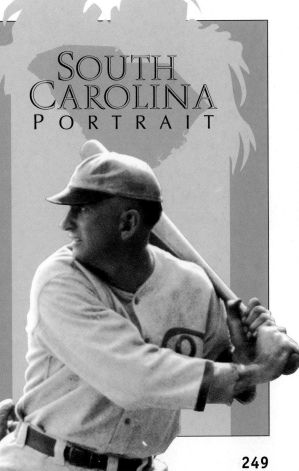

SOUTH CAROLINA PORTRAIT

"Shoeless" Joe Jackson
1888-1951

One of the most famous textile players was "Shoeless" Joe Jackson. He played for Brandon Mill in Greenville. He went on to play for three big-league teams. He got the name "shoeless" after he bought a new pair of baseball shoes. The new shoes hurt his feet, so he took them off and played barefoot! Can you imagine watching a baseball game today with an outfielder playing without any shoes?

"Shoeless" Joe was one of the greatest players of his day. Only two men in the history of baseball have higher batting averages than he did.

Then a sad thing happened to "Shoeless" Joe. Some people said he and seven other Chicago White Sox players accepted money to lose the 1919 World Series. Because of this, he was kicked out of baseball forever. This means he is not allowed to be in the Baseball Hall of Fame. Some people think he did not take the money. Nobody got more hits in that World Series than "Shoeless" Joe. Today, some people still try to clear his name. They think he should be in the Baseball Hall of Fame.

Into a New Century

Reform

Some things were getting better, but South Carolina still faced problems. One big problem was that many people did not know how to read or write. If adults could not read or write, they could not get very good jobs. There were other problems, too. As cities grew, water systems and sewers were needed. Paved streets and roads were needed. Many people didn't have electricity. People in mill villages needed help, too.

People could see that the old ways of government would not take care of the new problems. These people wanted to make progress. They were called progressives or reformers. **Reformers** wanted to improve life for people.

Better Schools

South Carolina's schools were not very good. They did not have enough money to operate. There were not enough teachers. Many children who did go to school spent three months or less a year in class. Some went to school for only one month a year. Nearly half of all the people over 10 years old could not read or write.

Ten-year-old Henry worked before school, after school, and Saturdays to shuck oysters. He started working when he was seven years old.

SOUTH CAROLINA PORTRAIT

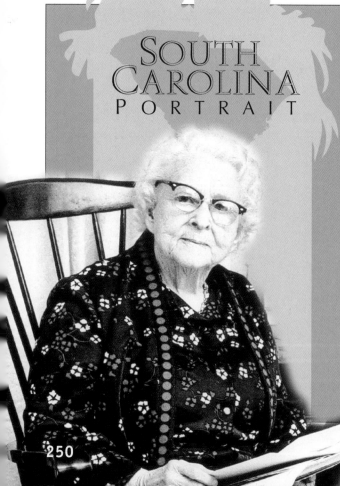

Wil Lou Gray
1883-1984

Even though schools for children improved, there were still many adults who could not read or write. What could be done? The State Department of Education decided to start an adult school program. They asked Wil Lou Gray to lead this program.

Wil Lou Gray was born in Laurens County. She taught school in Greenwood County and Laurens County. At both schools she was the only teacher. Later, she became a school principal. She saw the need to teach adults how to read and write. This became her life's work.

Gray started the first night school in our state. Four years later, she headed the South Carolina Illiteracy Commission. **Illiteracy** means not being able to read. This group taught adults how to read and write. Gray started the "Write Your Name" campaign. She wanted everyone to be able to write his or her name. It did not matter to her if a person was poor. It did not matter to her what color a person's skin was.

Gray believed adult education meant more than just teaching people to read and write. As long as people kept learning, their lives could improve. She set up Opportunity Schools to teach other skills to adults.

Wil Lou Gray spent her life trying to improve the lives of others. Today, there is a Wil Lou Gray school in Columbia.

Reformers helped adults learn how to read and write.

Jenkins Orphanage Band

The Reverend Daniel Jenkins saw that many young African Americans in Charleston needed help. They were **orphans.** They had no parents or family. They lived on the streets of the city and had to beg for food.

Jenkins started an orphanage for the children. He raised money to build a house where the children could live. He thought of a way to pay for the cost of taking care of the children. He asked people to donate musical instruments, and he started a band. He hired teachers to help the children learn how to play.

The Jenkins Orphanage Band played in the streets of Charleston. It also traveled to cities in the North and to England. People gave money to listen to the band. It took a lot of work, but the band earned enough money to keep the orphanage going.

Reformers knew the real key to progress was better education. They worked for better schools and more schools. They also worked for a new law that said every child had to go to school.

Schools began to improve. Spartanburg County soon had the most school buildings, teachers, and students in the state. Dillon County spent more money on its schools. Calhoun County had the first six-month school year. Schools for white children improved the most. Schools for black children received very little money to make improvements.

More Improvements and More Problems

Reformers worked to solve many other problems. They helped cities plan for growth. They laid water lines and sewer lines. Streets were paved. Streetlights were put up. New hospitals were built.

South Carolina was becoming modern, but there were some problems that were not faced. Segregation and the Jim Crow laws were still affecting people.

Memory Master

Lesson 1

1. Choose something that was invented during this time, and describe how it affected South Carolina.

2. Describe life in a mill village.

3. What is illiteracy?

PEOPLE TO KNOW
Freddie Stowers
Woodrow Wilson

PLACES TO LOCATE
Austria
England
France
Germany

WORDS TO
UNDERSTAND
veteran

A President From the South

People in South Carolina celebrated when Woodrow Wilson was elected president of the United States. He wanted to help reform things in our state and our country.

Woodrow Wilson was the first president from the South since the Civil War. He had lived in South Carolina as a teenager. It had been many years since our state and the South had felt like an important part of the country. Southerners were happy to have some say in U.S. government.

The United States made progress under President Wilson. He worked with U.S. Congress to outlaw child labor and unfair business practices. He helped pass a law for an 8-hour workday. Before, people worked for 10 or 12 hours a day.

World War I

Soon, our country faced a new problem. In Europe, a large war had broken out. Germany and Austria were fighting England and France. Other countries were in the war, too. There were so many countries fighting that it was called a world war. In time, it would be called World War I.

The United States did not want to fight in the war. Woodrow Wilson did all he could do to stay out of the war, but things changed when German submarines started sinking U.S. ships. Germany wanted to stop us from trading with England. President Woodrow Wilson knew it was time for our country to go to war.

I WANT YOU
FOR U.S. ARMY
NEAREST RECRUITING STATION

Woodrow Wilson

1856-1924

Woodrow Wilson was born in Virginia. When he was 14 years old, his family moved to Columbia. His father taught in a school that trained ministers. You can visit the home where Woodrow Wilson lived when he was a teenager. It is now a museum in Columbia.

When Wilson grew up, he taught at Princeton University in New Jersey. Later, he became the president of the university. He was also elected governor of New Jersey. While he was governor, he began to work for reform. When he became the U.S. president, he kept helping reform our country.

President Wilson did not want our country to fight in World War I. Then Germany attacked our ships, and we entered the war. Wilson said that we were fighting to "make the world safe for democracy."

Fun Facts About President Wilson:

- He was in the first filmed campaign ad.
- He spoke into a new invention called a microphone.
- He was president when radio was a new invention.
- His picture was on the $100,000 bill. (They are no longer used.)
- His family had a pet cat named Puffins in the White House.
- He let sheep graze on the White House lawn to help the Red Cross raise wool for the war effort during World War I.

South Carolina Helps the War

In South Carolina, people helped the war effort. Many young men joined the armed forces. Nearly half of the South Carolinians who served in the war were African American, but they were segregated from whites.

Soldiers trained at Camp Wadsworth in Spartanburg.

Our state helped build ships and weapons for the war. The Charleston Navy Yard built ships. The ships carried soldiers across the ocean. The ships were also used in battles.

People helped the armed forces in other ways. At home, there was less food, and fuel supplies ran low. People had "heatless" Mondays, "meatless" Tuesdays, and "wheatless" Wednesdays. This meant that people at home made sacrifices. This helped our soldiers have more supplies. Everyone did what he or she could to help win the war. People in South Carolina helped raise about $100 million to help fight the war.

Training in South Carolina

New soldiers had to be trained. Three army bases were built in our state to train soldiers from all over the country. They were Camp Sevier in Greenville, Camp Wadsworth in Spartanburg, and Camp Jackson in Columbia. After the men were trained, they were sent to Europe to fight.

Our Soldiers

Many of our National Guard units went into the army. These units were made of local men who kept ready in case of an emergency. They fought in many battles during the war. Seven soldiers from South Carolina received the highest military award—the Congressional Medal of Honor. This medal is given to soldiers for going "above and beyond the call of duty."

James P. Heriot was one of South Carolina's soldiers who received the Medal of Honor.

The South Carolina Adventure

The War Helps Farmers

The war helped cotton farmers. Soldiers needed many things made of cotton. With all this demand, prices for cotton went up. Even sharecroppers started to make money. With the chance to make money, farmers planted more and more cotton. Some had money to buy new farm machines. Their families now had many of the things they had lived without.

Peace at Last

Peace came when Germany surrendered. The countries agreed to stop fighting on November 11, 1918. The news that the war was over arrived by telegraph. In South Carolina and across the nation, people celebrated. Towns held parades to honor the soldiers. Troops marched through the streets as people cheered. November 11 is now celebrated as Veteran's Day. A *veteran* is a person who has served in the armed forces.

SOUTH CAROLINA PORTRAIT

Freddie Stowers
1896-1918

One night during World War I, Freddie Stowers led his men in a charge against the Germans. Stowers and his men were shot at, but Stowers pushed his men on until they had taken over the hill. Freddie Stowers died on that hill from his many gunshot wounds.

Many black soldiers fought bravely during World War I, but none were awarded a Medal of Honor. At that time, many people in our country were prejudiced against blacks. Over 70 years after the war ended, our country realized its error. A Medal of Honor was awarded to Freddie Stowers. He had died years before, so the award was presented to his two sisters.

In the ceremony, President George Bush said, "Today, Corporal Freddie Stowers becomes the first black soldier honored with the Medal of Honor from World War I. He sought and helped achieve the triumph of right over wrong. He showed. . . that an inspired human heart can surmount bayonets and barbed wire."

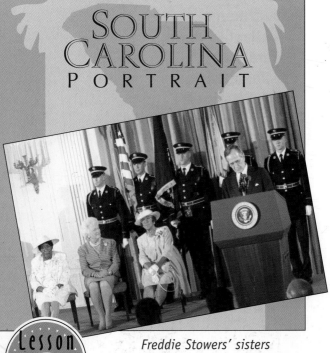

Freddie Stowers' sisters received his Medal of Honor in a special ceremony.

Lesson 2

Memory Master

1. What did President Woodrow Wilson do about child labor?
2. Name two ways South Carolinians helped in World War I.
3. How did World War I help cotton farmers?

PLACES TO LOCATE
Chicago
Cleveland
Detroit
The Pee Dee River
Pittsburgh

WORDS TO UNDERSTAND
convenience
emigrate
nutrition
pellagra
rural
sanitation
sewer system

The Roaring Twenties

For most of the United States, the years after the war were good. Many people had more money. They could buy radios and telephones for the first time. Families in small towns got electricity for the first time. They could keep food in a refrigerator. People wanted to forget about the war and have fun. They went to dance contests to see who could dance the longest. People listened to the new sounds of jazz. This lively time became known as the Roaring Twenties.

Women who wore the new styles and cut their hair short were called "Flappers."

Women Win the Right to Vote!

In the 1920s, South Carolina had a large group of new voters. The Nineteenth Amendment was added to the U.S. Constitution. It gave women the right to vote. Women from South Carolina and other states had worked for a long time to get the right to vote.

Nothing to Roar About

During World War I, people in our state enjoyed good times. But in the 1920s, many people did not have good times. During the war, farmers had been paid more for their cotton, and army bases like Camp Jackson had brought in lots of money. When the war ended, cotton farmers stopped making as much money. Times were hard again.

Jim Crow Stays

African Americans had fought in the war. Those who stayed home had supported the war. They played an important role in the war, but their rights at home were still denied. African Americans from around the state held a meeting where they spoke out against the unfair voting laws. They wanted the voting laws to be changed. They called for the end of the Jim Crow laws. They asked for better schools.

The war had not changed the ideas of most whites. They wanted things to stay the same. Riots broke out between whites and blacks. In Charleston, three people were killed.

Finally, a group of whites spoke out for the fair treatment of blacks. They said the two races should get along. But they wanted whites to rule the state. In the end, nothing really changed. There was still segregation. There were still Jim Crow laws. Black schools were still far behind white schools.

What do you see written on this Coke machine that you would not see today?

The Fall of Cotton

During World War I, the price of cotton was high. Farmers planted more and more, hoping to make more money. After the war, cotton was no longer needed for the army. Other places were not buying it as much either. This caused the price of cotton to fall from 40 cents a pound to 13 cents a pound. Farmers lost a lot of money.

Cotton farmers were also hurt by a bug called a boll weevil. It was a tiny bug, but it destroyed most of our state's cotton plants. The bugs ate the cotton bolls, and the plants died. It took many years before farmers found a way to get rid of the boll weevil.

What About Food?

For most farmers, cotton had been their only cash crop. Even though they were not getting much money for it, they kept planting more and more cotton. This meant they planted less and less food.

Tobacco in the Pee Dee

Farmers needed to find other ways to make money. What could they do? Could they grow other cash crops?

In the land near the Pee Dee River, farmers grew tobacco. Unlike cotton farmers, tobacco farmers had done well. Before the war, they had made much more money than cotton farmers. But tobacco could not be grown everywhere in South Carolina. It needed the special soil of the Pee Dee to grow.

This young man's family worked as sharecroppers. They grew cotton near Chesnee.

The South Carolina Adventure

South Carolina had to get food from other states. This was odd for a state that had so many farms. But people could not eat cotton. They could not eat tobacco, either. People had to buy their food. Most people did not have a lot of money. The cheapest foods were pork, cornbread, and molasses. This became the main diet for many poor South Carolinians. It did not give people all the *nutrition* they needed.

Because of their poor diet, many people were in poor health. They developed a skin disease called *pellagra*. Many babies and small children died because they didn't get the food they needed.

"Five cent cotton and forty cent meat How in the [heck] can a poor man eat."

—Bob Miller

The Textile Market Struggles

Early in the 1920s, textile mills were still doing well. They led the country in production of fabric and other cotton goods. People felt that the textile mills would always do well. But that was not the case.

Mill owners had a hard time getting high prices for their products. Many of the textile workers did not want to work long hours. They wanted to be paid more. After a while, work at the mills slowed down. The mills produced fewer products. The textile boom ended.

Blooming on the Vine

Cotton Prices

1. In the 1920s, did cotton prices rise or fall?
2. If cotton prices were lower, did farmers have more or less money to spend?
3. If you were a cotton farmer and cotton prices were low, how would you choose to make more money? You could:
   - Plant other crops and hope they make money.
   - Keep your cotton and hope that prices go up.
   - Work for someone else until next year.
   - Leave the farm and work at a mill.
4. After you choose one of these, explain what you think might happen because of your choice.

After four years of cotton picking, this family of 16 wanted to move on to a better life. They left Springfield, South Carolina and headed north to Ohio.

Another Great Migration

In the 1920s, half of our counties lost people. Both blacks and whites left the state. So many blacks left that for the first time in over 100 years, there were more whites than blacks in our state.

During the 1920s, our cities made progress. Charleston, Columbia, and Greenville had electricity and telephones. They had water lines and *sewer systems,* or ways of getting rid of human waste. Many of the streets had been paved.

For people in the countryside, there was not much progress. People still lit their homes with lanterns. They cooked on wood-burning stoves and pumped water by hand. Life for farmers kept getting worse.

Reasons People Left

Most people who left South Carolina were from *rural,* or farming, areas. They were looking for a better life somewhere else. Other states had more to offer people. Some of the reasons why people left were:

Unemployment

People had a hard time finding jobs. They hoped to find jobs in the big cities of the North and Midwest.

Poor City Services

Many rural areas had poor *sanitation* services. They did not have good ways of getting rid of human waste. This made people sick. Many towns and cities did not have good transportation, either. People wanted to live in places that were better developed.

No Electricity

Most small towns had no electricity. It was one modern *convenience* that people wanted. With electricity, people could have new washing machines. They could have electric lights. People felt life would be easier if they could have some of these inventions.

The South Carolina Adventure

People were tired of working so hard to earn a living. They decided to look for a better life somewhere else. Families packed up their things and left their farms and homes. They *emigrated* to the big cities of the North, like Chicago, Cleveland, Detroit, and Pittsburgh.

Many African Americans left our state. During eight months of 1922, more than 50,000 black farmers left South Carolina. This move to the North is called "the Great Migration."

Visitors Help

While many people were moving away from our state, people were also coming here to visit. So many people came that it helped the tourist industry grow. Tourism is the business created by visitors. People from all over came to visit Charleston. They wanted to visit one of the oldest cities in the country. They came to Fort Sumter to see where the Civil War had started. The shore at Folly Beach also became popular. When they visited these places, the people spent money at hotels, shops, and restaurants. This helped the economy. Tourism created new jobs for people.

Soon, a whole city called Myrtle Beach, was planned for tourists. The Ocean Forest Hotel was the first hotel in the new city.

The Ocean Forest Hotel was very fancy. It had marble floors and staircases. It had lights made of crystal. It had grand ballrooms. Men and women had to wear tuxedos and evening gowns to enter the dining room.

Lesson 3

Memory Master

1. Why did farmers struggle to get food?
2. What happened to the cotton industry in the 1920s?
3. Describe two reasons why people emigrated from South Carolina.
4. How did tourism help South Carolina?

PEOPLE TO KNOW
Franklin D. Roosevelt

PLACES TO LOCATE
Cheraw State Park
Lake Marion
Lake Moultrie
Santee Cooper Dam

WORDS TO UNDERSTAND
dam
depression
turbine

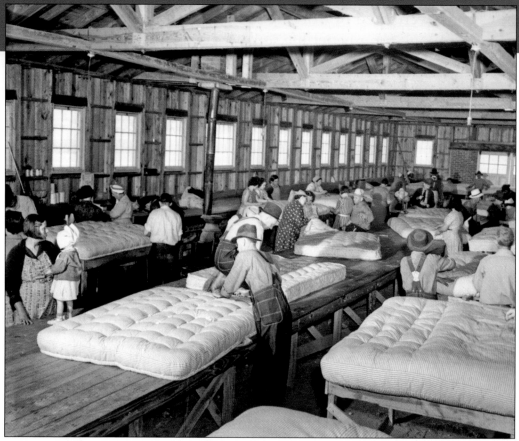

Finding jobs was not easy. These men and women made mattresses near Newberry.

The Great Depression

South Carolina and the nation were moving toward some hard times. There were growing problems in business. A *depression* is a time when many people can't make enough money to care for their families. They want to work, but they can't find jobs. The depression of the 1930s was the worst the United States has ever known. It is called the Great Depression.

Unemployment

In South Carolina, things got even worse. Cotton prices fell even more. Farmers were now making less than five cents a pound. Many of the cotton mills let workers go. Some of the mills just shut down.

People who borrowed money from banks couldn't pay the money back. This meant that banks didn't have any money, so they closed. They could not give people their money. Many people lost their life savings.

Poverty

People were out of work and hungry. Where could they go for help? Back then, there were no laws that let the government give aid.

Poverty was everywhere. In many counties, one out of every three people was out of work. Many families lost their homes. Many moved in with relatives. A newspaper in Columbia reported that over 100 people were living in the city dump.

The depression was very hard on African American families. Their incomes had been low even before the depression. Often, black workers lost their jobs before white workers.

People tried to help each other as much as they could. They opened soup kitchens to serve meals to hungry people. Local police and firemen collected food and gave it to families who had no money.

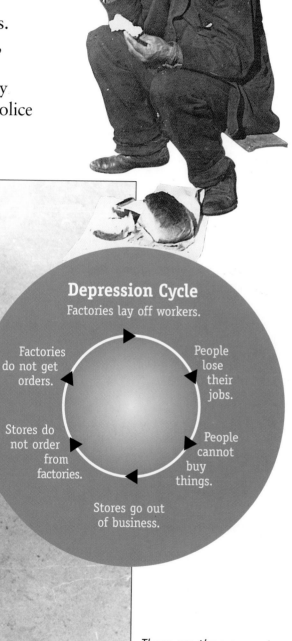

One out of every four workers in the United States was without a job.

Depression Cycle

Factories lay off workers.

People lose their jobs.

People cannot buy things.

Stores go out of business.

Stores do not order from factories.

Factories do not get orders.

These are the worn-out shoes of a sharecropper. How do they show what poverty was like?

The New Deal

People began to think the depression would never end. Then the government decided it must take action. President Franklin Roosevelt had a plan. He called his plan the New Deal. As part of the plan, the government hired people to do all sorts of jobs.

If people had jobs, they would have money. If they had money, they could buy goods. The stores where they bought the goods could order new goods to put back on their shelves. The factories that made the goods could hire people to work in the factories. It would take many years before times would be good again.

The government set up agencies to hire people to work. The agencies were called by the first letters of their names. They had names like CCC, WPA, and REA. There were so many agencies that people said Roosevelt had turned the government into a bowl of alphabet soup!

The CCC Repairs the Land

These CCC workers are planting pine trees in Newberry County. This helped the land and created jobs for people.

One agency in the New Deal was the CCC. These letters stood for the Civilian Conservation Corps. The CCC hired young men to work with the environment. Farmers had hurt the land by growing too much cotton. The CCC workers repaired the land. They planted crops that held the soil in place. This stopped the soil from washing away.

WPA workers provided health care for school children in our state.
These children are having their teeth looked at.

The CCC also built our first state parks. Some of the parks they built were Hunting Island Park, Paris Mountain Park, Poinsett State Park, Cheraw State Park, and many others. Have you ever been to any of these parks?

The WPA Makes Progress

The WPA was another New Deal agency. It stood for the Works Progress Administration. The WPA paid workers to build highways, bridges, and schools. The workers dug trenches and laid water and sewer pipes. The WPA even hired writers. They researched and wrote state and county histories.

The Slave Narratives

One of the WPA projects was the Federal Writers' Project. Writers interviewed blacks who had once been enslaved. They wrote down the stories and created the *Slave Narratives*.

The *Slave Narratives* was an oral history project. The WPA writers talked to over 2,000 former slaves. The former slaves were very old. From their true stories, we know what it was like to be a slave.

These people all had different stories to tell. Some had lived on large plantations with more than 1,000 slaves. Some lived on farms where there were only a few slaves. Others said they were the only slaves owned by their masters. Some told of how terrible their lives were. Some said that life was not so bad. It depended on where they lived and who their masters were.

Homes were moved to make way for the Santee Cooper Dam.

Santee Cooper Dam

Getting Power to the People

People in rural areas did not have electricity. The New Deal had a plan to bring them power. It paid workers to set up power poles and string electric wires throughout the countryside.

But where would the power come from? It would come from large *dams* built across rivers. Inside the dams were turbines. When water was let through the dams, it turned the turbines. *Turbines* are like large fans. As the turbines turned, they made electricity.

Santee Cooper Dam

Construction began on the largest New Deal project in our state. Large dams were built on the Santee and Cooper Rivers. Two lakes were formed behind the dams as the water backed up. They were called Lake Marion and Lake Moultrie. This great project became known as Santee Cooper.

To build the dams, land had to be cleared. This meant cutting trees down and moving homes, people, and whole towns. Today, we have two big lakes where people used to live.

Electricity helped people in rural areas. For the first time, this woman had electric power to run her water pump. Getting fresh water became a lot easier.

Many Still Suffered

Not everyone could work for the CCC or the WPA. Many people were still hungry and out of work. The government gave money to our state so people could have food and clothing. For the first time, some schools offered a lunch program. Many children who had no food at home could now have something to eat at school.

Memory Master

Lesson 4

1. What is a depression?
2. Describe one of the New Deal agencies.
3. What was the New Deal's plan to bring electricity to people in rural areas?

Palmetto Detectives in
LISTENING TO A STORY

"I'm tired of eating this cafeteria food," Ben said.

"Yeah, it's getting pretty yucky," Kevin said between bites of his sandwich.

"Then why didn't you get the spaghetti?" Christina asked Ben.

"Because I don't like the spaghetti, either."

After lunch, the class met a special guest in their classroom. "This is Mrs. Colson," Ms. Izard said. "She has lived in South Carolina all her life. She is going to talk to you about what it was like in the 1930s during the Great Depression."

"I was born in Abbeville, South Carolina, in 1925. My daddy was a cotton farmer. Unlike many of our neighbors, daddy did all right. We owned our own land, so we were a little better off. About the time I was four years old, daddy paid a man to take a picture of our farm. I still have that picture."

Mrs. Colson held up an old photograph. There was a little child standing on the porch in front of a house. "This is the house I grew up in, and that's me. When I was six years old, I started school. It was a one-room school. All the grades were together in that one room. I lived about two miles from the school. Can anyone guess how we got to there?"

Hands went up all over the class. Someone said by bus and another said by car.

"No, we walked. I walked with my older brother. Some schools had buses, but not mine."

Mrs. Colson also talked about the toys she played with when she was young. "Can anyone guess how many dolls I had?"

The girls all took a guess.

"One," Mrs. Colson said. "I had one doll."

"Your parents would only let you play with one doll?" Erin asked.

"No," Mrs. Colson said. "I only owned one doll. Times were hard back then, and money was spent on things we really needed. I got my doll when I was four or five. By the time I was 10, I had worn it out. Momma sewed it up and fixed it a number of times."

Mrs. Colson talked about her neighbors and the people she grew up with. She talked about her friends and the things they used to do for fun. "We made our own fun. We swam in the creek. The boys played a lot of baseball in the summer. Everyone enjoyed watching the games. Since people couldn't find jobs, they had a lot of free time. My brother got a job working for the CCC. Do you know what that was?"

"Yeah, that was one of the programs President Roosevelt set up. The CCC built some of our state parks," Carter said.

When Mrs. Colson finished telling her story, she asked if there were any questions. Ben's stomach grumbled, and he remembered how he had complained about the cafeteria food. He raised his hand.

"Mrs. Colson, what were the school lunches like back then? Were they better than they are today?"

"Oh, there were no school lunches. Not at first anyway. We brought our lunches from home. We carried them in a can. We brought whatever we had left over from home. Sometimes it was just hard boiled eggs, but I always had something to eat. I don't remember ever going hungry at school. During the Great Depression, things got so bad that some kids were lucky to even eat at home. Because of the New Deal, some schools got money to serve lunch. My school was one of them."

Mrs. Colson paused for a minute as if she was remembering something. "There were two brothers who went to our school. I can still see their faces. They were very thin boys. They had to take turns eating breakfast. One morning, one boy would eat, and the next morning the other boy would eat. They were lucky they could eat lunch at school. I don't think they cared how the lunch tasted. They were just happy to get it."

Ben's grumbling stomach didn't seem so hungry now. Those two boys must have been really hungry. Tomorrow, he decided, he would eat his lunch without complaining.

ACTIVITY

What Did You Learn?

We can learn history by listening to people tell stories about the past. Show what you learned from Mrs. Colson's story by answering these questions:

1. What year was Mrs. Colson born?
2. Why was her family a little better off than others?
3. Describe one thing Mrs. Colson shared about her childhood.

Chapter 10 Review

Geography Tie-In

Expanding Railroads

Railroads helped our state's economy at the beginning of the 20th century. They created new towns. They provided a faster, easier way for farmers to ship their goods to places around the state. Look at the map of the railroads on page 245, and answer the questions.

1. How many different railroads are shown on the map?
2. Which railroad had the most routes?
3. Which railroad had the shortest route from Cheraw to Florence?
4. Which railroad had the shortest route from Greenwood to Anderson?
5. Did you notice that the railroads covered most of the state? Write a paragraph to explain why that was important for farmers and other people who had goods to sell.

Genuine Genius!

Investigate With Oral History

Think about the adults you know. All of them have a story to tell. There may be someone who lived during the Great Depression. Or maybe you know someone who fought in a war. Your grandparents might remember segregation. You could talk to them for an oral history project.

When you do an oral history project, you have to prepare. Before you talk to the person, write down some of the questions you will ask. Try not to ask questions that can be answered with "yes" or "no." Ask questions that will get the person talking. Pay attention to what the person is saying, and always look at the person when he or she is talking. If you can, record your conversation. Make sure to keep notes about what he or she said.

After you have spoken with the person, write a summary of what he or she said. What new things did you learn about the past?

Blooming on the Vine

Advertising Electricity

Businesses write ads to tell people about their new products. Have you ever seen an ad for a new toy or a new kind of computer? Answer the questions about this ad.

1. What is being advertised?
2. Do you see ads for this today?
3. What group of people is the ad addressing?
4. According to the ad, how has electricity helped farmers?
5. Think about an invention people use every day that uses electricity, and write an ad for it. Describe all the good things about the invention, and list the ways it helps people. Then draw a picture of the invention, and decorate the ad to make it look exciting.

Visit Clemson College's Farm Labor Saving Exhibition Here Nov. 17th

ELECTRICITY

Has Brought Many Labor Saving And Comfort Providing Devices To The Farm.

SANTEE-COOPER

AND THE

BERKELEY ELECTRIC COOPERATIVE

Are Cooperating To Provide The Power To Operate These Appliances At The Lowest Possible Cost In Order That Berkeley County Farms May Enjoy The Full Benefits And Greater Efficiency Now Possible In This Wonderous New Electric Age.

S. C. PUBLIC SERVICE AUTHORITY

R. M. JEFFERIES, Gen. Mgr.

Board of Directors

JAMES H. HAMMOND, Chairman
W. G. JACKSON, 2nd Vice-Chairman
WILLIAM C. JOHNSTON

W. L. RHODES, Vice-Chairman
JAMES E. POWE
ROBERT S. LAFAYE

JAMES G. LEWIS

PRINCIPAL OFFICE: MONCKS CORNER, S. C.

Activity

Primary Source: Moving to a Mill Village

Many people were glad to have work in a mill. The passage below was written by Lola Derrick. Her family moved to a mill village when she was a young girl.

My family came down from a farm in the Dutch Fork section of Richland and Lexington Counties. We lived on a farm so poor it would grow nothing but rocks, my daddy cut cord wood on the side to buy food. He had heard about the mills opening in Columbia and one day he just decided to load up all our belongings and us onto the wagon and come to Columbia. He drove that old wagon onto the ferry at the Broad River and crossed. We went straight to the Granby Mill Village in 1898 and he went to the mill to get a job. I was 8 years old and worked at the Granby Mill until the Olympia Mill opened and then went to work there. We got one of those nice houses on Fifth Street. I was an experienced worker when I reached twelve years of age . . . I had two new dresses and plenty of good food.

1. Why did Lola's father want to move his family to Columbia?
2. How old was Lola when she began working at the mill?
3. What are two good things that happened to Lola's family after they began working at the mill?

Into a New Century

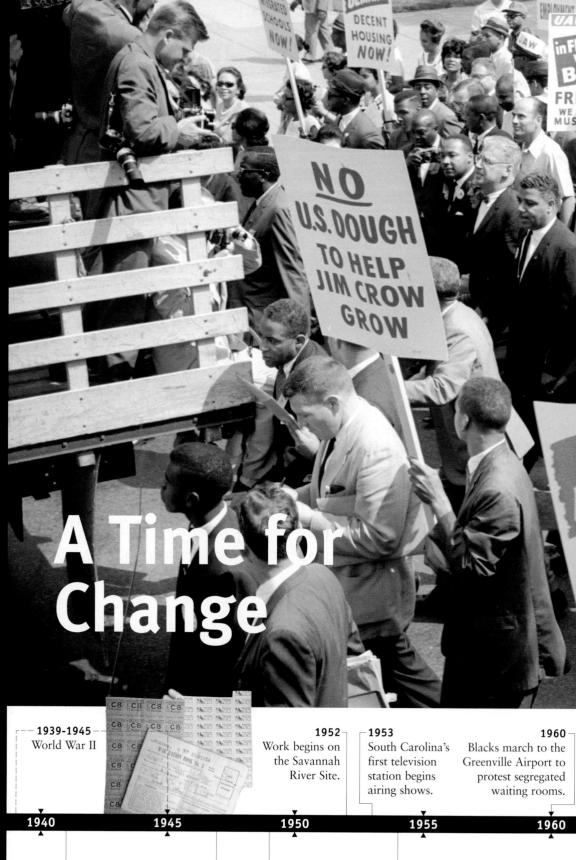

"*Some say there has been no progress, but they have forgotten where we started. Some would stop here, for they cannot see how far we still have to go.*"

—*Charles Joyner, 1994*

A Time for Change

Timeline of Events

1939-1945
World War II

1941
Japan attacks Pearl Harbor, Hawaii. The United States enters World War II.

1947
Judge Waring rules that blacks can vote in primary elections.

1949
Briggs v. Elliott case begins.

1952
Work begins on the Savannah River Site.

1953
South Carolina's first television station begins airing shows.

1954
In *Brown v. Board of Education*, the U.S. Supreme Court rules that school segregation is against the law.

1960
Blacks march to the Greenville Airport to protest segregated waiting rooms.

1940	1945	1950	1955	1960

After World War II, many people in our country felt it was time for change. African Americans still faced much discrimination. They called for equal rights and better treatment. This photograph shows people who marched in Washington, D.C., for the cause of civil rights. In our state, groups held protests and spoke out for change.

1963
Over 200,000 people gather in Washington, D.C. for the cause of civil rights.

1970-1971
South Carolina public schools are desegregated under federal court order.

1992
James Clyburn becomes first African American elected to U.S. Congress from South Carolina in the 20th century.

2000
South Carolinians celebrate the beginning of the 21st century.

| 1965 | 1970 | 1975 | 1990 | 1995 | 2000 |

1964
Civil Rights Act.

1965
Voting Rights Act.

1963-1975
Vietnam War

1990s
New industries and tourism help our state's economy.

73

PEOPLE TO KNOW
Jimmy Doolittle
Adolf Hitler

PLACES TO LOCATE
Asia
China
Europe
France
Great Britain
Italy
Japan
Pearl Harbor, Hawaii
Poland
Soviet Union (Russia)

WORDS TO UNDERSTAND
bomb
defense
dictator
recycle

A Second World War

The New Deal helped end the Great Depression. Then something happened that ended the depression for good. A war began. It was called World War II. It brought a great need for our farm products and textiles. People pulled together, once again. Many South Carolinians fought, and others stayed at home to help our country.

Fighting Overseas

World War II began in Europe and Asia. Dictators took over the government in these places. A *dictator* is a ruler who has all the power. Adolf Hitler was the dictator of Germany. Italy also had a dictator. The dictators stopped holding elections. They killed people who were against them. In Japan, the army took over the government.

The rulers of these countries wanted to conquer their neighbors. When the German army invaded Poland, all of Europe went to war. On the other side of the world, Japan invaded China.

The United States did not get involved in the war at first. Then something terrible happened. The U.S. Navy had a base at Pearl Harbor, Hawaii. One morning in December, Japanese airplanes dropped *bombs* on the navy base. The bombs blew up ships and killed people. After this attack, the United States entered the war. We fought against Germany, Italy, and Japan. We fought with Great Britain, France, and the Soviet Union (Russia).

After the Japanese attacked Pearl Harbor, the United States entered World War II.

TOP SECRET

Doolittle's Raiders trained at the Columbia Air Base.

TOP SECRET MISSION

Soon after the attack at Pearl Harbor, men at the Columbia Air Base volunteered for a secret mission. These men flew special planes called B-52s that carried bombs. General Jimmy Doolittle led these men. They trained for their mission in South Carolina.

After a few weeks, Jimmy Doolittle and his men headed to the Pacific Ocean. They landed on an aircraft carrier and waited for permission to perform their secret mission. An aircraft carrier is like a floating airport.

At the right moment, Doolittle's Raiders, as they were called, took off in their B-52s and headed for Japan. They bombed Tokyo, the capital of Japan. Doolittle's Raiders did not do much damage to Tokyo. But America had answered the attack on Pearl Harbor with an attack of its own.

South Carolina Helps the War Effort

Thousands of South Carolina's young men went off to fight. They served in the army, navy, and marines. Black and white soldiers served in separate units.

Women were photographers, office workers, nurses, drivers, and pilots. Doctors and nurses joined the armed forces to care for sick and wounded soldiers.

At home, South Carolinians worked hard to help the war effort. Our state had many training bases. Soldiers came here to prepare for battle. The Charleston Navy Yard built battleships. They made special ships called destroyers. The military opened air bases in Greenville and Columbia.

Red Cross volunteers marched in a parade in Rock Hill. They wanted to get people excited to help in the war effort.

People used ration stamps like these to get food and other items.

Making Things Last

People at home had to make sacrifices. They wanted to help our soldiers win the war. Soldiers needed lots of things, so people at home bought things in rations. That means they could only buy a small amount of things at a time. They could only buy so much gas for their cars. They could only buy so much sugar or meat. Even chocolate was rationed.

Each family got a certain number of ration stamps each month. They used ration stamps to buy things. They could not buy very many things at once. When the stamps ran out, families had to wait until the next month to get more. Rations helped our soldiers win the war.

Some people planted gardens to grow their own food. These were called "victory gardens." The more food a family grew, the less food they had to buy. This saved more food for our soldiers.

People took care of what they had. They patched old clothes. They made their own clothes. They threw nothing out. They found new ways to use what they had. Today, we *recycle*, or reuse, some things. During World War II, people recycled almost everything!

The South Carolina Adventure

Demand for Cotton and Textiles

Although people did without many things, parts of our economy were growing. The war created a large demand for cotton, textiles, and food. Our country needed ways to feed and clothe soldiers.

Cotton prices went up because the demand for cotton went up. Cotton farmers made more money. The cotton had to be turned into cloth to make all the items soldiers needed. This meant that textile mills had to run around the clock to make enough cloth. The mill workers worked in shifts. There was a day shift, an evening shift, and a night shift.

Cotton warehouses and textile mills were busy during World War II.

Other Jobs

The war created good jobs in **defense** plants. That is where people made things needed for the war such as bombs. With so many men off to war, women began to work in jobs that used to be for men only. Blacks also filled some of the jobs, but they were not paid as much as white workers.

The War Ends

After years of fighting and millions of deaths, World War II finally ended. Both Germany and Japan lost.

The war brought many changes. South Carolina now had an economy with good jobs. The soldiers and sailors returned to jobs with better pay. One thing had not changed though—South Carolina was still segregated.

Memory Master

1. What event caused the United States to enter World War II?

2. Name one way South Carolina helped in the war.

3. How did World War II help cotton farmers and textile mills?

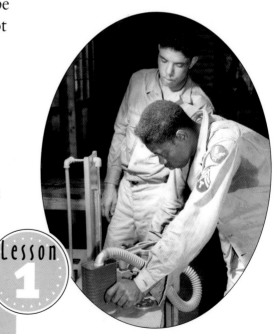

Lesson 1

During World War II, African Americans often worked and fought separately from whites. These men are testing gas masks at the air base in Columbia.

Lesson 2

PEOPLE TO KNOW
James F. Byrnes
J. Strom Thurmond

PLACES TO LOCATE
Charleston
Edgefield
Ellenton

WORDS TO UNDERSTAND
nuclear plant
suburb

After World War II, there was a baby boom.

A Booming State

When the war was over, thousands of men and women came home to South Carolina. They had served their country in many parts of the world. The war gave them a new view on life. Most did not want to go back to their old jobs of farming or working in mills. These veterans wanted something better. Many went to college. Some started their own businesses.

The world was at peace, and the future seemed safe. There were plenty of jobs. Couples started having more babies. So many babies were born during this time that those babies are called "baby boomers."

Attracting Industries

The war had boosted our economy and world trade. Our shipping ports were good places to send products all over the world. Our leaders looked for new companies. They wanted different types of companies, not just textile mills. Leaders like James F. Byrnes and Strom Thurmond pushed for more industries to come to South Carolina.

Big Companies

Some big companies did come. They came for many reasons. South Carolina had good workers who were not part of labor unions. Unions wanted high pay for their workers. They cost companies more money. Also, our state had low taxes for companies. This helped businesses save money.

Companies such as Michelin came. They built factories in the upcountry. People worked at Michelin making tires. Then the companies shipped their products from our ports. As our ports became busier, there were new jobs there, too.

Military Bases

Many military training bases stayed open after the war. Soldiers got basic training at Fort Jackson. There were air force bases in Lexington and Sumter Counties. Because many jobs opened at the Charleston Naval Base, thousands of workers moved to the Charleston area. These bases were important for our economy. They brought many people.

Spending Money

Most people had enough money to buy new things. They bought washing machines, dryers, refrigerators, stoves, furniture, cars, and toys. Many people bought their first televisions in the years after the war. All the TV programs were in black and white. People enjoyed watching Milton Berle and Howdy Doody. They also liked to watch sports and game shows.

People spent money on music, too. They bought record players and records. The most popular music was something new called rock and roll.

J. Strom Thurmond
1902–2003

J. Strom Thurmond was a well-known leader in our state. He fought in World War II. After the war, he was governor of South Carolina. As governor, he brought new industries.

In 1948, he ran for U.S. president, but he did not win. He became a U.S. Senator and was the longest serving senator until he was surpassed by Senator Robert Byrd in 2006. He was also the oldest senator in our country's history.

Thurmond was devoted to the people of our state. He saw South Carolina go through many changes and was able to help the state change with the times. He lived to be more than 100 years old.

Thurmond is buried in Edgefield. Many buildings and places in South Carolina are named after him.

Savannah River Site

←200 AREA   MI.
↑ C. SHOPS   MI.
↑ 100-L   MI.
↑ 100-P   MI.

The Savannah River Site

The government chose to build a new kind of plant in our state. It was called the Savannah River Site. It was a **nuclear plant** that would make material used in powerful bombs. It would provide jobs. Some people were excited by this news. Others did not like it. They did not want to live near a nuclear plant because they thought it was not safe.

People living in this area had to move. Small tenant farms were in this area. There were also six small towns. Over 6,000 people had to leave their homes.

People moved their homes and churches to new places. Entire houses were loaded on trucks and moved away. The people of Ellenton moved to a new town called New Ellenton. Many people did not want to move. They did not want to leave their homes.

Thousands of people worked to build the nuclear plant. After it was finished, many people worked at the Savannah River Site.

I can even see it now, see these huge houses moving down the road. It was just amazing, a whole big chunk of houses moving.

—Phyllis Tisdale Boyd, former Ellenton resident

Things Slow Down at Farms and Mills

Industries were becoming more and more important. Farms were changing. Farmers had new machines to pick cotton. Since machines did most of the work on farms, not as many people were needed to work the land. Because of this, sharecroppers moved away. Thousands of people left South Carolina to find better jobs.

Cotton was no longer king, even though some people still grew it. Tobacco became our leading cash crop. Soybeans and pine trees became important crops, too.

Mills were also changing. Mill villages were becoming a thing of the past. Mill owners began selling mill village houses before World War II. This continued after the war, too. Sometimes, mill workers bought the houses.

Activity

Charting Change

The chart below shows some changes in agriculture. Use it to answer these questions:

1. What two years are shown on the chart?
2. After looking at the chart, what can you say about agriculture during this time? Did it grow or slow down?

Agricultural Change	1945	1974
Number of Farms	148,000	32,000
Farmland	11 million acres	6.3 million acres
Cotton Harvest	1 million acres	252,000 acres

Cars, Roads, and Suburbs

More and more people were buying cars. Our government paid for better roads to be built. During the 1940s, over 5,000 miles of new roads were built in South Carolina.

Cars changed the way we lived. People could live farther away from work. New *suburbs* were built. People had homes in the suburbs, and they traveled to work in the cities. Suburbs popped up near every big city.

Memory Master

Lesson 2

1. Why did people in Ellenton have to move away?

2. Why did people leave our state?

3. Name one way cars changed the way people lived.

PEOPLE TO KNOW

Harry Briggs
Septima Clark
George Elmore
Martin Luther King Jr.
Benjamin Mays
Jackie Robinson
Donald Russell
J. Waties Waring

PLACES TO LOCATE

Clarendon County
Georgia
Orangeburg
Washington, D.C.

WORDS TO UNDERSTAND

Briggs v. Elliott
civil rights
custom
desegregate
petition
primary election
protest
public facility

The Civil Rights Movement

Civil rights are the basic rights of every citizen of our country. After World War II, many African American soldiers came home to a country that still did not treat them equally. They had just fought for freedom, and they wanted more freedom at home. They took part in the civil rights movement.

Challenging Jim Crow

Both laws and customs kept blacks and whites separate. *Customs* are the ways people do things. There were separate neighborhoods, schools, and *public facilities.* It was the custom in many towns for black people to shop on Saturdays. That was the only day stores were open for them.

Things were not equal. For example, black teachers did not get the same pay as white teachers. Jim Crow laws kept black people from their basic rights. Black people were tired of being treated like second-class citizens. They decided to change things.

A group called the National Association for the Advancement of Colored People (NAACP) worked to help blacks. People joined this group to help make life better for African Americans. They went to the courts to push for changes in the laws.

Public facilities like water fountains and restrooms were separated. What do the signs say in this photograph?

For the first time, African Americans were allowed to participate in primary elections. They waited in long lines, like this one in Columbia, to cast their vote.

Voting Rights

During this time, black people were not able to vote in primary elections. ***Primary elections*** decide the final people to run for a political office. A man named George Elmore wanted blacks to be able to vote in primary elections. He went to court and challenged the law.

A judge named J. Waties Waring ruled that black people could vote in the primary. He said, "It is time for South Carolina to rejoin the Union. . . [and] adopt the American way of conducting elections."

Soon, there was a primary for the Democratic Party. Thousands of blacks stood in long lines to vote. Some waited hours so they could use their new right.

Judge Waring's decision shocked white people in the state. They were very upset that a judge had ruled in favor of George Elmore. Many people did not like Judge Waring. They damaged his home and treated his family badly. Judge Waring was brave for making such an important decision.

What do you think?

Why do you think people were willing to wait in long lines to vote?

Segregated Schools

Can you imagine walking nine miles to school? That's what some children had to do. In 1947, there were no school buses for black children in Clarendon County. There were 30 school buses for white children.

A group of parents spoke out against this. Their children went to a black school called Scott's Branch. The state would not buy any buses for the school. The parents decided to buy a bus with their own money. Sometimes, the bus broke down. It cost a lot of money to repair.

The schools for black children were rundown. Often, there was no heat or indoor plumbing. Classrooms were crowded, and there were not enough teachers. There were not even janitors to help keep the schools clean. The schools for white children had all of these things and more.

Briggs v. Elliott

It was time to do something about the segregated schools. Harry Briggs was the first to sign a *petition* that listed many problems with black schools in Clarendon County. Because he was the first to sign it, it was called the Briggs Petition. The petition also compared black schools with white schools. It was clear that they were not equal. Other black parents signed the petition, too. They wanted better schools for their children.

The parents were brave to sign the petition. Some of them were treated cruelly by the white community. Harry Briggs lost his job. He also lost credit to buy supplies from the local store. Other signers faced the same problems. After the petition was given to the school board, the case went to court. This case was known as *Briggs v. Elliott.*

This is one page of the Briggs Petition. Can you find Harry Briggs' name?

This painting shows the judges of the Supreme Court who made the decision in Brown v. Board of Education of Topeka.

To the U.S. Supreme Court

The court ruled that the schools were unequal. The state promised to create a school system that would be separate and equal. The parents thought that more needed to be done. They took their case to the U.S. Supreme Court.

When *Briggs v. Elliott* went to the Supreme Court, there were similar court cases from other states. Together these cases were known as *Brown v. Board of Education of Topeka.* It was one of the most important court cases in the history of our country.

The U.S. Supreme Court ruled that public schools had to be **desegregated.** This meant there would no longer be separate black and white public schools. The judges said the color of a child's skin could not affect where he went to school.

Blooming on the Vine

Briggs v. Elliott

1. Who was the Briggs Petition named after? Why?
2. What happened to this person after he signed the petition?
3. Do you think the people who signed the petition were doing it for themselves or for their children?
4. Do you think they also signed the petition for you? Why or why not?
5. Would you have the courage they had to make things better for children?

A Time for Change

One way people protested was to wear signs in public places. This woman is protesting in Columbia. What does her sign say?

Change Comes Slowly

Brown v. Board of Education of Topeka made segregation in schools against the law. But in South Carolina, segregation was also a custom. Some people still wanted to keep black and white people separate.

Even though the law said otherwise, schools remained separate. Other public buildings did, too. These places had signs that said "White Only" or "Colored Only." A black person could not go to a place that said "White Only." The places for black people were usually not as nice. What could be done to change these things?

Protests

People wanted to end segregation, but they did not want violence. That means they did not want to hurt anybody. They did not want to break the law. Many black and white people decided to protest. To **protest** is to complain about something in public. A protest can take many forms. People can march as a group down the street. They can boycott certain businesses. People found new ways to protest.

"I Have a Dream"

Young black leaders worked hard to end segregation. One leader was Dr. Martin Luther King Jr., a minister from Georgia. He led peaceful marches and protests. He reminded everyone that our nation was founded on the belief that "all men are created equal."

Dr. King led a large march in Washington, D.C. Over 200,000 white and black people joined in the march. Dr. King gave a powerful speech. "I have a dream," he said, "that one day this nation will rise up and live out the true meaning of its creed: 'We hold these truths to be self-evident, that all men are created equal.'" He called on everyone in our country to work, so people of all races could be free.

Thousands of people gathered at the Lincoln Memorial in Washington, D.C. to hear Dr. Martin Luther King Jr. speak about equal rights.

Benjamin Mays
1895-1984

Benjamin Mays was born in South Carolina. He lived near a town called Epworth. His father was a sharecropper, so his family did not have much money.

Mays grew up to be a very important man. He became president of a college and did a lot for the civil rights movement. Some people call him the "Grandfather of the Civil Rights Movement." He was an advisor to other leaders. Even though Mays grew up poor, he accomplished many things. He said:

I am happy, I am glad, in fact I am extremely proud that my native state has done so much to honor Benjamin Mays, son of the soil, son of the farm, son of slaves.

—Benjamin Mays, 1981

Help From a Baseball Player

Have you ever heard of Jackie Robinson? He was the first black baseball player in the major leagues. Before Jackie Robinson, baseball was segregated. Today, people see him as a hero because he helped improve civil rights.

One time, Jackie Robinson visited South Carolina. He gave a speech at a meeting with the NAACP. He believed in equality for all people. As part of a protest, he tried to enter the white waiting room at the Greenville Airport. He was not allowed inside because he was black. When people heard about this, they were upset. It started our state's first civil rights protest. About 350 people marched to the airport to show their support for Robinson.

Jackie Robinson was a famous baseball player who helped in the civil rights movement.

Sit-ins

Another type of protest is a sit-in. People had sit-ins at lunch counters. These places were supposed to be for whites only. If black people sat at a lunch counter, they would not be served. Protesters held sit-ins all day. This hurt business for the restaurant. It also drew attention.

Sit-ins took place all across the state. Many lunch counters closed down for a time. There were sit-ins in Charleston, Columbia, Greenville, Spartanburg, Rock Hill, Manning, Sumter, and Orangeburg.

This photograph shows a sit-in at a Columbia store.

Violence at a Bowling Alley

The protests made some people angry. Sometimes there were fights, but most protesters did not fight back. They believed in peace. Many times they were arrested. In Charleston, a march turned into a small riot. Policemen and firemen were injured.

Fighting also took place in Orangeburg. Some black college students wanted to go bowling, but the bowling alley was for whites only. These students were tired of segregation, so they led a protest. The protest led to a clash with the police. Three students were killed, and 27 people were injured. This event became known as the "Orangeburg Massacre."

Good Changes

In 1963, Governor Fritz Hollings gave his farewell address. He urged everyone to obey the law. He wanted our state to, "remember the lessons of one hundred years ago." He knew we must not resist integration.

The new governor agreed that segregation was becoming a thing of the past. His name was Donald Russell. He supported civil rights. To show his support, he hosted a picnic at the governor's mansion. He invited everyone in the state. The picnic had black and white people eating together. No governor had ever done this before.

Changes took place at our colleges. Harvey Gantt became the first black student at Clemson University. Soon, all public colleges in the state had black students.

Two Important Laws

Congress finally passed the Civil Rights Act that gave all citizens "equal protection of the laws." Segregation became illegal. No restaurant, hotel, school, library, or other public facility could be segregated. This was a huge moment for civil rights in our country.

Congress also passed the Voting Rights Act. This act required that voting be made fair. No state could have unfair tests or other methods to stop blacks from voting. Because of this, the number of black voters increased.

Lesson
3

Memory Master

1. What were some of the customs that separated blacks and whites?
2. What decision did Judge Waring make?
3. Why did people sign the Briggs Petition?
4. Name two ways people protested.
5. What decision did the Supreme Court make in *Brown v. Board of Education?*

The BMW factory in Spartanburg provides many jobs.

Into the 21st Century

Since the civil rights movement, South Carolina has continued to grow and change. More people moved back to the state. Relations between blacks and whites have improved. During the civil rights movement, women struggled for equal rights, too.

Our country also fought in many wars. Soldiers from South Carolina and the rest of the United States fought in Asia and the Middle East.

People in South Carolina celebrated the beginning of the 21st century with fireworks and parades. They looked back at the history of our state and the world. They also looked forward to our future.

Industries

In the early days of our state, most people made a living from farming. Agriculture is still important, but other industries play a larger role in our economy.

Today, our leaders still look for new companies to move to South Carolina. BMW and Honda have plants here. Honda is from Japan. BMW is from Germany. The BMW plant has a museum that shows many of its cars. You can also tour the assembly line to see how cars are made.

At the same time, some industries are leaving the state. Many textile mills have closed. These mills are moving to other countries. The closing of a mill means a lot of people lose their jobs.

PEOPLE TO KNOW
Charles F. Bolden Jr.
James Clyburn
Pat Conroy
Larry Doby
Althea Gibson
John B. "Dizzy" Gillespie
Joseph L. Goldstein
Jonathan Green
Jesse Jackson
Jasper Johns
Richard W. Riley
Charles Townes

PLACES TO LOCATE
Allendale
Beaufort
Camden
Cheraw
Germany
Japan
Silver
Sumter

WORDS TO UNDERSTAND
astronaut
enrich

Tourists come to South Carolina to enjoy our beautiful beaches.

Have you tasted a fresh praline? Tourists in Charleston like to buy this special candy.

Tourism

Tourism is a big industry for our state. Millions of people visit South Carolina each year. Most people come to the coast. They enjoy our beaches, resorts, and golf courses. They also visit historic sites. Charleston, Hilton Head Island, and Myrtle Beach are popular places for tourists. Many other areas also attract tourists. People come to visit the mountains, lakes, rivers, and small towns in the upcountry.

Linking the Past to the Present

Air conditioning was an important invention that helped tourism grow. People could escape the hot, humid climate and keep cool. Air conditioners still keep South Carolina's homes and businesses cool. How would your life be different if you didn't have air conditioning?

Education

Schools are important to South Carolina. Our state gives more money to education than ever before. Our leaders know that good schools help everyone. They work hard to improve our schools. Business leaders know that good schools are important for training good workers.

The South Carolina Adventure

South Carolinians Enrich Our Lives

In recent times, many talented South Carolinians have **enriched** the lives of people in our state and around the world. They have written stories and poems, made music, painted pictures, played sports, worked for better government, and helped scientific progress. Let's meet a few of them.

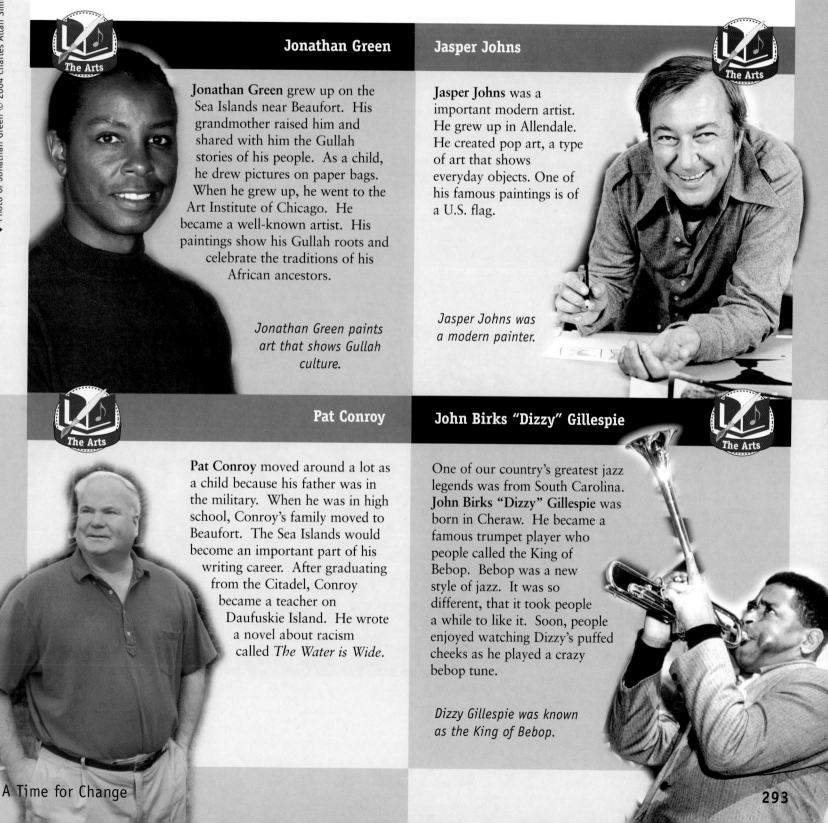

Jonathan Green

Jonathan Green grew up on the Sea Islands near Beaufort. His grandmother raised him and shared with him the Gullah stories of his people. As a child, he drew pictures on paper bags. When he grew up, he went to the Art Institute of Chicago. He became a well-known artist. His paintings show his Gullah roots and celebrate the traditions of his African ancestors.

Jonathan Green paints art that shows Gullah culture.

Jasper Johns

Jasper Johns was a important modern artist. He grew up in Allendale. He created pop art, a type of art that shows everyday objects. One of his famous paintings is of a U.S. flag.

Jasper Johns was a modern painter.

Pat Conroy

Pat Conroy moved around a lot as a child because his father was in the military. When he was in high school, Conroy's family moved to Beaufort. The Sea Islands would become an important part of his writing career. After graduating from the Citadel, Conroy became a teacher on Daufuskie Island. He wrote a novel about racism called *The Water is Wide*.

John Birks "Dizzy" Gillespie

One of our country's greatest jazz legends was from South Carolina. **John Birks "Dizzy" Gillespie** was born in Cheraw. He became a famous trumpet player who people called the King of Bebop. Bebop was a new style of jazz. It was so different, that it took people a while to like it. Soon, people enjoyed watching Dizzy's puffed cheeks as he played a crazy bebop tune.

Dizzy Gillespie was known as the King of Bebop.

A Time for Change

Jesse Jackson

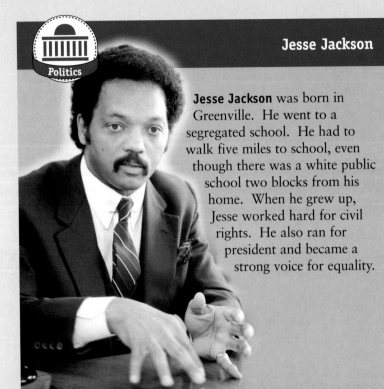

Jesse Jackson was born in Greenville. He went to a segregated school. He had to walk five miles to school, even though there was a white public school two blocks from his home. When he grew up, Jesse worked hard for civil rights. He also ran for president and became a strong voice for equality.

James Clyburn

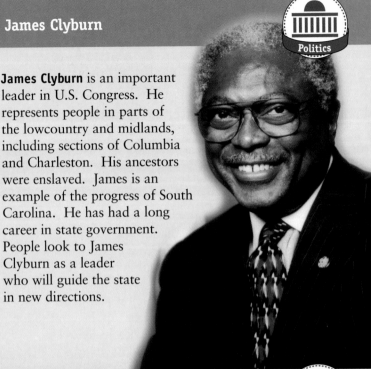

James Clyburn is an important leader in U.S. Congress. He represents people in parts of the lowcountry and midlands, including sections of Columbia and Charleston. His ancestors were enslaved. James is an example of the progress of South Carolina. He has had a long career in state government. People look to James Clyburn as a leader who will guide the state in new directions.

Richard W. Riley

Richard W. Riley, born in Greenville, served as governor for eight years. He helped raise money to improve schools. He visited all 91 school districts in South Carolina. Riley said:

A new South Carolina . . . is struggling to be born. We will not build the new South Carolina with bricks and mortar. We will build it with minds. The power of knowledge and skill is our hope for survival in this new age.

Richard Riley also served as U.S. secretary of education. He did important things, and he was known for his work in improving education across the country.

Charles Townes

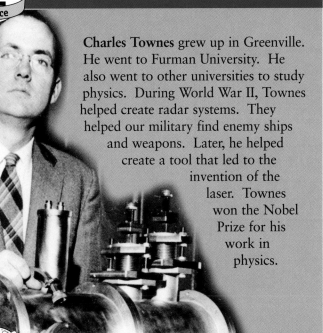

Charles Townes grew up in Greenville. He went to Furman University. He also went to other universities to study physics. During World War II, Townes helped create radar systems. They helped our military find enemy ships and weapons. Later, he helped create a tool that led to the invention of the laser. Townes won the Nobel Prize for his work in physics.

Charles F. Bolden Jr.

Charles F. Bolden Jr. grew up in Columbia. He dreamed of being an *astronaut*. After high school, Charles went to the U.S. Naval Academy. He studied electrical science. He joined the marines and fought in the Vietnam War. After the war, he went back to school to get a master's degree. His parents always told him to "study, work hard, and never be afraid of failure." His hard work paid off. Soon, his dream of being an astronaut came true. He went into space on a shuttle called *Columbia*.

Joseph Leonard Goldstein

Joseph Leonard Goldstein was born in Sumter. He studied chemistry in college and became a medical researcher. Goldstein won the Nobel Prize for his research. He discovered a cause for many heart attacks and strokes.

Althea Gibson

Althea Gibson is the first African American to win the U.S. tennis championship and Wimbledon. She was born in the small town of Silver. Her family moved to Harlem, New York, when she was young. She did not have an easy life, and her family was very poor. She worked hard to become a great tennis player.

Larry Doby

When Jackie Robinson began to play baseball, **Larry Doby** joined the American League. He was the first African American to do so. Larry Doby was from Camden. White players did not want him to play with them. His first year was not good, but in his second year, Larry became a star. He helped the Cleveland Indians win the World Series. He is in the Baseball Hall of Fame.

Memory Master

Lesson 4

1. Name two companies that have factories in our state.
2. What can happen when a textile mill closes?
3. Name one person from our state who has enriched our lives. Describe what he or she did.

Palmetto Detectives in THE ADVENTURE CONTINUES

It was close to the last day of school. Outside it was a beautiful spring day. It was the last day for South Carolina history. Ms. Izard looked at her class.

"So what do you think? Does South Carolina's story have a good ending?" she asked the class.

Everyone agreed that it did. "For a while there, I didn't think it would," said Christina. "There were a lot of bad times."

"I felt sorry for the slaves," said Kevin. "I was glad when they got freedom and better schools."

"The farmers had it bad, too, and the mill workers," Grant added. "Now most of the mills are gone."

"Yeah," Ben agreed, "but life got better for many people. Now people have good jobs and nice schools like ours."

"It's nice that people get along better now," Erin said.

"Yes it is," Ms. Izard added, "but we still have a long way to go. There is still some inequality. Sometimes people still judge others because they don't look the same."

Ms. Izard took a folder from her desk.

"Do you remember the state seals I had you draw back in the fall? I still have them, and I am going to hand them back to you."

When everyone had their seal, Ms. Izard asked the class if they would choose the same seal now that they had drawn earlier in the year.

Carter raised his hand first. "I still think the palmetto is the best symbol for our state. The hard times this state went through show that we can bounce back again and again."

Ms. Izard looked at the class. "Do the rest of you agree with Carter?" Most of the class shook their heads no.

"Well, what would you choose as your state seal?" Ms. Izard asked.

Erin stood up. "We would all choose Kevin's telescope."

"What is so special about his telescope?" asked Ms. Izard.

"Well, you see things in it." Grant spoke up. "Kevin, show Ms. Izard."

Kevin went back to his cubby and got his telescope. "Put it up to your eye," he said. "Do you see something that happened in the past?"

"No, I don't," she said.

The class was disappointed.

"I see all of you in here." Funny, the kids thought. She was looking out the window.

"I see all of you . . . in the future!"

WHAT'S IN YOUR FUTURE?

Now, for your last assignment, write what you think happens to Kevin, Grant, Carter, Erin, Christina, and Ben in the future. Make your story good because these kids are you!

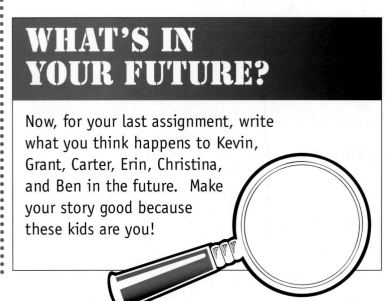

Chapter **11** Review

Genuine Genius!

Make an Illustrated Biography

Many people from South Carolina grew up to do important things. You have read about some of them in this chapter. Now, you can learn more about one person. Choose a person from this chapter, or think of another important person from our state.

1. Use library books and the Internet to read about the person's life. As you read, look for answers to these questions:
   - When was the person born?
   - What town or city did he or she come from? Locate it on a map.
   - What did the person do to make history?
   - What things happened in the person's life that led to that?

2. Make a list of the big events in the person's life. Draw a picture for each event. Below each picture, write what happened. Put all the pictures in order on a poster to make a colorful biography.

3. We don't know everything about everyone from the past. Often, there are pieces of the story that no one knows. Think about the person you chose. What DON'T you know about his or her life?

Activity

A Timeline for the Civil Rights Movement

Many things happened during the civil rights movement. A timeline is a good way to organize the events. Look at the timeline at the beginning of this chapter. There are eight events on the timeline that were part of the civil rights movement.

Make a list of the eight civil rights events. Right the date of each event. Then, make your own timeline with these events. Make sure the marks between the events show equal amounts of time. You can choose to make your timeline read from top to bottom or from left to right.

Then choose one event in the civil rights movement that you think was very important. Write a paragraph, draw a picture, or prepare a speech to show why the event you chose made a difference in the civil rights movement.

Where Were the Wars?

The United States went to war several times after World War II. Our soldiers fought in Korea, Vietnam, and the Persian Gulf region. Soldiers went to Afghanistan and Iraq, too. Locate these places on a world map. On what continents are they located? What can you learn about the people who live there?

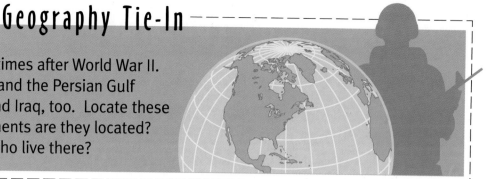

Activity

The Census: It Counts!

Every 10 years, the government has a census. It is a way of seeing who lives in our state and our country. The adults in each house or apartment fill out a special form. The form asks questions about how many people live in the house, the ages of the people, and what jobs the adults have.

Census forms also ask people what race they are. Look at the graph to see what the census said about South Carolina for the year 2000. Then answer the questions below.

1. How many groups are on the graph?
2. Which group is the largest?
3. Which group is the second largest?
4. If your ancestors lived here before European explorers came, what group would you belong to?
5. If you moved here from Japan, what group would you belong to?
6. If you moved here from Mexico, what group would you belong to?

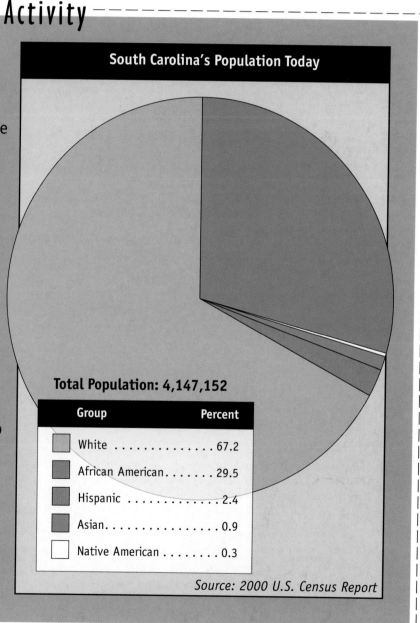

South Carolina's Population Today

Total Population: 4,147,152

Group	Percent
White	67.2
African American	29.5
Hispanic	2.4
Asian	0.9
Native American	0.3

Source: 2000 U.S. Census Report

United States, Political

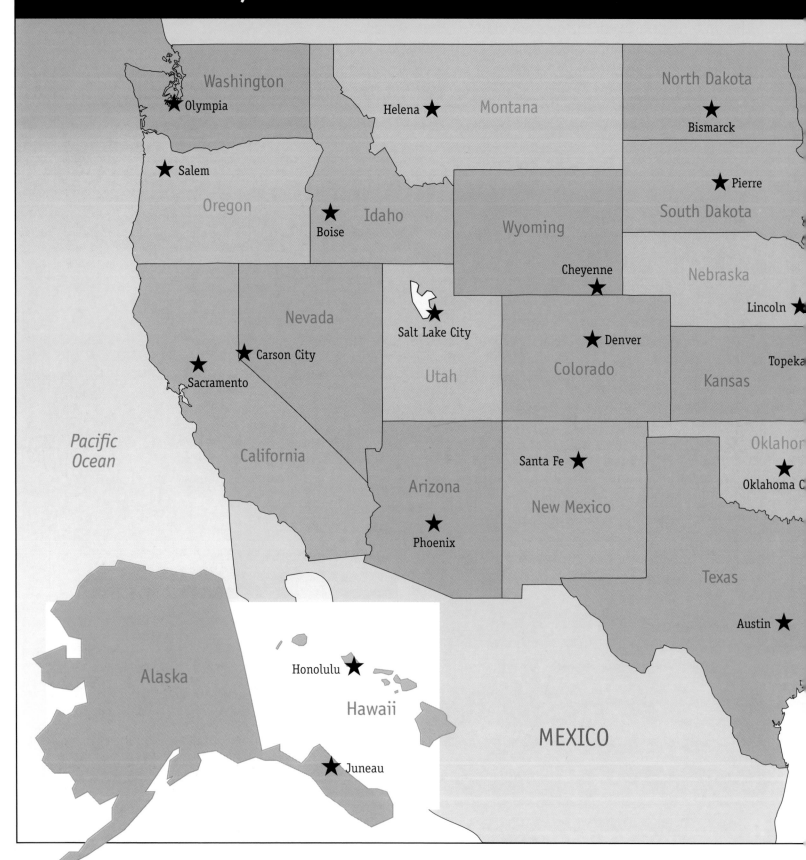

Washington
★ Olympia

Helena ★

Montana

North Dakota
★
Bismarck

★ Salem

Oregon

Idaho

★
Boise

Wyoming

★
Pierre

South Dakota

Cheyenne
★

Nebraska

Nevada

Salt Lake City
★

Denver
★

Lincoln ★

★ Carson City

★
Sacramento

Utah

Colorado

Topeka

Kansas

Pacific
Ocean

California

Arizona

Santa Fe ★

Oklahor

Oklahoma C
★

★
Phoenix

New Mexico

Texas

Alaska

Honolulu ★

Austin ★

Hawaii

Juneau ★

MEXICO

The South Carolina Adventure

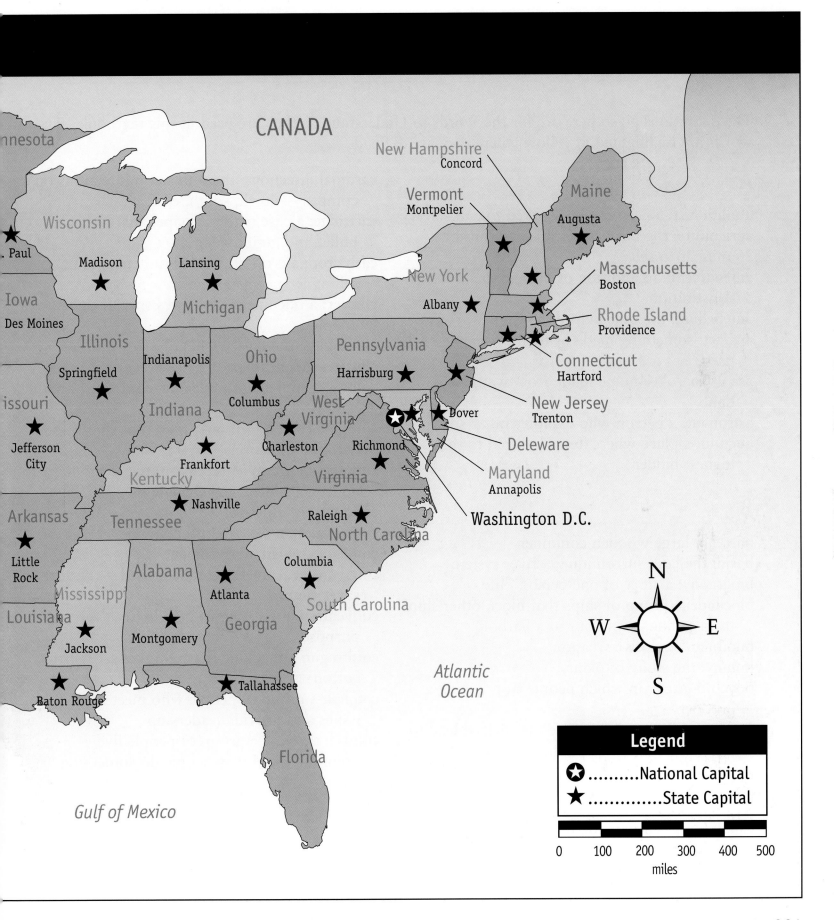

CANADA

Minnesota

Wisconsin

St. Paul

Madison ★

Iowa

Des Moines

Lansing ★

Michigan

Illinois

Missouri

Jefferson City ★

Springfield ★

Indianapolis ★

Indiana

Ohio

Columbus ★

Arkansas

Little Rock ★

Kentucky

Frankfort ★

Tennessee

Nashville ★

Mississippi

Louisiana

Jackson ★

Alabama

Montgomery ★

Georgia

Baton Rouge ★

Tallahassee ★

Florida

Gulf of Mexico

New Hampshire
Concord

Vermont
Montpelier

Maine

Augusta ★

★

★

New York

Albany ★

Massachusetts
Boston

★

Rhode Island
Providence

Pennsylvania

Harrisburg ★

★

★

Connecticut
Hartford

West Virginia

Charleston ★

Richmond ★

★ Dover

New Jersey
Trenton

Deleware

Maryland
Annapolis

Virginia

Washington D.C.

North Carolina

Raleigh ★

Columbia ★

South Carolina

Atlantic
Ocean

N

W ● E

S

Atlanta ★

Glossary

The definitions given here are for the **Words to Understand** as they are used in this textbook. The words are highlighted in yellow where they are defined.

A

abolitionist: a person who worked to end slavery

agriculture: the business of raising crops or animals to sell

amendment: an addition or change to a constitution

antebellum: the time before the Civil War

artifact: something made or used by people of the past

asi: a Cherokee home made from wattle and daub

astronaut: a person who explores outer space

auction: a place where items are sold to the highest bidder

B

barrel: a large wooden container

basin: the land surrounding a river system

biography: a story of one person's life

blockade: a group of ships that block other ships from sailing in and out of a harbor

bomb: an explosive weapon

botany: the study of plants

boycott: an act in which people stop buying a product

Briggs v. Elliott: a court case that helped lead to the desegregation of public schools

C

canal: a waterway made by people

cannon: a big gun that can shoot large shells and balls across long distances

cardinal directions: the four main directions on a compass—north, south, east, west

cartridge: a case made of paper that holds a bullet and gunpowder

cash crop: a crop grown for the purpose of selling it

charter: a document that gives special rights to people

civil rights: the basic rights of every citizen

climate: the weather of a place over time

colony: a settlement under the control of another nation

compass rose: a tool on a map that shows the cardinal directions

congress: a group of representatives who meet to address problems or write laws

conquer: to take over

constitution: a set of written laws

contract: a written agreement

convenience: something that provides comfort or saves time

convention: a meeting of people for a certain purpose

cotton gin: a machine that removes seeds from cotton

council: a group of people who meet to discuss issues and provide leadership

culture: the way a group of people live

custom: the usual way people do something

D

dam: a wall that holds back a body of water

daub: a mixture of clay and grass used to make asis

debt: the state of owing money to someone else

decision: a choice

declaration: an announcement

defense: something used to protect something else

delegate: a representative

depression: a time when many people can't make enough money to take care of their basic needs

desegregate: to end segregation by race

dictator: a ruler who has all the power

dike: a large fence used to keep rivers from flooding rice fields

document: a paper record

draft: to force someone to join a war

E

economy: the way people make a living

elite: a social class of people who are wealthy and powerful

Emancipation Proclamation: a document issued by Abraham Lincoln that said all slaves in the southern states were free

emigrate: to move from one's home to a new place

enrich: to make richer or more meaningful

enslaved: to be made someone else's property

executive: the branch of government that carries out the laws

experience: what you learn from things you have done

experimental: something being tested

explorer: a person who goes to new places to learn about them

F-H

federal: a term used to describe national government

flexible: when something can bend without breaking

gang system: a system to grow cotton in which slaves worked in a group from sunup to sundown

geography: the study of Earth's land, water, people, and other living things

goods: things that people make to sell

government: a person or group of people who rule or have control

Gullah: a mixture of African and English languages; a culture

heroic: brave

history: the record and story of the past

human feature: something on the land made by people

human system: a way people use and change the land

hurricane: a big storm that comes from the ocean

husk: the hard shell surrounding a rice grain

I-J

illiteracy: the condition of not being able to read

imports: goods coming into the country from other places

independence: freedom from another's control

indigo: a plant used to make a blue dye

industry: a type of business

integrate: to bring together

intolerable: when something is unfair and should not be allowed

invention: a new creation that often changes the way people live

island: a piece of land with water on all sides

Jim Crow laws: local and state laws set up to keep whites and blacks segregated

journal: a book of someone's thoughts and feelings

judicial: the branch of government that decides what the laws mean

L

landform: a physical feature of the land, such as a mountain or hill

legend: a story that tells about the past

legislative: the branch of government that makes the laws

leisure: relaxation

loom: a machine that weaves thread or yarn together to make cloth

Loyalist: a person who wanted the 13 colonies to remain loyal to England

M-N

manual: done by hand

manufacturing: the act of making something with machines

mica: a shiny rock

migration: when many people move to a new place at the same time

militia: a group of men who fight together

missionary: a person sent by a church to try to help people

monument: a structure built to honor something or someone

mortar: a tool that holds rice as it is ground with a pestle

motive: a reason

motto: a saying that tells a goal or an idea

museum: a place where historical objects are put on display

nation: a large community of people who have many things in common

national government: the government of a country

natural resource: something found in nature that people use

nickname: another name for a person or place

nuclear plant: a place where nuclear bombs and energy are produced

nutrition: the food and materials needed for life and growth

O-P

oath: an agreement

oral history: the stories of the past shared by telling them to others

orphan: a child who does not have parents or a family

overseer: a person who watches over other people as they work

palisade: a tall wall made from logs

palmetto: South Carolina's state tree

Patriot: a person who wanted the 13 colonies to be independent from England

pellagra: a skin disease caused by poor diet

peninsula: a piece of land surrounded by water on three sides

pestle: a tool used to grind rice in a mortar

petition: a written request for something from the government

physical feature: something found in nature

plain: an area of flat land

plantation: a large farm

plunder: to steal

port: a place where ships can load and unload goods

poverty: the state of not having enough money to provide the basic things needed to live

precipitation: any type of water that falls to Earth

prejudice: making judgments about people because of their race, religion, or social class

primary election: the election that decides the final people to run for a political office

privacy: the state of being left alone

promote: to make known; to advertise

protest: to complain about something in public

public facility: something like a restroom, water fountain, or library that is for public use

Q-R

quarter: the chance to surrender

rammer: a long rod used to push cannonballs into a cannon

ratify: to approve

ration: a set amount of food or supplies

rebellion: an organized fight against those who are in power

Reconstruction: the federal government's plan to rebuild the South after the Civil War

recycle: to reuse something

reformer: a person who wanted to improve life for people

region: an area made up of places that have things in common

representative: a person who acts or speaks for a larger group

resist: to go against

revolution: a fight to replace one government with a different government

river system: a system of rivers emptying into other rivers

rural: having to do with the country, not the city

S

sacrifice: to give up something

sanitation: relating to health and cleanliness

sapling: a young tree

scale of miles: a tool on a map that stands for actual distances

scrip: paper money printed by mills to be used in mill villages

seal: a stamp used to mark important government papers

secede: to break away from a country

segregate: to separate

services: work that people do for other people to earn a living

sewer system: a way of getting rid of human waste

sharecropper: a farmer who worked the land owned by someone else

spindle: an object that holds thread

submarine: a boat that travels under water

suburb: a place outside the city with houses, yards, and shopping malls

surrender: to give up

swamp: a flooded forest

symbol: something that has a special meaning and stands for something else

T

tan: to stretch animal skin to make it lighter

tariff: a special tax on imports

tax: money the government collects from people

technology: the science of improving tools, machines, and electronics

temperature: a measure of how hot or cold the air is

tension: uneasiness

textile mill: a factory that turns cotton into cloth

threaten: to aim to harm

tide: the rising and falling of the ocean level

timeline: a tool for learning history that uses dates to show the order of when things happened

tourism: the industry of making money from people who visit a place

tradition: a way of life handed down from parents to children

traitor: a person who acts against his country

transportation: the ways people travel

treaty: an agreement

tributary: a river that empties into another river

truce: an agreement to end a war

turbine: a large fan

U-Z

unstable: able to fall apart

veteran: a person who has served in the armed forces

violent: the state of using force to hurt someone

volunteer: a person who helps others without being paid for his or her time

wattle: bark and branches used to make the roofs of asis

wayside hospital: a hospital set up near railroad lines by women during the Civil War

wigwam: a Native American home made from wood, bark, and grasses

Index

Credits

Amon Carter Museum, Fort Worth, Texas 112-113, 132 (top)

AP/Wide World Photos 28 (bottom left), 103, 147, 293 (top right and both bottom), 294 (bottom), 295 (top left)

Architect of the Capitol 69, 122, 138-139

Avery Research Center for African American History and Culture 174

BMW 291

Board of Public Works, Gaffney 36 (right)

Carrie Gibson 38 (bottom right), 41 (right), 42 (top), 80, 81 (top)

Charles Allan Smith 293 (top left)

Clemson University 88 (bottom), 188 (right)

Courtesy of South Caroliniana Library, University of South Carolina, Columbia 144 (top, middle two), 163, 166-167, 169 (right), 170 (left), 188 (left), 199 (top), 203, 205 (bottom), 208, 211 (top), 212-213, 234, 244, 250 (bottom), 251, 260, 261, 265, 279, 283, 286, 289

Courtesy South Carolina Confederate Relic Room and Museum 204

Darby Erd, South Carolina State Museum 10, 11 (top), 48 (bottom), 56, 70 (bottom left)

David Blanchette 48-49

Drayton Hall 100 (left), 130

Elloree Museum 171 (right)

Eric Horan 2-3, 18-19, 28 (bottom right), 39, 40, 42, 105, 292 (top)

Folklife Resource Center, McKissick Museum, University of South Carolina, Columbia, South Carolina 104, 177 (bottom)

Fort Sumter National Monument 194

From the Collection of the State of South Carolina 128, 201

Gary Rasmussen 12-13, 50-51, 53 (bottom), 55, 58, 62, 114

Georgetown County Library 98 (top), 245

Gibbes Museum of Art/Carolina Art Association 78 (bottom), 88 (top), 98 (left), 100 (top), 110, 164

Historic Columbia Foundation 178 (left)

Howard University 288 (left)

James Clyburn 294 (top right)

Jennifer Petersen 44-45

Jon Burton 14, 15, 44, 74-75, 108-109, 134-135, 148-149, 150-151, 153, 154-155, 180-181, q 214-215, 236-237, 268-269, 296-297

Kindra Clineff 81 (right), 187

Lexington County Museum 202

Library of Congress 7 (bottom left), 83, 97, 111 (top), 126, 129, 132 (bottom), 136, 144 (top far left), 170 (middle), 171 (top), 179, 184-185, 190, 191, 192, 206, 207, 209 (right), 211 (bottom), 213 (top), 216, 220, 224, 225, 227, 228, 230, 231, 232, 240-241, 246, 247, 248, 249, 250 (top), 252, 253, 254, 257, 258, 263, 266, 272, 274, 275, 277, 287, 288, 294 (top left), 295 (bottom right)

NASA 295 (top right)

National Archives 144 (2nd from right), 162 (left), 218-219, 221, 223, 262, 264, 267

North Wind Picture Archives 66-67, 78-79, 86, 91, 92, 106, 117, 118, 123, 125 (top), 127, 131, 158-159, 173, 195, 197, 198, 205 (right), 229 (left)

Pat and Chuck Blackley 292 (left)

Pocumtuck Valley Memorial Association, Memorial Hall Museum, Deerfield, Massachusetts 17 (bottom)

Robert Clark 6, 30 (top), 37, 38 (top, and bottom left and middle), 41 (left), 48 (right), 63, 89

Shawna Kawasaki 4

South Carolina Department of Archives and History 7 (bottom right), 82, 90, 99 (bottom), 107, 140, 160, 209 (top), 235, 271, 284

South Carolina Farm Bureau 24, 36

South Carolina Historical Society 99, 142, 161 (bottom), 175, 193

South Carolina State Museum 70

Southeastern Expeditions 35

Sumter County Museum 125 (right)

Suzanne Chapelle, Courtesy of the Irvine Nature Center 61

The Charleston Museum 177 (left), 178 (right), 243

The Granger Collection 57 (bottom), 59, 64, 72, 94, 102, 165, 169 (top), 176, 210, 222, 233, 282, 285

The Peabody Museum of Archaeology and Ethnology 53 (top)

Tom Blagden/Larry Ulrich Stock 34, 60

U.S. Army Art Museum 121

U.S. Army Corps of Engineers 30 (bottom)

U.S. Department of Energy 280

Winthrop University Archives 276 (top)